To

_____

From

_____

Date

_____

365 Spirit-Lifting Devotions for Women

ISBN-10: 0-8249-4502-6
ISBN-13: 978-0-8249-4502-2

Published by Guideposts
16 East 34th Street
New York, New York 10016
Guideposts.org

Distributed by Ideals Publications, a Guideposts company
2636 Elm Hill Pike, Suite 120
Nashville, TN 37214

Guideposts and *Ideals* are registered trademarks of Guideposts.

Acknowledgments
Every attempt has been made to credit the sources of copyrighted material used in this book. If any such acknowledgment has been inadvertently omitted or miscredited, receipt of such information would be appreciated.

A Note from the Editors
Guideposts, a nonprofit organization, touches millions of lives every day through products and services that inspire, encourage and uplift. Our magazines, books, prayer network and outreach programs help people connect their faith-filled values to their daily lives. To learn more, visit Guideposts.org or GuidepostsFoundation.org. For more information about *Daily Guideposts*, visit DailyGuideposts.org.

Unless otherwise noted, Scripture references are from The Holy Bible, New International Version®, NIV®. Copyright © 1973, 1978, 1984 by Biblica, Inc.™ Used by permission of Zondervan. All rights reserved worldwide. Other Scriptures are taken from The Holy Bible, King James Version (KJV). The New King James Version (NKJV). Copyright © 1982 by Thomas Nelson, Inc. Used by permission. The New American Standard Bible® (NASB), Copyright © 1960, 1962, 1963, 1968, 1971, 1972, 1973, 1975, 1977, 1995 by The Lockman Foundation. Used by permission. The New Revised Standard Version Bible (NRSV). Copyright 1989, 1995, Division of Christian Education of the National Council of the Churches of Christ in the United States of America. Used by permission. The Holy Bible, New Living Translation (NLT), copyright 1996, 2004. Used by permission of Tyndale House Publishers, Inc., Wheaton, Illinois. The Message (MSG). Copyright © 1993, 1994, 1995, 1996, 2000, 2001, 2002 by Eugene Peterson. Used by permission of NavPress, Colorado Springs, CO. The Living Bible (TLB) © 1971. Used by permission of Tyndale House Publishers, Inc., Wheaton, Illinois 60189. The Good News Translation (GNT) Second Edition © 1992, American Bible Society. Used by permission. All rights reserved.

Cover and Interior design by Thinkpen Design, Inc., www.thinkpendesign.com
Typeset by Mullerhaus

Printed and bound in China

10 9 8 7 6 5 4 3 2 1

DAILY GUIDEPOSTS

365 SPIRIT-LIFTING DEVOTIONS FOR

Women

Guideposts

INTRODUCTION

*G*iven the many hats women wear every day, it is often difficult to carve out a little quiet time for meditation and prayer. We do so much for others that we often forget to take time for ourselves. *365 Spirit-Lifting Devotions for Women* can help. This life-changing book is a collection of devotions by and for and about women. All women. Young and old, mothers and daughters (and grandmothers, too), wives and widows and brides-to-be, homemakers and career women, neighbors from far and wide. All bound together by faith and by the unique perspective women bring to life.

Unlike other collections of devotionals, *365 Spirit-Lifting Devotions for Women* is a book for any year and for every year, even Leap Year. Start reading today and you will keep reading day after day and year after year. You will be inspired by devotionals on special religious and commemorative days and smile at the occasions that are just plain fun. Go ahead. Take a peek at your birthday or one of your own special days.

Each day's reading begins with a Scripture to help you focus your meditations for the day. Next comes a real-life story by one of the best loved inspirational writers of our time. Each woman shares her experience and ends with a personal prayer for the day and the message. It doesn't stop there, however, since each of these authors prays for their readers—and asks that you keep them in your prayers, too.

365 Spirit-Lifting Devotions for Women will draw you into this very special prayer chain of women praying for each other. This caring and nurturing is typical of the strength with which we approach life's challenges. It is in all women. Tap into it and let your spirit soar.

—Marie Gangemi

January

*"See, I am sending an angel ahead of you to guard you
along the way and to bring you to the place I have prepared."*
—EXODUS 23:20

I sometimes think New Year's Day comes at the wrong time of year. I'm usually facing a bunch of tasks left over from the old year, such as taking down the Christmas tree and putting away all the decorations, writing thank-you notes, and dealing with decisions about what to do with the stack of Christmas cards. Throw them away? Save the ones with pictures? Check the addresses? Then there's the thought of trying to catch up with all the work I put off during the holidays. I'm behind before the New Year even starts.

"Who can think about new beginnings or inspirational goals in the midst of old concerns?" I asked my husband Lynn as he came in the door after a quick trip to the office to complete a couple of year-end responsibilities.

"Let me show you a gift I just received," he said, pulling out an attractively wrapped package from his briefcase. On it was a card: "To Lynn. May this gift encourage you in the coming year." It was signed by a friend in his Bible study group.

Lynn tore off the paper and lifted out a beautifully framed message, penned by a professional calligrapher. The message read:

Lynn, Trust Me. I have everything under control. Jesus

He set down the frame amidst the clutter on the kitchen counter so I could see the simple message as I went about my tasks. Slowly those words began to change my frame of mind. If I needed something to help me carry my old concerns into the New Year, I'd just found it...the determination to face each day's concerns, trusting in the words of this promise from the Source of all comfort and strength.

*Father, each day in this new year, please help me
remember that You are in control of everything.*
—CAROL KUYKENDALL

January 2

Jesus...departed again into a mountain himself alone.
—John 6:15 (kjv)

In this small mountain village where my husband Robert and I live, many of the residents are summer people. Our good friends the Kramers left for California at the end of September, the Actons left for Arizona a couple of weeks ago, and one by one many of our other neighbors are disappearing, their summer places tightly closed for the winter. The village lake is dotted with skaters now, while in summer its banks were lined with people fishing, families picnicking, and frequent weddings held in the gazebo on an island at its center. The main street looks practically deserted, with only two small businesses still open.

Though we miss our friends and the neighborhood get-togethers that are part of summer life here, we're not lonely. We keep in touch with our families and close friends by phone or e-mail, and God's beautiful creations keep us company. This morning, I can gaze out at Mount Dewey through the window by my desk and enjoy its snow-covered, Christmas-card pines. Large, fluffy snowflakes are slowly, gently falling, as I sit inside our cozy house. Robert is baking bread, and the scent surrounds me like a hug. Tonight we'll sit by the fire and read to each other. Then we'll end the day with our nightly prayer time by candlelight.

When I'm lonely, O God, I'll find gratitude in simple things, reach out to distant loved ones, and spend time with You in prayer.
—Marilyn Morgan King

In the world ye shall have tribulation:
but be of good cheer; I have overcome the world.
—JOHN 16:33 (KJV)

*E*ach year in early January we invite all our godchildren and extended church family over for a potluck meal and one last singing of Christmas carols. Last year we included our ninety-four-year-old adopted grandma, whom we fondly call "Baba Draga." She bubbled with joy to be with all us "young people." (We middle agers were pleased to be considered young.)

At one point my husband Alex was at the piano taking requests for everyone's favorite carols. Baba Draga astonished us all by requesting "Home on the Range." As we searched for the music, Baba Draga explained it was her very favorite song because of the line, "Where seldom is heard a discouraging word, and the skies are not cloudy all day." She said, "I taught this to my boys, and when they would get into scraps or start complaining, we would sing this song." Chuckling, we sang "Home on the Range," while Baba Draga beamed and waved her arms conducting us.

A few months later Baba Draga asked me to take her to the eye doctor. Her eyesight had been diminishing, and she was anxious to get some test results. To our disappointment, the doctor confirmed the diagnosis of macular degeneration. It was getting worse, and nothing could be done to stop her loss of vision.

Baba Draga insisted on taking me out to lunch afterward and surprised me by her good humor. When I commented on her happy mood despite the doctor's grim prognosis, she peered across the booth at me. "You know," she said, "everyone at my age has some loss or pain to bear. But I memorized something years ago that I tell myself every day: 'When cheerfulness is kept up against all odds, it is the finest form of courage.'"

Dear God, thank You for Baba Draga and her example of courage. Today, and all year long, please help me refrain from discouraging words or thoughts.
—MARY BROWN

Mine arm also shall strengthen him.
—Psalm 89:21 (KJV)

I t wasn't working. In spite of the fact that my daughter Joanna was wearing ankle braces and high-topped basketball shoes, every few games she'd hurt one ankle or the other again.

We took Joanna to a physical therapist, who suggested ankle strengthening. He told us something odd: Joanna's ankles needed to be "retrained" to land correctly when she jumped. Each ankle had been sprained so often that her foot came down off center, making the foot roll and thus reinjuring the ankle. To our amazement, Joanna's exercises strengthened and "retrained" her ankles, and she was injury-free the entire season.

Since then, I've begun noticing in how many ways I "brace" my life instead of strengthening and retraining my character. So in this new year, I've begun spiritual therapy. Rather than just apologizing for the hurtful things I've said, I'm determined to exercise the discipline of tongue control. Instead of occasional spurts of organizing closets and drawers, I've resolved to keep them tidy. Along with my emergency support of quick prayers, I'll work on the daily exercise of Bible reading and quiet time. With my thoughts centered on God, I'm bound to land right!

Father, help me in this new year to dispose of braces that weaken me, and strengthen and retrain my spirit instead.
—Marjorie Parker

To every thing there is a season, and a time to every purpose under the heaven.
—ECCLESIASTES 3:1 (KJV)

*A*s a child in Pennsylvania, I loved winter. So when the time came to move to Southern California, where the weather might occasionally include rain but would never permit that rain to solidify, I decided I had to take some snow with me. The winter before I moved, I filled an empty jelly jar with snow from our backyard, the home of numerous snow angels and snowmen over the years of my growing up. I closed the jar tightly and sealed the lid with duct tape to be sure not to lose a drop. I wanted to keep my winter memories intact.

Southern California lived up to my expectations. I found a good job, a wonderful husband, and lots of sunshine. Still, I made sure my jar and the memories of my childhood winters were never far from reach.

One year Keith suggested we go to the Grand Canyon for Thanksgiving, and I agreed enthusiastically. On Thanksgiving Day, it snowed. For the first time in years, real snow and I were in the same place at the same time. I danced around like a kid, and sometime during the dance, I realized that my time for memory-making was far from over. The snow hadn't gone from my life!

Back in Los Angeles, I peeled the duct tape off the jelly jar, unscrewed the lid, and poured out the melted snow from Pennsylvania. If I kept my winter memories sealed up so tightly, how would I slip in the new ones?

God of childhood and maturity, You are with me
all the stages of my life, ready to surprise me in every one.
—RHODA BLECKER

JANUARY 6

The Gentiles shall come to thy light, and kings to the brightness of thy rising.
—Isaiah 60:3 (kjv)

*W*e Southerners joke about the fact that our seasons are not reflected in changing leaves but rather in the food we eat. We have crawfish season, strawberry season, Creole tomato season, Vidalia onion season, and—my favorite—king cake season.

Only available during the Mardi Gras holidays, king cake is made in an oval shape from braided strands of cinnamon dough, topped with icing and sprinkled with purple, green, and gold sugar. There's a small plastic baby baked inside, and whoever finds it must bring a king cake to the next gathering.

My daughter loves king cake as much as I. She called from New York City to ask me to send her one.

"Sure!" I replied.

The next day I stopped at the bakery to order one. On the way out I picked up a brochure on the counter titled *The History of the King Cake*.

"The Mardi Gras season officially begins on the Twelfth Night of Christmas, January 6, also known as Epiphany," it said. "It marks the day the wise men brought gifts to the Christ Child. By doing so they 'revealed' or 'made known' Jesus to the world as Lord and King.

"The New Orleans custom, begun in the late 1800s, celebrates Epiphany with cakes that are baked to honor the three kings. The oval shape signifies their circular journey to confuse King Herod. The plastic baby represents Jesus. And the search for the baby is represented by the mystery of who will get the slice with the plastic baby in it."

So even if you've never been to Mardi Gras, why not share in a beloved New Orleans custom? Bake a king cake or have one shipped to you, and celebrate one of the biggest *Aha!* moments in history.

> *Wise Father, on this Epiphany, thank You*
> *for revealing Yourself to us in Jesus Christ.*
> —Melody Bonnette

JANUARY 7

*May grace and peace be multiplied to you
in the knowledge of God and of Jesus our Lord.*
—2 PETER 1:2 (RSV)

By January 7, Christmas seemed a dim memory. My husband Alex had left for a conference overseas. I dreaded the lonely week ahead and the dark months of winter. But it's a family tradition to join our friends Bill and Melanie, Serbian Orthodox Christians who observe Christmas today, so I bundled up the children and headed to their Victorian farmhouse in rural Williamston, Michigan.

Driving there, I remembered our evening together last year. Alex, as the first male guest to arrive, represented the Christ Child and scattered wheat, nuts, and coins in the four corners of the room, wishing the family good health and prosperity. Later we talked by the fire, sipping hot spiced cider.

This year the house bustled with people I didn't know—farmer neighbors and university students from former Yugoslavia. After helping in the kitchen, supervising the kids sliding down the banister of the grand staircase, and catching snatches of conversations, I felt frazzled by the time dinner was served.

As we gathered around the "manger"—the long mahogany dining-room table with straw scattered underneath—quiet descended. Melanie lit a candle, symbolizing the coming of the light of the world. We sang a beautiful old hymn, first in Serbian, then in English, proclaiming the glory of Christ's Nativity. Listening to the young man next to me heartily singing, I no longer heard a thick-accented immigrant, but my brother in Christ.

Passing around a common cup, each person said to the next, "Peace from God. Christ is born." As we gently spoke those words, the Prince of Peace Himself seemed present with us.

Later, as I drove slowly home, I no longer dreaded the days ahead. The message echoed softly in my heart: "Peace from God. Christ is born."

*O Lord, how quickly I forget You! Please help me continue
to rejoice in Your coming, to see You among us and find Your peace
within me each day this year.*
—MARY BROWN

"You are my lamp, O Lord; the Lord turns my darkness into light."
—2 SAMUEL 22:29

Last year I worked hard to rid myself of a bad habit—gossip. I decided that I'd try to measure my speech by the old rule of "Is it true? Is it necessary? Is it kind?" Although it took a lot of prayer to keep my lips clamped together, I discovered a certain peace in my relationships that wasn't there before.

Then one cold winter morning I felt a chill in the office that had nothing to do with the weather. *Maybe I'm imagining it*, I thought. I ignored it for a week, but by the eighth day I knew that I had to approach my coworker Mary. *God, I prayed, give me the guts to talk with her directly.* "Is something wrong?" I ventured. "I noticed you've been chilly toward me."

"I heard that you said I wouldn't be a good manager because I had no brains," she said.

"What?" I couldn't believe that such an ugly rumor had gone around, especially since I'd been so good about not gossiping. "I never said anything of the sort—" and then I stopped, remembering. "I said promoting you to management would be a no-brainer!"

Mary and I both had a good laugh over that one, and I realized that eight days of coldness, hurt feelings, and worry could have been avoided with one straightforward discussion. But at least I had my new personal resolution for the new year cut out for me: Don't let things fester. If something seems wrong, speak up.

God, with Your help, let me courageously face whatever I'm afraid of.
—LINDA NEUKRUG

To every thing there is a season...a time to keep, and a time to cast away.
—ECCLESIASTES 3:1, 6 (KJV)

The day that I always wish would never come has arrived. I am "downloading" the Christmas tree. I love putting the decorations on, and I loathe taking them off. But the sanitation service will only collect trees through this week. That means I have a deadline.

An empty box sits on the floor, waiting to hold the ornaments until next season. First, there's my angel collection. One perches on a red ceramic heart that bears my name. My friend Mary sent it the year I moved away. The handblown indigo glass angel with translucent wings came from our daughter Kelly on the last Christmas before she married. My friend Cathy from Montana sent the felt cowgirl angel. The frowning, yellow-painted wooden one was purchased by another friend Mary, who saw me admiring it in an airport gift shop. Mary died just two months ago.

Then there is a cheerful alpine fellow whom Mom brought back from a trip to Germany. The white-threaded alpaca wearing a woven blanket is from Janet, who owns an alpaca farm. A smiling, rosy-cheeked boy wrapped in a knitted muffler and cap stood on our son Phil's twelfth birthday cake. It has a trace of frosting still stuck to its foot. Our daughter Brenda gave me the pink porcelain fairy rising from a flower after competing at Disney World with her high-school cheerleading team.

Each ornament tells a story; many bring to mind someone dear to us who is no longer nearby. Maybe that's why I'm sad when it's time to take down the tree: I feel like I'm packing away my family and friends. I'm a lingerer, but even a lingerer must move ahead. If I don't, I'll have no new ornaments to add to my tree, no new stories, no new friends.

Okay, Lord, now that I'm done talking about taking down the Christmas tree, help me to quit dawdling and go do it! New possibilities await!
—CAROL KNAPP

January 10

Listen! The Lord is calling to the city.
—Micah 6:9 (niv)

I've never considered the incessant ringing of bells throughout my day a blessing, but I've recently learned otherwise. Not long ago I was having lunch with friends at a family-style restaurant when the phone—mounted on a post right behind my head—rang. It rang again. And again. Then, across the room, a cell phone rang. Then a beeper sounded at the next table.

"Would you ever have thought we'd have to live with so much ringing?" my friend Kathy asked.

"And that bells ringing could be so annoying?" I said. Just then Kathy's watch alarm began beeping. We all burst out laughing.

The next day, when our bell choir played in church, the bulletin carried a brief history of church bells. Centuries ago, monks attracted a gathering by ringing bells, calling the people to worship. By the eighteenth century, some clergy referred to bells as "messengers of God," and inscribed on them *Vox Domini*, Voice of the Lord, as though their glorious sound were God's own voice calling the people to Him.

Though I wouldn't go so far as to call the ringing of a cell phone glorious (although I do like the ones that play Mozart), all that ringing carries a different message for me now. When I hear a bell ring, I pause for a moment and think of *Vox Domini*, the Voice of the Lord, calling me to remember Him throughout the day.

While it's good to silence the phone when I need to be alone with God, much of the day I can't escape the ringing. So now I've made it a reminder that no day is so busy that I can't stop to praise God and thank Him for His daily blessings upon me.

Dear God, fill my day with small reminders that You are the Lord of all things.
—Gina Bridgeman

The Lord was my support. He brought me out into a spacious place.
—PSALM 18:18–19 (NIV)

I t seemed to be taking a while for my son to take his first steps. A fast crawler, Solomon had turned into a leaner, walking in endless circles around the coffee table, holding my hand, and keeping a pinky on the table. It was obvious that he could carry his own weight; the only thing holding him back was uncertainty about his footing. He still needed someone to lean on.

We were at my mom's for brunch one cold January morning when Solomon leaned on a chair and picked up his boots. A small snow boot in each hand, he stood up, and in a moment took his first solo step toward me. "One, two, three," a roomful of my relatives whispered along with me as Solomon made it across the living room rug. In eight steps, he reached me and put his boot in my lap, unaware that he had let go of the chair. For the next few days, Solomon walked—but only with his hands full and outstretched, as if the things he held gave him grounding.

Solomon had found his balance, but I know he still had Someone to lean on, holding those boots, leading him step by step.

Lord, thank You for being there to lean on
when I launch out into the unknown.
—SABRA CIANCANELLI

"Let them construct a sanctuary for Me, that I may dwell among them."
—EXODUS 25:8 (NASBB)

*Y*ears ago, a newcomer arrived at our church in Stone Mountain, Georgia. Dawn smiled a lot and was more excited about prayer than anyone I'd ever known. One day she told my friend Joann and me, "I believe God wants the three of us—with help—to erect a small prayer chapel here at the church. Let's pray about it." A few weeks later, Dawn said, "I believe God's spoken to me. The prayer chapel is to be an old log cabin. He'll show it to us, and then we'll move it here."

The three of us looked everywhere for a log cabin. Then one day Dawn drove Joann and me down a red dirt road we'd traveled countless times before in our search. Suddenly, she stopped in front of an old two-story pink-shingled house that leaned to the left and was nearly covered in vines. She ran to the house as though it were an old friend. Joann and I followed politely. Dawn pulled off a few shingles and exclaimed, through laughter and tears, "Look! Here's our log cabin!"

Dawn located the owners—a huge company in another state—and they decided to donate the building to our church. "We'll haul it log by log and reconstruct it at the church," Dawn explained. She prayed some more, and found an expert in reconstructing log buildings. He lived out of state, but he accepted Dawn's enthusiastic invitation to donate his time.

It took months, of course, to reconstruct the house. But the three of us were so eager to pray in this new shelter—an answer to prayer—that we met there one wintry Wednesday morning. The roof wasn't on yet, and it snowed on us as we prayed together, huddled close to one another for warmth.

Father, teach me again how to seek Your will in prayer.
—MARION BOND WEST

I will restore health unto thee.
—JEREMIAH 30:17 (KJV)

Last year my agency began a staff wellness program. Each participant agreed to do three things: increase the daily number of footsteps walked by five hundred to one thousand; eat four to six fruits and vegetables per day; and meet one personal health goal. My personal goal was to take forty-five thousand footsteps per week.

I ate a healthy diet and walked on my treadmill nearly every day. So I was shocked (and embarrassed) when I reviewed my first two weeks on the program: I hadn't met my steps goal. And one day the only vegetable I ate was french fries.

Fortunately, our wellness coordinator, Pilar, helped me spot the problem: travel habits. At home I was fine, but when I traveled I ate mainly fast food and walked less than a third of my target amount. Pilar shared three tips that helped me establish and maintain good health habits at home and on the road:

1. Give the program thirty days of real effort. According to experts, that's the minimum time required to change eating and exercise patterns.

2. Write it down. Writing down what I ate and the number of steps according to my pedometer provided argument-proof data—and an incentive to walk into a restaurant and eat a salad instead of gobbling a burger while I drove.

3. Keep on keeping on. I still travel a lot, and there are days when I don't meet my goals. But I've learned to forgive myself and get right back on the program.

At year's end I'd met my goals more than 90 percent of the time. My physical and mental health improved. This year I've set a higher goal: ten thousand steps per day, the surgeon general's recommendation for healthy men and women.

Divine Teacher and Healer, guide me as I seek
wholeness and wellness in every area of my life.
—PENNEY SCHWAB

"You are the God who sees me."
—Genesis 16:13

Our college-age son Jeff received a new gadget for Christmas, a small camera to attach to his computer so he could broadcast live shots of his dorm room on his web site. One January evening my husband Gordon beckoned me to the computer to see this new technological marvel—a live look at Jeff's room nearly three hundred miles away. The first shot showed Jeff's head in the foreground. In the background, a pair of legs extended from the top bunk and rested on a chest of drawers nearby. In the second shot, the legs were standing on the chest of drawers.

Gordon immediately telephoned Jeff. His roommate Paul answered. "This is the World Wide Web furniture police," Gordon teased. "We've seen you standing on the furniture."

There was a long, startled silence, followed by a meek, "Yes, sir?"

"Just kidding," Gordon replied. "This is Jeff's dad."

Apparently Paul didn't remember the new webcam. "Oh. Are you here looking in our window?"

The next time we visited Jeff's dorm room, I noticed a piece of tape on the carpet that said, "Now entering webcam zone. Be careful!"

It's easy to forget that, wherever I am, Someone is watching me. No matter how careful I am to keep up appearances, God always sees deep down inside my heart. And even in my darkest, loneliest moments, God is there, watching me with loving eyes. Sometimes it takes a newfangled gadget to remind me of an age-old truth.

Dear God, help me always to remember that
You see me better than I can see myself.
—Karen Barber

Here there is no...slave or free, but Christ is all, and is in all.
—COLOSSIANS 3:11

My nine-year-old John ordered a paperback from the school book club titled *I Have a Dream—Dr. Martin Luther King Jr.* I was quite surprised when the book arrived to find that it was not a book about Dr. King, but an illustrated edition of the actual text of his most famous speech. I had been John's age myself when this historic speech was delivered.

As John and I looked through the book together, we came to a picture of a white mob pouring ketchup on the heads of African-Americans seated at a lunch counter. John had many questions, and I had to admit the sad truth about our society's history of race relations. *What faith Dr. King must have had to believe that such monumental changes were possible*, I thought.

Then I read aloud a simple yet moving paragraph from the speech: "I have a dream that one day on the red hills of Georgia, the sons of former slaves and the sons of former slave owners will be able to sit down together at the table of brotherhood."

A shiver went down my spine as the words hit me like a prophecy fulfilled in my own life. We lived in the red clay hills of Georgia, and as difficult as it was to admit it, some of my ancestors had owned slaves. Yet Dr. King's dream had become a reality every time my family had sat down around our turn-of-the-century mahogany dining room table to share a meal with African-American friends, coworkers, and neighbors.

Finally I understood something of Dr. King's faith. Yes, he worked hard for new laws to bring about justice and change, but he also knew that the laws of the heart are the ones that revolutionize the world. Even monumental changes start small—one dining room table at a time.

Father, remake our life together in the image of Your love for us,
one heart at a time—beginning with mine.
—KAREN BARBER

*In returning and rest shall ye be saved; in quietness
and in confidence shall be your strength.*
—ISAIAH 30:15 (KJV)

had been away from the office for some weeks due to illness, and when I returned to work I was full of the anxieties typical of editors. Did those proofs get sent out in time? Was this freelancer doing a good job on the art for that project? Is editor X on top of project Y? In and out of different offices I trotted, asking questions, worrying about the answers, feeling that I would never catch up with all that I had missed, feeling sure we were headed for some kind of corporate train wreck.

Finally, on my third day back, I flopped down exhausted in the office of my colleague Elizabeth and asked, "What am I missing? I'll never get this all straight. What do I need to make sure all this gets done on schedule? How can I get that report for the board done by Friday?"

She was silent for a moment, looking as though she were reluctant to answer my barrage of questions. Finally, she said slowly, "Well, there are two things that would help."

"Great," I said. "What are they? I'll get right on it." I stood up, almost ready to run out of her office before I had the magic recipe.

"Patience and trust," said Elizabeth quietly. "I think they are what you need right now."

I gulped and sat down again. As her words sank in, I realized that all the staff had been working hard and conscientiously in my absence. My questions were just taking up their valuable time, making them feel second-guessed. And I realized, too, that impatience, my old enemy, had crept up on me as I lay unable to work and now was busy upsetting everybody, including me.

"Thanks," I said, and I went to sit in my own office repeating to myself silently, *Patience and trust. Patience and trust.*

Lord, teach me to trust others and to approach every situation with patience.
—BRIGITTE WEEKS

*Now He was telling them a parable to show that at all times
they ought to pray and not to lose heart.*
—Luke 18:1 (NASBB)

Time to give up praying," I told myself sadly. My prayers were for someone I loved very much. But after ten years, they were still unanswered.

Later that afternoon, a letter to the editor in the local paper caught my eye. "Time to take down the 'Annie Lost Dog' posters. Annie is back home!" Overjoyed, I could hardly believe the amazing news. I'd prayed for Annie for nearly a year because her stubborn owner refused to take his ad out of the paper. The ad explained that Annie was very shy and lost in unfamiliar surroundings. The owner seemed quite desperate. He'd been visiting his daughter in Athens, Georgia, when Annie ran away.

A few days later a full-length story ran in the *Athens Banner-Herald* with a picture of the black Labrador-retriever mix and her happy owner, who said he simply refused to believe his dog wouldn't be found. He'd returned to Athens on weekends, walking the streets calling "Annie" late into the night and sitting outside his daughter's home in thirteen-degree weather hoping to get a glimpse of his pet. When the daughter begged her father to relinquish his hope of finding the dog and begin the grieving process, he intensified his prayers.

Ten full months after her disappearance, Annie was discovered, still wearing her identification tags, twenty-five miles from Athens.

"I especially want to encourage others who have lost pets not to give up hope," Annie's ecstatic owner said.

The last five words seemed to leap off the newspaper and land right in my heart. Laying the paper aside, I resumed my ten-year prayer.

*Father, I praise You for caring about fallen sparrows,
lost dogs, and sons who've gone astray.*
—Marion Bond West

Give unto the Lord the glory due unto his name;
worship the Lord in the beauty of holiness.
—PSALM 29:2 (KJV)

Remember," our pastor said as he concluded the sermon, "worship is every bit as important to your spiritual well-being as breathing is to your physical health."

While he gave the closing prayer, I checked to see that the music for the postlude was in place and mentally reviewed the introduction to the last hymn. As I played the organ, a familiar feeling of guilt accompanied every note. I had a secret: Although I attended church every Sunday, I didn't worship. I was too busy concentrating on the details of the service.

I hope no one remembers I played the same prelude last month. Will the offertory be long enough? Should I slow down on the last verse of the hymn? I enjoyed the Christian fellowship with my friends and neighbors, was inspired and challenged by the sermons, and missing church left a hole in my week. But I didn't worship while I was there.

Finally, I confessed my feelings to an older friend who was a professional musician as well as a church organist. Her response was not what I expected. "Why do you think it's called the worship service?" she asked. "Because for many of us—the pastor, the acolytes, the musicians—it's definitely a time to serve. We worship through our work, too, you know. Still, it's important to find times when you're free of responsibility and can give your whole heart to worship."

Her advice helped me relax and let go of the guilt. I began to seek a few nontraditional opportunities for worship: an evangelism event, musical presentations, even an occasional TV service. And a strange thing happened— although most Sunday mornings still find me on the organ bench, and sometimes every head is bowed and every eye closed except mine, there are plenty of times now when heart-worship happens.

Dear Lord, thank You for pastors, musicians, ushers,
nursery workers, and all who worship through service on Sunday.
—PENNEY SCHWAB

He calleth his own sheep by name.
—John 10:3 (kjv)

I found a gift in a grocery sack today. I was putting away the food I'd brought in from the car, checking the items against the cash register receipt. Skim milk, orange juice, Earl Grey tea, carrots... How could three bags of groceries come to $62.07?

That's when I came to my gift—on that white strip of figures from the register. At the bottom of the long column, just below the dismaying total, I read: "Valued Customer 43220884464."

I gaped at the 11-digit figure. Was I really valued customer 43,220,884,464? Truly valued, as the receipt claimed, among so many?

It's a question I remember asking, many years ago, of God. In a universe with billions of galaxies, on a planet with billions of people, could He possibly care about me?

Staring at the register receipt, I recalled His answer. *I do not count My children,* He seemed to say, *I name them.* It was a new thought to me—the importance of names, all through the Bible. How genuinely valued a name makes us! To my heavenly Father I am not a number, but an individual. Not Valued Child 873972491, but Elizabeth. Known by name, called by name, written by His own hand in the Book of Life.

I'm so grateful, Father, that You count not in billions, but one by one.
—Elizabeth Sherrill

JANUARY 20

He hath made every thing beautiful in his time.
—ECCLESIASTES 3:11 (KJV)

*T*he scale didn't lie. Holiday indiscretions—the Christmas cookies, the fudge, a candy cane or two (or ten)—piled upon years of self-indulgence had pushed my weight well over what the optimistic height/weight charts recommended. Time and gravity had also begun their dirty work: wrinkles and ripples surfaced where there had been none five years before.

My gray mood matched that January morning as I set off to cover my beat as a reporter for the *Wyoming State Journal*. Today I was scheduled to cover an appearance of Miss Wyoming at a local elementary school. From the press release, I knew that she would perform on the piano and speak to the children about resisting drugs. I would be sure to recognize her by her slim figure, brunette curls, and trademark tiara.

Arriving at the school a little early, I snapped the top fastener on my bulky parka and pulled my woolly hat low over my ears for better protection from the bitter chill. The kindergartners were lined up by the front door. I hesitated for a moment, trying to determine whether the children formed a welcoming committee for the beauty queen or were simply waiting to go inside. Suddenly a little girl broke rank, clasped me around my legs, and arched her back, the better to smile into my startled face.

"Are you Miss Wyoming?" she inquired sweetly. I nearly dropped my camera bag.

"No, honey, I'm from the newspaper."

"Oh." She continued hugging me and smiling until her teacher shepherded her back into line.

That afternoon, I couldn't help but smile—and I walked a little taller as I completed my assignment.

Lord, thank You for the people who see past the physical wear
and tear and help me to rejoice in my true beauty.
—GAIL THORELL SCHILLING

January 21

So God created man in his own image.
—Genesis 1:27 (KJV)

*T*he snow started Wednesday afternoon and didn't stop for forty-eight hours.

The storm was widespread. On Thursday my husband phoned from Chicago to say O'Hare International was closed and he wouldn't try to get back before going on to Phoenix. Snowbound and alone, I reminded myself how much I had to be grateful for: plenty of food on hand; phone and electrical lines intact; warmth and dryness while a blizzard raged outside.

Sunday morning dawned dazzlingly bright on a pristine white world. And oddly, this was the hardest day of all. Church services were canceled—I couldn't have gotten out of my driveway anyway—and the feeling of isolation was like an ache. *Where are You, God?* I prayed. I told myself not to be silly. God was just as near to me here at home as He is when I'm in church. Why did He seem so far away?

The road crews were slow to reach our street. It was already dark on Monday afternoon when our plow service got through and cleared the driveway. Cabin fever propelled me into the car and through streets tunneled between six-foot white walls. The grocery store parking lot was jammed, the lines at the check-out counters twenty carts long.

I pushed my own cart down a crowded aisle; I didn't care which one. I wasn't looking at the shelves; I was looking at people. A woman's face framed in a blue scarf. A man's face, ruddy beneath his woolen cap. I was listening to voices: "....shovel a path to the bird feeder." I was watching gestures. A mother lifting a child from a cart, a teenage clerk loading shelves.

I was seeing God.

God in every face, every voice, every action. God in the people I so seldom really look at, whose glory it had taken a snowstorm and five housebound days to show me.

Show me Yourself, Lord, in Your human likeness.
—Elizabeth Sherrill

*King David said…"I will not take for the Lord what is yours,
nor offer burnt offerings which cost me nothing."*
—1 CHRONICLES 21:24 (RSV)

Recently I brought several casseroles over to church to be stored in the refrigerator for that evening's fellowship dinner. When I opened the appliance's door, I recognized "The Church Refrigerator." No matter what the denomination, it's always the same.

Every church refrigerator contains a bottle of Welch's grape juice, five bottles of partially used salad dressing (three without labels), two nearly empty jugs of Kool-Aid, a jar half-full of pickle juice with a couple of slices swimming in it, a dried piece of cake, and several plastic containers of something no longer identifiable. In the freezer section, there are three ice trays (two empty) and a carton of Neapolitan ice cream, sagging because the appliance had already seen its best days before it was donated, probably as a tax deduction.

When I turned to a nearby closet to store the cardboard box I'd carried the casseroles in, I recognized "The Church Missionary Barrel." I didn't paw through it, but I assumed that it contained items that their previous owners claimed "still have some good in them."

It was then that I recalled the Old Testament verse in which King David refused to offer something that cost him nothing to give to a holy, loving God.

*Father, help me always to remember that what I give in Your name
is being given to You, not merely to "someone less fortunate."*
—ISABEL WOLSELEY

Pride goes before destruction, and a haughty spirit before a fall.
—PROVERBS 16:18 (RSV)

I was still in college when I married a serviceman. I hadn't yet met his family, and because I'd heard stories about the in-law problems of other army wives, I was plenty apprehensive about meeting mine.

After my husband's discharge, we'd settled into our own home for a month or so when my mother-in-law phoned. "I've invited the relatives to Sunday dinner so you can meet them all," she said.

"How nice," I politely answered, then stunned myself by adding, "I'll bake a cake to bring for dessert."

I say stunned because my kitchen experience was nil—we'd lived in room-and-board army quarters all our married life. But I'd spotted a recipe on a sugar sack that said, "Impress guests with this elegant cake." *How hard can it be to measure ingredients?* I thought.

Well, I was so busy concentrating on how impressed my mother-in-law and all the guests would be with my cake that I unknowingly turned the sack and finished the second half of the recipe before I had finished the first half, printed in a comparable spot on its opposite side.

When I pulled the cake from the oven an hour later, its top looked like a mini-mountain range. What'll I do now? Then I had an idea: frosting will cover the flaws.

It worked. At least it did until dessert time, when we discovered the cake's center had collapsed. There was stunned silence at the table...until someone giggled, precipitating a chain reaction, with me joining in.

True enough, pride goes before a fall, but laughter is the best medicine. And laughter was the surest sign that I was an accepted member of my in-laws' clan.

Give me the ability, Lord, always to laugh at myself.
—ISABEL WOLSELEY

The people read it and were glad for its encouraging message.
—Acts 15:31

*T*was waiting anxiously at the repair shop while a mechanic checked out my car. The estimate for repairs I'd received from another mechanic was more than nine hundred dollars. It was more than I could afford, so I was getting a second opinion.

But how would I know this mechanic was telling the truth? I was clueless when it came to cars. *God, please guide me*, I prayed.

I tossed aside the magazine I'd been reading and scanned the bulletin board directly in front of me. One small note caught my attention. "Dear manager," it read, "thanks to your mechanic Jim, my 1978 Nova is in excellent running order once more." My heart did a double take. Jim was at this very moment looking at my car! With peaked interest, I continued to read. "I appreciate that Jim is not interested in involving me in needless repairs. He does only what's essential for the efficient operation of my car." It was signed, "Ed, a grateful customer." I had seen Ed's signature in our local newspaper at the end of many letters to the editor. He was an octogenarian whose judgment I respected.

When Jim returned to give me his verdict on my ailing car, I met him with a confident smile. Thanks to Ed's note, I knew I could count on Jim to tell me the truth and to give me a fair price.

What a beautiful service Ed did for me, I mused. *I must tell him.* At home I wrote a thank-you for his thank-you note. In a few days his wife phoned me. "You have no idea how your note encouraged my husband," she said. "He so often feels that his days of service are over."

As long as we're here, there's always something we can do.

Father, help me to be alert to people who need a word of encouragement today.
—Helen Grace Lescheid

JANUARY 25

Let the children come to me...because the
Kingdom of heaven belongs to such as these.
—MATTHEW 19:14 (GNT)

All New England was prepared for the "Blizzard of the Century." Technically, so was I. I'd bought groceries, waxed the shovel, gassed the car, posted mail, and taken out the garbage. I was safely ensconced like everyone else in the region, fortified against the onslaught.

My emotions were a different story. There are no pre-blizzard grocery runs to stock up on faith and cheer. The snow this season had started before Thanksgiving and continued through Christmas. It seemed appropriate during the holidays. With Christmas two weeks past, this storm was different. Starting on Sunday, the snow continued falling through the night and into the next day. When it finally ended Monday night, snow filled the streets, sidewalks, and yards, transforming even the darkness with an eerie glow. And it filled me as well, numbing my mind and quenching my spirit.

Sleepless, I wandered to my window. It faced a parking lot, uncharacteristically empty for the past forty-eight hours except for maintenance trucks. At 4:00 a.m., they'd been plowing now for nearly two full days. Two trucks plowed endless rows in a seemingly impossible task. The monotony was hypnotizing, further deadening already paralyzed senses as I continued watching.

Suddenly, both vehicles swung dramatically around to face each other. Simultaneously, their bright lights beamed on. In one concerted movement, they began to whirl around like dervishes in tight, wild circles in the snow. I felt an incredulous spark that grew into delight, until I heard myself laughing aloud at their antics. The two weary, dispirited drivers had become children on a joyous ride. For ten minutes they kept it up, until I was dizzy with laughter.

I finally fell asleep, knowing that God had been there all the time, smiling, and just waiting for me to notice Him and smile back.

Lord, help me to gaze on Your world with childlike delight.
—MARCI ALBORGHETTI

And God saw every thing that he had made, and, behold, it was very good.
—GENESIS 1:31 (KJV)

My husband David and I were nervous as we set up our easels and laid out our supplies for our first-ever painting class. "How can someone who can't draw a straight line or a round circle expect to paint something like this?" I whispered to him as we studied the paintings our teacher, John Knox, had brought to share with us.

"Now, I want you all to cover your entire canvas with a thin coating of red paint," John said.

Red paint! Paint my lovely new canvas red? I don't even like red.

"This will be the undercoating of your first work," John explained to the class. Soon David's canvas was a bright red, and my canvas was a deep pink. "Great," John said as he walked by.

"John, I just don't get it," I shot back. "How in the world does this mess of hot-pink paint have anything at all to do with the pear we're supposed to be painting?"

"I was just getting around to that, Pam," he said. John went on to explain that these varying shades of red would underpin the rest of our painting. It would strengthen lines, creep out of cracks, show through thinner paints and bring energy to our finished work. "When your painting's done, you might forget about this red undercoating, but it will be there, breathing underneath everything you put on the canvas."

The background of my painting turned out to be yellow, but John's predictions were true. Somehow the red really did give life to all that came after.

Not so different, I thought to myself, from God's plan for us. In the beginning, He undercoated His creation with good. No matter what gets brushed or poured or splattered across the canvas of our life, God's good is always there, ready to shine through. Reason enough to live our lives in bright joy!

Father, everything You make is good. Let me look for the pattern of Your goodness in all the happenings of my life.
—PAM KIDD

January 27

Is not my word like as a fire? saith the Lord.
—Jeremiah 23:29 (KJV)

One blustery, icy day, unable to escape the piles of paper on my desk any longer, I sat down to work—sorting mail, paying bills, catching up on correspondence. Next to me was a warm crackling fire. Several times I felt like quitting, but as I stirred the coals, my mind cleared and I tackled the next pile. Halfway into the afternoon, the fire appeared to be completely out. I added kindling, then blew till the ash-covered coals flamed again. When I brought in a couple of logs from outdoors, I was rewarded with a roaring fire for my last batch of letters.

The next morning I picked up the stack of envelopes to take to the post office. Seeing the empty fireplace, I fondly remembered the warmth it had provided, as constant and comforting as God's love. *I wish I could experience God's presence with me today like that warm fire*, I thought, but I would be in and out of the car, running errands, going to work.

An idea came. I sat down, still clutching the pile of envelopes, and before I headed out I took a little time to read Scripture. My spiritual fire was built. Then in order to have some "fuel" with me, I grabbed an index card and jotted down a few verses from the day's reading: Rejoice always, pray constantly, give thanks in all circumstances (1 Thessalonians 5:16–18, RSV). I set that card on the dashboard. At the post office a man hobbled by with a cane, and the card inspired me to pray for him and for other people I encountered during the day. As I dealt with the demands of work and family, God's Word kept me aglow.

Dear God, thank You for the comforting fire of Your presence.
During my tasks today, rekindle my awareness of You.
—Mary Brown

JANUARY 28

This is the Lord's doing; it is marvellous in our eyes.
—PSALM 118:23 (KJV)

As I write this, a soft, white snow is falling on eastern North Carolina. Here along the coast in Richlands, we seldom see snow. It's an unusual event, one we are ill-equipped to handle. We have no plows to clear the roads and no chains for our tires—and we Southerners are notoriously poor drivers in the snow. So the area schools close, and most of the businesses, too, and we find ourselves with the unexpected gift of a day at home.

In my excitement over this unusual turn of events, I'll keep the phone lines busy, calling friends and neighbors, sharing my joy and amazement at having been caught unaware by the beauty of it all. I don't have boots or proper clothes for snow, but that won't keep me indoors. With old socks on my hands and plastic bags over my sneakers, I'll take advantage of the chance to build a snowman in the yard. Later, as the gray day fades into darkness, I'll scoop clean snow from the tops of cars, stir it together with eggs, sugar, and cream, and eat it by the warmth of the fire. I'll savor every mouthful of the special homemade concoction, even though my head will throb with the chill of it.

It won't last long, this snow. It will probably melt by morning, and we'll go back to business as usual. But today, this unexpected gift of a day, I'll play—and give thanks. Maybe that's what God had in mind when He sent it.

My heart overflows with gratitude, Father, when I remember all the unexpected gifts You've sent my way. May I never take them for granted.
—LIBBIE ADAMS

January 29

That our daughters may be as corner stones,
polished after the similitude of a palace.
—Psalm 144:12 (KJV)

easonal affective disorder: SAD. Every year I think I'll escape it, yet every autumn it ambushes me. My energy level drops as the days shorten. After work I slink home to flop on the couch, snooze, and nibble snacks I don't need until the trees bud once again.

Last year I felt more discouraged than ever, facing SAD along with an empty nest—my first autumn alone in thirty-three years. By January I had moved out of the woods to a town twenty times larger, with dozens of opportunities to motivate me. But the first week in my quaint but drafty and echoing one-hundred-year-old apartment, the temperature plunged to twenty-five degrees below zero. With no rugs or drapes to insulate against the cold, gasping radiators made little difference. Alone, cold, and new to town, I spent my first few evenings in my new home wrapped in a blanket, weeping. It was only January. How could I last until spring?

My daughter Tess noticed that I needed a lift and arrived with five-year-old Hannah for a weekend. Tess rearranged the living room furniture and added brick-red pillows and a small bright rug to match. After cooking grilled cheese sandwiches and soup, she popped in a silly Muppets video as all three of us snuggled under a blanket on the sofa. Once Hannah was asleep, Tess and I shared tea and confidences. That night I slept soundly and woke cheerfully, knowing that I had precious company in my chilly new home.

Later, as Tess and I hugged good-bye, I thanked her for taking care of me. "Mom," she assured me, "you know I always will." Winter would last another three months, but my daughter's love would last forever.

Thank You, Lord, for the blessing of children.
—Gail Thorell Schilling

January 30

*[Jesus] gave them power...to heal all manner of sickness
and all manner of disease.*
—Matthew 10:1 (KJV)

The feeble line etched by the fetal monitor told the grim story: the baby wasn't doing well. As first-time childbirth coach for my daughter Tess, in labor with her first child, I sensed a growing uneasiness in the hospital room.

Normally chipper Nurse Leah wasn't smiling. "We'd like to see more baby activity," she explained. Every few minutes she would check the monitor, then slip out to the nurses' station to phone the doctor.

We had met Dr. Culwell, the obstetrician on call, only once. Trim, white-haired, slow-talking, he had seemed pleasant enough during our brief office visit. But could he handle what was fast becoming an emergency?

The doctor strode into Tess's room, chatted calmly, checked the fetal monitor, and quickly made his decision. "We need to do a Caesarean section so we don't compromise this baby. She might have trouble with ten or twelve more hours of labor."

Major surgery and we don't even know this guy!

As the nurses began to prepare Tess for the operating room, Dr. Culwell confided to me on his way out the door, "I started praying about this at home."

"You're the man for us!" I said. My tension melted away.

A few minutes later, I held Tess's hand in the operating room. Suddenly, our praying doctor whisked a tiny baby the color of cement through the air to the warming table. As the pediatrician deftly suctioned her, she began to turn pink as a sunrise. Her throaty wail assured us all was well.

The next day as Tess snuggled her tiny Hannah, I met Dr. Culwell in the hall. "I don't know how to thank you," I said haltingly.

"Oh, it wasn't just me," he drawled, looking heavenward with a grin. "I had a lot of help."

*Merciful Father, thank You for skilled professionals
who humbly put their trust in You.*
—Gail Thorell Schilling

Will what is molded say to its molder, "Why have you made me thus?"
—Romans 9:20 (RSV)

While waiting for my son Ross at the library, I picked up a book and started reading about James Naismith. In the 1880s, he spent three years in a seminary but never became a pastor. He earned a medical degree but never practiced. As a teacher at the YMCA Training School in Springfield, Massachusetts, he invented a game he hoped would hold his students' interest in the gym during the long winter months. With a soccer ball and a couple of peach baskets nailed to the balcony above the hardwood floor, Dr. Naismith invented basketball and changed the world of sports.

I'm intrigued by his story for a couple of reasons. One, he didn't become what he set out to be. His life moved in an entirely different direction from what he had planned. I can't help but think of the direction my own life has taken. I'm not starring in a Broadway musical or hosting a morning talk show. Those were dreams of mine at one time as I studied singing and then later began a career in TV news. But God led me in other directions. Some days I wonder what might have been, but I can't say I'm disappointed. God knew that marriage and children were in my dreams, too, and those have come true beautifully. Now my stage is the church's fellowship hall, and I host some lively Cub Scout meetings.

Still, as I'm midway along life's adventure, I'm trying to imagine where God's plan for me is headed. That's where the second and even more intriguing aspect of Dr. Naismith's story comes to mind. When "The Father of Basketball" died in 1939 at age seventy-eight, he had no idea what he had created. The game's phenomenal appeal was still decades away. Like Dr. Naismith, I may never know how what I've done on earth reaches into the future, but God does. On days when I can't see beyond the end of my driveway, I'm comforted by this: God knows well the road I'm on because He set me on it, and He knows where I'm heading because He's leading me there.

God, light my way along Your path so that all I do leads me toward the destination You have in mind.

—Gina Bridgeman

February

February 1

The God of hope fill you with all joy and peace in believing.
—Romans 15:13 (KJV)

The road ahead was dark and deserted. My car's wipers whined as they pushed a mixture of snow and ice back and forth across the windshield. I grasped the steering wheel with white knuckles and prayed silently. My daughter Keri and I were driving toward Birmingham, Alabama, where she was to participate in a scholarship competition the next morning. Winter storms are an oddity in the South, and I was terrified. I didn't want Keri to know.

She sat silently beside me, eyes straight ahead.

"If you want, you can turn on the radio," I said. Static followed, then a jumble of voices and music, and finally Elton John filled the car with a love song.

My heart melted, thinking of the child beside me. Then, in the midst of my anguished prayers for all the dark unknowns, the presence of God filled my heart with a confident knowing. "Keri," I said, "someday we'll remember this moment and everything I'm about to say will already be true. You are going to get a good scholarship. You are going to excel in college. Someone very wonderful is going to fall in love with you, and all the scattered, confusing pieces of your life will fit perfectly together. I know this because God has put it in my heart to say this to you.

"Someday we'll be dancing at your wedding, and we'll remember this night, and we'll laugh with happiness. Who knows? I might even get Elton John to sing this very song as you walk out onto the floor for the first dance!"

Five years later, I pick up the phone. Keri gives me a glowing report of her first class in graduate school. She speaks of the teenage girls she will be counseling and offers an update on her boyfriend, who attends another graduate school nearby. "Mama, have you written to Elton John yet?" she says with a chuckle. And with those words she tells me everything a mother needs to know.

Dear God, in my scariest moments, You point me to the place where, in Your time, You fit the pieces of my life together into a perfect whole. Thank You.
—Pam Kidd

FEBRUARY 2

A light to lighten the Gentiles, and the glory of thy people Israel.
—LUKE 2:32 (KJV)

I'll admit it. I've never looked forward to or enjoyed Groundhog Day. No matter what that groundhog sees when he comes out of his hole, we Wisconsin realists already know that we're going to have at least six more weeks of winter. Probably more like twelve weeks of cold, dreary weather, if the truth be known.

Personally, I like the other holiday that falls on February 2 much better: Candlemas Day. Candlemas commemorates the presentation of the infant Jesus in the temple by Mary and Joseph. As Luke tells the story in his gospel, the old man Simeon, who has been waiting to see the deliverance of Israel, takes the baby in his arms and declares that He is the light of the nations and Israel's glory. Since the eleventh century, candles have been blessed on Candlemas Day in many churches to recall Simeon's words.

In northern Europe, where Candlemas Day is celebrated with gusto, tradition says that dark, snowy skies on February 2 offer hope of a quick end to winter, much like the Groundhog Day tradition in the United States. An old Scottish couplet proclaims:

> If Candlemas is fair and clear,
> There'll be two winters in the year.

But if that happens, at least we'll have the warm, bright light from those candles to give us hope for an early spring and warmer weather.

Today, in my home in Oak Creek, I'm going to light candles on the table at supper time. I'm going to think about how the light of Christ shines bright in our lives no matter what the weather. I'll also dream about springtime and warmer weather and perhaps even plan a few warm-weather vacations. I'll leave Groundhog Day to those folks around the country who truly do have a chance for less than six more weeks of winter.

Heavenly Father, today as I light these candles, help me to spread the light of Your Son Jesus Christ into a few dark corners.
—PATRICIA LORENZ

FEBRUARY 3

Now our Lord Jesus Christ himself...stablish you in every good word and work.
—2 THESSALONIANS 2:16–17 (KJV)

When I visited my daughter Tamara's family in Barrow, Alaska, the spring whaling season was keeping the Eskimo village busy. Subsistence hunting was how many in this town of several thousand bordering the Arctic Ocean survived. Umiaks, small ribbed boats covered in sealskin, sat offshore on the Arctic ice, flying the captain's flag if the crew had been successful.

One cold overcast afternoon, I watched a flurry of activity from Tamara's apartment window. A forty-six-foot bowhead whale had been hauled onto the edge of the ice two miles out. Men and women bundled in parkas were loading supplies on sleds and towing them behind snowmobiles to the site. It would take the village several days to harvest the *muktuk* (blubber) and meat from the whale. I longed to ride with them and see this unusual event, but I felt hesitant.

Tamara knew I wanted to go. Before I could protest, she dragged her arctic gear from the closet, zipped me into it, and pointed me out the door.

I walked to the beach and asked two young men if they had room for me on their sled. They showed me how to sit holding on to the side ropes, and we bumped over the rough trail until the ice ended. Beyond us the blue-gray water stretched to the far horizon. Huge and black against the snow-covered ice lay the whale that would provide food for the villagers.

Later, I hiked back to town with the villagers across the same rough trail—keeping an eye out for polar bears. "I am walking on the Arctic Ocean," I kept telling myself. "This is unbelievable!"

It was an unforgettable experience, and it happened because Tamara thought I could do it. She pushed an undecided me out the door and pointed me in the direction of an amazing adventure.

Thank You, God, for the people in my life who
get me moving in the directions I ought to go.
—CAROL KNAPP

FEBRUARY 4

God is not a man, that he should lie.
—NUMBERS 23:19 (KJV)

One time my husband Keith and I were driving to Yosemite National Park in the late winter. We had reached the town of Fresno, California, when we encountered signs on the sides of the road that chains would be required before we could proceed. We didn't have chains, having driven up from Los Angeles, where snow is nonexistent. So we pulled into the parking lot of an old auto parts warehouse and went in to ask for chains for our VW Bug.

The man behind the counter wore a red plaid flannel shirt, overalls with frayed suspenders, and a huge mustache that hadn't been trimmed recently. When he smiled, he was missing a front tooth. His hands were big and greasy, and he looked like he would be more at home tinkering with a tractor than greeting us.

We told him what we needed, and he turned to the computer terminal on the counter. "Let's see what this thing says," he said. He input his request and then stared at the monitor screen for a long time.

Then he looked up at us. "We just put this in a couple of weeks ago. It says we don't have any of those chains, but you know, I just don't believe it. You folks wait here."

He vanished into the cavernous depths of the warehouse and emerged in a minute with our chains in his hands. "I don't never fall for false prophets," he said with satisfaction.

In this age of high technology, dear God, keep me grateful for the human touch.
—RHODA BLECKER

February 5

How can I repay the Lord for all his goodness to me?
—Psalm 116:12

As I drove to church that January morning, I was still stewing over the financial reports I'd received earlier that week. Seems my 401(k) had seen yet another abysmal quarter. My investments were shrinking faster than a cheap blouse in hot water!

When I walked into church, an usher handed me a white envelope. "Your giving report for last year," he said. I tossed the envelope into my purse and settled into a pew near the back. While I waited for the service to begin, I scanned the bulletin. So much was going on! A Bible study for women was beginning Tuesday night. The teens were holding a fund-raiser for their mission trip next summer. The singles were having a dinner after the morning worship service. Indoor soccer was starting for children ages six to twelve. A new transportation ministry was being formed to serve anyone who needed a ride to church or to doctor appointments.

Music swelled as the choir filed in and the opening anthem began. And as the congregation—many of them visitors and new members—began to sing, I glanced down at the contribution report sticking out of my purse. Not all of my investments had done poorly last year. Some of them had yielded a hundredfold!

Father, in difficult financial times, give me wisdom. And help me never to neglect the surest investment of all—Your kingdom.
—Mary Lou Carney

FEBRUARY 6

Great peace have those who love Your law, and nothing causes them to stumble.
—PSALM 119:165 (NKJV)

*M*y son Chase and I walked away from our townhouse. Neither of us was talking. I was terrified, unsure that I'd done the right thing. My daughter Lanea had said she wanted to be alone. "Please, just leave the house!" she pleaded, a hint of hysteria in her voice.

Earlier that day, Lanea, home on a college break, had gone to the doctor for a checkup. The doctor found a lump in her breast. A mammogram showed a large mass that needed to be removed—immediately, the doctor said. She was only nineteen!

How could this happen to my little girl? Something that I can't fix? Anxious thoughts tripped over each other in my mind. Shutting them out, I said, "It's going to be all right. We just have to trust God."

Lanea's icy voice cut through my optimism. "You don't have to trust anybody," she said. "I'm the one with the lump." We rode home in silence. Now, Chase and I were walking out the door, praying she'd be all right when we got home.

When we did get home, Lanea was smiling. "I just needed to scream at God," she said. "No matter what, I know it's going to be all right." And it was. When Lanea went to the hospital for surgery, she found herself cheering the ministers who came to encourage her.

It's been nine years since her surgery, but Lanea still tells people about the peace God gave her then. She learned to really trust Him, because she had to.

Thank You, Lord, for teaching me to find peace amidst the storms, to find my way even through the shadows.
—SHARON FOSTER

"I, the Lord, have called you in righteousness;
I will take hold of your hand I will keep you."
—ISAIAH 42:6

*D*uring a time of great difficulty in our family, friends continuously encouraged me, "Keep hanging in there. Hold on to God and His promises. He'll see you through." Like a terrified child, I clung to the Lord Jesus, but sometimes I felt my strength was slipping. I wondered how much longer I could hold on to God's hand.

At first, I saw my part-time job as a registered nurse as a good diversion. For eight hours in this other world, my own problems could disappear into the background.

One day after finishing my rounds, I checked on Mr. Jones. He was in the last stages of throat cancer, and he was blind. I found him propped up in bed, struggling for breath. He was starving, yet afraid of the pain of swallowing. I took his thin, veined hand in mine. "Nurse," he croaked in a hoarse whisper, "like you're holding my hand, Jesus is holding on to me."

He motioned to the Bible lying on the bedside table, and I read from the place he had marked. "I, the Lord, have called you in righteousness; I will take hold of your hand. I will keep you."

A flush of joy washed over his face. "Yes! Yes, that's it. He's holding me."

Driving home that night, I thought about Mr. Jones's words. Could anything be worse than what he was living through moment by moment? Yet in his extreme weakness and pain, he'd found peace, strength—even joy. How?

Slowly, it dawned on me: it's not how hard we hang on to God's hand, but how tightly He holds on to ours that counts.

As I contemplated this wonderful fact, peace replaced my panic. No matter what lay in the future, all would be well with me and my children as we are held safe in the hand of almighty God.

Thank You, Father, that when I stumble and fall,
I am upheld by Your loving hand.
—HELEN GRACE LESCHEID

FEBRUARY 8

Judge not, and ye shall not be judged.
—LUKE 6:37 (KJV)

*T*he first time I saw the Lost and Found room at work, I was dumbfounded. I ran my hands through the mounds of stuff, saying, "How can people be so careless?"

There was a huge box containing a Kitchen-Aid mixer attachment, a bottle of spray perfume, seven pairs of gloves and thirteen individual gloves, three unmatched shoes, a baby blanket, seven pacifiers, four stuffed animals, seven pairs of eyeglasses, six pairs of sunglasses, and eleven umbrellas, seven of them black. All we were missing was a partridge in a pear tree.

"I can't believe this!" I insisted. "How can someone lose a shoe in a bookstore? And how can we throw all this stuff out?" I was in fine form, judging people for being careless and us for being wasteful.

"Oh, we don't throw it out," my coworker said, apparently shocked that I should think so. "We give all the glasses to the Lions' Club, we donate the pairs of gloves to the homeless shelter, along with the T-shirts. And the baby stuff always goes to the crisis nursery."

"And what about the umbrellas?" I asked.

"We put a big barrel of them near the front door when it's pouring, and tack a sign on it that says, FREE. TAKE ONE. People are very thankful, believe me."

"I believe you," I said. "I just don't understand how people can be so—"

"What?" he asked, hearing me stop abruptly.

"Nothing," I said quickly, but then admitted, "I just spotted my plaid folding umbrella with the wooden handle. Guess I got so involved in reading the last time I was here that I forgot to take it with me." I gathered some of the baby stuff together. "Here," I said, "let me help you take this batch to the crisis nursery."

Lord, let me look at my own faults before I criticize another today.
—LINDA NEUKRUG

A merry heart maketh a cheerful countenance.
—PROVERBS 15:13 (KJV)

I looked around on that chilly February day at my fellow travelers. It was evening rush hour on the New York City subway. Even making the homeward trip, this is nobody's favorite place to be. The lucky few were seated, and the rest of us clung together like stranded seamen. All around me were frowns heavy with strain. There were circles under a frail woman's eyes, and a large man snored in the corner seat, his hands tightly locked around his backpack. The faces were blank, cut off from the world by earphones or weariness.

I began to wonder where the blessings of the day and the light of the Lord were hiding in this scene. *Where is Norman Vincent Peale when we need him?* I thought ruefully. *This subway car could do with a large dose of positive thinking.*

Then I noticed two women, both I guessed in their thirties, holding on to the same pole, moving with the train as it swayed. They were deep in conversation. I could only hear the odd word: "terrific," "thrilled," "let's go," "then he said...." It was obvious they were friends; their faces lighted up with laughter as they struggled to hear each other through the din.

Their happy, mostly inaudible chatter was strangely contagious. I found myself smiling with affection for two total strangers who brightened the world that day between the 33rd Street and 14th Street stations.

Thank You, Lord, for leading the way to small joys
when the daily routine seems dark.
—BRIGITTE WEEKS

FEBRUARY 10

For God so loved the world that he gave his only Son.
—JOHN 3:16 (RSV)

The first Valentine's card came in the mail today. Because my birthday is on Valentine's Day, I've probably received more than my share of these over the years! When I was growing up, I saved them in a heart-shaped candy box covered in red satin, marveling that there could be so many different rhymes for the same message.

How many ways are there to say "I love you"? I look around and see the footstool with my mother-in-law's needlepoint cushion, the hammered-brass kettle from her home in Holland that Corrie ten Boom brought us on her last visit, the quilt on the wall that family members worked in secret for a year to give us on our fiftieth anniversary.

How many means of expressing love? On the bed upstairs is the green bathrobe made by my friend Mary Lynn Windsor. On the dresser, the photo our friend Sandy LeSourd took of my husband and me in Florida; before sending it, Sandy glued two dozen seashells to the frame.

Since January 1, I've been trying to be more aware of the things around me every day. But the blessings, I realized as I carried the valentine from room to room, are so much more than the physical things themselves! Object after object evoked a face, a voice, a loving hand. Next to the seashell frame on the dresser is a wooden plaque with a single word: Jesus. Of all the ways there are to say love, God chose the One that says it best.

In this month of valentines, Lord, help me find
new ways to speak Your language of love.
—ELIZABETH SHERRILL

I have learned, in whatsoever state I am, therewith to be content.
—PHILIPPIANS 4:11 (KJV)

*D*uring my first year back in New Hampshire, I discovered that with no big sky sun to brighten spirits, winter dragged on and on and on. By mid-February, the lichen on a birch tree offered the only fleck of color in a landscape that ranged from gray to grayer to grayest.

For four months, I had slept in sweat suits and woolen socks in an uninsulated cabin. Everything I wore seemed dark, bulky, or boring. Even a shopping trip to perk up my mood—and wardrobe—seemed out of the question. Much too often, our secluded roads were smothered in snow drifts or glazed by freezing rain; we were housebound for sure. Increasingly crabby and out of sorts, I recognized all the symptoms of cabin fever.

Then I remembered how Kathryn had coped with the same ailment more than twenty years before.

At that time my husband and I ran an appliance repair shop in Wyoming. One wintry afternoon, an elderly widow called us to fix her hot-water heater. Knowing she was alone, we responded the same day, easily locating her small log cabin in deep snow, tucked under creaking cottonwood trees.

As our client's head appeared in the door's small window, I glimpsed her wrinkled cheeks and the white braids wound on top of her head. We must have looked startled, however, when she opened the door wearing an ancient ivory evening gown, high heels, and a gray wool cardigan. She noted our surprise, smoothed her satin skirt, and muttered, by way of explanation, "I get so tired of winter clothes." Without further preamble, she led us to the faulty heater.

Kathryn passed away several years ago, but I still smile when I remember her refusal to cave in to the winter doldrums.

Heavenly Father, forgive me when I focus on what I lack instead of what I have.
—GAIL THORELL SCHILLING

"Is not wisdom found among the aged? Does not long life bring understanding?"
—JOB 12:12

*W*hen I drive U.S. Route 11 back home from Harrisonburg, Virginia, I pass a gray metal historical sign in the curve just before Lacey Springs: BIRTHPLACE OF ABRAHAM LINCOLN'S FATHER. Here in the heart of the South was born the father of the man who would write the Emancipation Proclamation and the Gettysburg Address.

When I did some research, however, I found that Lincoln wasn't close to his father Thomas; he didn't attend his funeral in 1851. Thomas was a farmer through and through; he may not have understood his son's intense desire to read and learn more than was necessary to run a farm.

But whatever Lincoln thought of his dad as a child and young man, Thomas Lincoln did at least a few things that affected his son's life in wonderful ways: he married two excellent, God-fearing, loving, laughing women (Nancy, Abe's mother, and Sarah, his beloved stepmother), he gave himself to his community in service (as a jury member, road-petitioner, and guard for county prisoners), and he chose as his church one that renounced slavery.

In 1860, when president-elect Lincoln made his last visit to Sarah in Illinois, they went to the cemetery where Thomas was buried. I like to think that whatever had been amiss between Abe and his father was healed then, and that the good Thomas had brought into his son's life was freed to work for America's good in the years just ahead.

Lord, thank You for Abraham Lincoln, who held us together as a nation in the roughest of times. May the healing he hoped to begin be accomplished in our lives.
—ROBERTA ROGERS

"I will go before you and make the rough places smooth."
—ISAIAH 45:2 (NASB)

Okay, everybody, outta those nice warm beds! You've got square tires this morning!"

It was a jovial disc jockey's way of warning commuters that the weather was extremely cold, traffic would be slow, and they had better allow themselves a few extra minutes for defrosting windshields before slowly rumbling along frozen streets on their way to work.

Those of us who live on the Canadian prairie know all about "square tires." At temperatures of twenty-five to thirty degrees below zero, tires become so stiff after a car has been sitting outside overnight that it initially makes for a bumpy ride. After driving a few hundred yards, the rubber becomes flexible again and the ride smoothes out.

I know what it is to get up in the morning and experience a bumpy ride—and not only in a car. This morning was one of those days. I just didn't want to climb out of my warm, cozy bed. Negative thoughts had drifted in that obscured the vision through my spiritual windshield. My tough resistance to a new project made it difficult to shift gears and get going. My rigid insistence of wanting things to go my way made for a square-tire start to my day.

I can tell you what smoothed out the ride though. It was committing my plans and attitude and direction to God before I ever left the driveway. In reading portions of His Word and remembering His promises, I felt my reluctance thawing out and my spirit warming to whatever He had in store down the road.

Lord, when it comes to Your leading, make me flexible. Amen.
—ALMA BARKMAN

FEBRUARY 14

"Haven't you heard...'the two will become one flesh'?
So they are no longer two, but one."
—MATTHEW 19:4–6

Long-stemmed red roses, thick boxes of chocolates, huge stuffed bears holding plush hearts—it was easy to see that Valentine's Day was just round the corner! But as I stood in the card aisle of the grocery store that morning, I wasn't there to buy sentimental verse or romantic humor. I was there to choose a get-well card for our friend Jan who had suffered a bad fall, breaking both her arm and pelvic bone.

Jan and her husband Dwight work together, building beautiful homes in our community. They had been finishing up one that they were going to move in to when, late one evening, Jan misjudged the position of the second-story stairway and fell eleven feet onto the hardwood floor below. Dwight called for help and stayed beside her until the ambulance arrived.

When my husband Gary and I went to visit her, we found Jan sitting in a wheelchair in the kitchen of the duplex where they were living. "Oh, Jan, we're so sorry you're hurt!"

Jan laughed. "Oh, it could have been lots worse!"

A hospital bed took up most of the living room. Dwight hovered nearby, eager to get her a glass of water or reposition her cushions. He spoke in hushed tones about how scared he had been when she fell. Then, as we were leaving, I noticed a small mattress leaning up against the wall by the front door. Dwight smiled. "That's my bed. I put it on the floor beside her in case she needs anything in the night."

Flowers and cards and even plush bears are fine. But I knew that what I'd just witnessed went way beyond those. This was true romance. I slipped my hand into Gary's. "Happy Valentine's Day," I whispered.

You are the source of all real love, God. Thank You!
—MARY LOU CARNEY

February 15

Establish the work of our hands for us—yes, establish the work of our hands.
—Psalm 90:17

*E*very time I take out my mother's rings, I can see her hands. They were elegant hands, with long fingers, the nails perfectly shaped ovals. She painted them with brightly colored nail polish—usually red—that chipped and wore off so that the spots of color that remained were like ruby islands floating on her pale pink nails.

I look at my own hands and remember that I could only write a little after she was diagnosed with lung cancer late last fall, and that my pencil stopped when she died the following January.

Close to the end, I see my hands moving tentatively to lay a cool towel on her forehead. I see my hands lying on the arms of the recliner where I slept next to her bed.

Suddenly I laugh when I remember my daughter Lanea's young hands fussing over her grandmother, moving with twentysomething rhythm to find music to comfort her or putting my mother's favorite movie into the video player.

Finally, I feel my son Chase's hand on my shoulder, keeping me steady and reassuring me while he and I sang "How Great Thou Art" at her funeral. His hands were no longer a little boy's hands; they were big and strong enough to keep me upright.

When I'm done reminiscing, I put away the rings. I grab my laptop and begin to work. The hands I see before me are my own. They are alive, and they are strong—just like my mother's hands.

Lord, thank You for generations who comfort, teach, and strengthen one another.
—Sharon Foster

Our Father.... Give us this day our daily bread.
—MATTHEW 6:9, 11 (KJV)

As I was saying the Lord's Prayer several years ago, I was struck by two words: *Give us*. How late in the prayer it comes, this very first request for our own needs—halfway to the end! Since the words Jesus gave His disciples were the pattern for the entire life of prayer, He must have been telling them, "Your own needs must always come second."

That certainly hadn't been my order of business! My prayers usually led off with a cry for help: "Give me the words to write her," when Maude's husband died. "Protect Andrew on his trip." "Guide the doctors during Fran's surgery."

Jesus has different priorities. Start by honoring God, He tells me. Hallow His name. Pray for His kingdom. Seek His will. Spend half your prayer time—the first half—putting the Father first. Jesus was all too aware of the wrenching human need He was sending His disciples to confront. Yet He didn't tell them, "Here's how to ask for God's aid in difficult situations." He said, "Worship God."

So I set out to follow this model. The very first week of the experiment, the prayer chain at our church learned of a college student threatening suicide. *Make her answer her mother's phone calls, God!* I wanted to cry. *Have the dorm staff force her door open! Get her boyfriend to apologize!*

Instead, using the sequence of the Lord's Prayer, I made myself start, not with the problem, but with God's all-sufficiency. I concentrated on the greatness of His name. I asked for His kingdom to come everywhere on earth, including that dorm room; for His will to be done in all situations, not this one alone.

And as I followed Jesus' pattern, a curious thing happened. The panic was gone. I found myself offering my intercessions while focusing on the nature of God, forever working toward the very best. The prayers of many people were in fact answered when the student at last picked up the telephone and spoke to her mother.

Looking at our need through the lens of God's love: that must be why, in the prayer Jesus taught, the words *Give us* come so late.

Our Father, come first in my prayers and actions today.
—ELIZABETH SHERRILL

February 17

*"Do not fear or be dismayed because of this great multitude,
for the battle is not yours but God's."*
—2 Chronicles 20:15 (NASB)

Lately, I've been asked to talk to groups of women about my depression. Back in 1994 when my illness began, I promised God that if He'd help me get better, I'd try to help others. I meant one-on-one, not speaking to crowds.

Each time I'm asked to share, I get nervous and clumsy. One Saturday morning at a brunch, I set up my visuals and then, while walking back down the four stage steps, I fell and landed on my bottom. Thank goodness the artificial plants hid me and no one noticed.

See, you can't do this. You can't even walk without falling.

The women at my table made polite conversation and ate their chicken salad. I couldn't eat because my hands were shaking. Someone introduced me, I teetered up those same four shiny wooden steps. *Help me, God. Too many faces are staring at me.*

Then the miracle happened. My hands steadied. I heard my shaky voice become strong. I told my story, and the group laughed and cried with me. Afterward, I asked God, "How could I have felt that I was soaring when earlier I couldn't walk down the steps without stumbling?"

God seemed to say, *You asked Me to help, Julie.*

Lord, when I ask You to help, I never have to face any difficulty alone.

—Julie Garmon

Casting all your care upon him; for he careth for you.
—1 PETER 5:7 (KJV)

I was leaving my parents' apartment after a daylong visit with them before heading to my sister's house. "We'll walk you to the bus stop," my mother said.

"Oh, that's not necessary," I began. "I'm sure I can find—"

They were already putting on their coats. We walked the few blocks, the snow crunching under our feet. But louder than the snow came the list of instructions. "Now, be extra careful that you get on the right bus. Both the N-20 and the N-21 stop here, and you don't want to get on the wrong one."

I'm sure I can figure that out, I thought. Then my mother held up her MetroCard—it was a new development since I'd last been in New York City, when I'd used a token. "Here," she said, "take my MetroCard. Just slide it in the money changer on the bus. Make sure you put it in with the arrow facing down."

"Thanks, Ma," I muttered, thinking, *Next, they'll tell me to look both ways before I cross the street!*

Sure enough, "And this is a busy intersection," my stepfather Joe instructed me. "Make sure to look both ways."

As soon as I was settled into a place in the line, I gave a sheepish smile to the lady in front of me, a stranger, who was cuddling a baby swathed in a yellow crocheted blanket. "Everybody was somebody's baby once," she said, looking lovingly at her own child.

Suddenly, I felt the love and caring that my parents' instructions conveyed. All they wanted was for me to be safe. I turned to look for them. I didn't have to look far—they were waiting to see that I got on the bus safely.

"Thanks!" I mouthed. "Thanks for caring about me."

God, today let me be grateful for, not grumpy about, the concern of those who love me. They are extensions of Your love.
—LINDA NEUKRUG

Behold, how good and how pleasant it is for brethren to dwell together...!
—PSALM 133:1 (KJV)

*W*hump! Tim's landing was perfect, just below my ribcage, an accidental Heimlich maneuver. As I struggled to catch my breath, he hopped onto my pillow, looking annoyed that I had ruined a perfectly good sleeping spot. I glared at him and rolled over. I still had another hour before my alarm was set to go off, and I intended to enjoy it.

I had just gotten back to sleep when Nickel launched her attack, sticking a paw in my ear. A shake of my comforter sent both cats scrambling. A moment later, I heard the toilet flush.

Not again! I had asked the cats very nicely not to drink out of the commode, and when they refused to listen, I closed the lid. Now, every few days, they have voiced their protests with toilet-flushing sprees. I abandoned my last hour of sleep and marched to the bathroom. There they posed, completely still, jet-black bookends. Tim was perched on the tank, looking angelic. Nickel faced me, her ear-probing paw poised on the handle, waiting for me to make the first move.

I struck quickly, scooping one cat in either arm, and dashed for the bedroom. I dropped the cats on the bed and hopped up myself. Then I pulled the comforter up over my head, trapping the three of us in a striped, downy tent. Slowly, Tim climbed into my lap and reached up with one paw to bat my nose. I scratched his nose. He pawed my stomach, so I tickled his. Satisfied, he curled up in my lap and began to purr. Nickel slithered into my lap and used Tim as a chaise longue, stretching out so I could tickle her stomach, too.

Quite suddenly, I opened one eye to the muted but insistent beeping of my alarm. I was curled in a ball around my two roommates.

Father in heaven, thank You for my extended "feline family." They are my friends and guardians and my foot-warmers, too. What a special gift!
—KJERSTIN EASTON

They have ears, but they hear not.

—PSALM 135:17 (KJV)

Several years ago I went through a difficult period. My husband was retiring from the Navy after twenty-two years, and we were in a time of transition. The future seemed uncertain, and Larry and I both were experiencing anxiety.

At the same time, my aunt came from Indianapolis to visit my grandmother here in Richlands, North Carolina. With her she brought a gift for me from my cousin, whom I very seldom see or hear from. There was no way Cheryl could have known that I was going through a tough time, but when I opened the package I found a small cloth angel with a wooden head and lacy wings. Attached was a little poem that read:

> *I'm a little coping angel, come to help you cope.*
> *When things are looking rather bleak,*
> *And you are out of hope,*
> *Then you will need a coping friend*
> *To chase those clouds away, to cheer you and be near you,*
> *And to brighten up your day.*
> *So through the trials yet to come, and trials always do;*
> *Remember I'll be by your side, just looking out for you.*

When I called to thank Cheryl for her kindness, I asked how she could have known I needed such a gift. She told me that God had prompted her to send it.

Now the little angel hangs above my work station as a daily reminder that I, too, can be a messenger of God's love, but only if I'm willing to open my heart and let Him lead me.

Lord, help me tune my listening ear to You, that I might be of service to others.

—LIBBIE ADAMS

> *"What else will distinguish me and your people*
> *from all the other people on the face of the earth?"*
> —EXODUS 33:16

*G*rowing up, I always went to Ash Wednesday Mass with my family early in the morning before school. Then I'd spend the rest of the day with that black smudgy cross on my forehead, hearing kids say, "You have dirt on your face." Some really didn't know what it was, others were teasing. But I didn't care. I liked having that mark to set me apart, a physical sign that helped me say, "I am a child of God."

So now it's almost Ash Wednesday, and once again I'll display the cross made of ashes on my forehead and wash it off a few hours later. After that, what will remain to show the world that I am still God's child? Will my eyes reflect the peace of the Lord in my heart? Will my hands reach out in compassion to someone in need? Will my smile share the joy of Jesus?

In the Lenten tradition I knew as a child, I can give up something for the next forty days—give up a part of myself to someone else as a tangible way of showing God's grace. I might look that store clerk in the eyes when I ask, "How are you?" and wait for the answer, even if it takes a little extra time. Or turn the other cheek the next time someone speaks harshly to me, instead of getting in the last word. The ashes may disappear, but I'll be showing an unmistakable sign that I belong to the Lord.

> *Dear God, inspire me to carry Your Spirit throughout this season,*
> *as I await Your glorious Resurrection.*

—GINA BRIDGEMAN

Just as we have borne the image of the man of dust,
we shall also bear the image of the man of heaven.
—1 CORINTHIANS 15:49 (RSV)

At age five, my son John is obsessed with the Revolutionary War. So it was no surprise that while we were in the Metropolitan Museum of Art today, he asked if we could go see *Washington Crossing the Delaware*. We took a detour through Medieval Art, passed Paul Revere's silver, and entered the picture galleries of the American Wing. The kids breathed a deep sigh of admiration as we walked in: the painting is quite large and very dramatic.

"Hey, that's George Washington, too!" John said, glancing at the opposite wall. "Who is he talking to?" We turned to study a painting of Washington and Lafayette on the porch of Mount Vernon. Curious about what else was in the collection, we wandered farther in until we came to a room chock-full of paintings of Washington. The kids sat down to take a better look.

"Which one do you like best?" I asked, as I glanced from one picture to another. In a full-length portrait, Washington looked debonair; in a smaller painting, he was commanding; in a third, he appeared serious and reserved. Each artist seemed to have captured a different person in paint.

Which is the real guy? I wondered. Over the years, I'd put my textbook image of him into a tidy little box labeled "Hero," and it was pleasantly startling to find he was much more human and complex than I'd imagined.

Sometimes, if I'm not careful, I can find myself doing the same thing with Jesus. Unfortunately, I'm quite capable of putting Him into a neat little box labeled "Lord," where I'm guided by my ideas about Him rather than by Jesus Himself. Yet Jesus wants more. He wants me to know Him in all His divine and human complexity. And He wants that knowledge to make me a living servant of the living God.

Lord Jesus, change my heart so fully that all who know me know You.
—JULIA ATTAWAY

In you they trusted and were not disappointed.
—PSALM 22:5

*S*everal years ago, inspired by a book I'd read, I made a list of thirty people I hoped to meet one day. The list was wide and varied, including writers, motivational speakers, and celebrities. Amazingly, over the past several years, I've met eighteen people on that list. Some of them were everything I'd expected and others were major disappointments.

Not long ago, after one such disappointment, I was complaining to God about how disillusioned I'd been. Then God spoke to me in my heart: *Debbie, you asked to meet these people, and I'm happy to send them into your life, but I want you to make another list.*

"Another list?"

This time leave the spaces blank. I'm going to send thirty people into your life whom I want you to meet, and I promise you none of them will be a disappointment.

This prayer-time conversation has had a curious effect on me. Now, whenever I meet someone, I look at him or her with fresh eyes and wonder if this is one of the people God is sending into my life. I find that I'm more open, more receptive, waiting expectantly for those God wants me to meet. Since then, I've been blessed in countless ways. I've still got my original list, but it's not nearly as important to me as the one God asked me to keep.

Father, thank You for the special people You have sent into my life.
Not a single one has ever disappointed me.
—DEBBIE MACOMBER

"This, then, is how you should pray: 'Our Father....' "
—MATTHEW 6:9

W hen I was four years old, my family went on an outing to Dale Hollow, a crystal-clear lake near the Tennessee-Kentucky border. One minute, I was lolling in the bow of the boat as we floated along; the next minute, I was being lifted up in my daddy's arms and tossed out into the water. I trusted my father completely, so I was not alarmed. I sank deep into the water, then swam straight up. As I broke the surface gasping for air, I sputtered, "Next time you do that, Daddy, tell me first."

A hundred such stories are stored in my memory: clinging to Daddy's back as he dove off a rocky cliff; jumping from a high tree limb straight into his arms. He wanted me to be confident. He didn't want me to be afraid. And because he was my daddy, I never was.

As I delve deeper into the practice of prayer, intent on developing an open, honest relationship with God, I find a particular strength in the way Jesus taught His disciples to pray. When Jesus tells us to call God our Father, He's telling us that God loves us, accepts us, wants to be with us. We can do nothing to make God love us more; we can do nothing to cause Him to love us less.

So when you pray, don't hide your fears and gloss over your feelings. Talk with God as though you trust Him enough to jump out of a tree and straight into His arms.

> *It's me, Father, Your daughter Pam. My day has turned chaotic.*
> *Earlier, I put my trust in a colleague and instead of doing what was right,*
> *she did what was easy and I was the one who lost. Now images*
> *of revenge are creeping into my thoughts. I crave a calm heart,*
> *a peaceful demeanor, a kind attitude. Help me, today,*
> *to remember to believe in my best self.*
> —PAM KIDD

But we had the sentence of death in ourselves, that we should not trust in ourselves, but in God which raiseth the dead.

—2 CORINTHIANS 1:9 (KJV)

*I*t was only February and not yet time for the King Alfred daffodils to be blooming. But there they were—the only ones in the neighborhood—in small beds on either side of my front steps, standing tall and straight and golden, with a very special message.

Two nights earlier my husband Bob had died. As we came home from the hospital, Emily commented that the daffodils had big buds on them. At that time I wasn't interested enough to even glance at them. Then, the next day, a visitor commented, "Your daffodils will be blooming soon. The buds are showing yellow." I had other things on my mind then, too.

But on the day of Bob's funeral, the first thing I saw when we turned into the driveway were the masses of wide-open daffodils filling the flowerbeds. They seemed to reach out to me.

"It's a message from God," I cried, springing from the car. My family gathered around me as I explained.

"Last year these flowers bloomed and were beautiful," I said. "Then they died. All that remained were the bulbs in the ground. But now they are alive again!" I caught Emily's hand in mine. "Your dad had a beautiful life. Then he died and was put in the ground. But now," I said as I swept my hand across the flowers, "he's alive again—this time in heaven! He is glowing and beautiful up there with God."

Dear Father, when the days are darkest and the pain most intense, how wonderfully You remind me of Your love and redemption.

—DRUE DUKE

Cleanse thou me from secret faults.
—PSALM 19:12 (KJV)

It was our friend Brother Andrew who started me on the adventure of seeing God in the people around me. "He can reach out to us," Andrew said, "through even the briefest contact." Then he told this story.

Andrew is a Dutchman who for decades ministered secretly to Christians behind the Iron Curtain. Yet this selfless man carried a burden of guilt he could not lay down. Years earlier, Andrew had been among the Dutch soldiers sent to Indonesia to put down the independence movement.

When the Cold War ended, Andrew decided to return to now-independent Indonesia to serve the people he once fought. Nothing he did for them, however, served to ease his conscience. The place he most dreaded revisiting was the town of Ungaran, where his army unit had been headquartered.

"At last," he said, "I forced myself to go back there." He made himself walk up the single main road, past the mosque, to the big U-shaped school building the Dutch had used as a barracks. The building had been turned back into a school; on the former drill ground inside the U, some children in ragged clothing were playing.

As Andrew stood watching, a little girl, maybe eight years old, suddenly broke away from her playmates and ran toward him. The other children stopped their game and stared after her, clearly puzzled. The child ran straight up to Andrew, put her small hand in his, looked up into his eyes, and smiled. Then she ran back to join her companions.

Andrew stood where he was, tears running down his face. "I knew who it was who'd come to me. It was Jesus. Jesus telling me, 'I forgive you, Andrew. Now forgive yourself and serve these beautiful people with joy.'"

Speak to me this year, Lord, in the people You will send me.
—ELIZABETH SHERRILL

FEBRUARY 27

Jesus himself drew near, and went with them.
—LUKE 24:15 (KJV)

Sister Janice handed me a white business card that read MINISTRY OF PRESENCE, followed by a telephone number. "Our desire is to be present with God's people in need," she said. "Please call if Sister Rosarita or I can help you or your clients."

"I will," I said automatically. Secretly, I doubted that two nuns would be of much help. The community was full of people with real needs—for food, decent housing, legal aid, and affordable medical care. Our church-sponsored service agency had trained staff to help meet those needs. Along with the Salvation Army, Emmaus House, and Family Crisis Center, we took care of just about everything.

Or did we? Sister Janice discovered that several families were without shelter on sub-zero nights. She found temporary housing, then organized a Winter Cold Shelter program. Sister Rosarita conducted a comprehensive survey of the poor that led to better access to daycare. Did a family need transportation? Both sisters would drive, and also listen and pray.

During His earthly ministry, Jesus preached to the multitudes and fed thousands—the same work as our helping agencies. But He was also fully present for people with special needs, just like Sisters Janice and Rosarita. He wasn't too busy to heal a bleeding woman who touched the hem of his robe (Luke 8:43–48). He took time to bless little children (Luke 18:16). He noticed a poor widow putting two mites into the temple treasury and praised her generosity (Luke 21:1–4).

The ministry of presence, I realized, doesn't need to be done by an agency or trained staff. Jesus gives the privilege of presence to anyone with a caring heart the willingness to listen, and a genuine desire to help.

Lord, who needs my ministry of presence today?
—PENNEY SCHWAB

FEBRUARY 28

To every thing there is a season, and a time to every purpose under the heaven.
—ECCLESIASTES 3:1 (KJV)

Several years ago, on a trip to China, my husband Robert learned that the Chinese think of life in twelve-year segments. Age sixty is considered a complete lifetime, and the sixty-first birthday represents the beginning of a new life. Worldly responsibilities are complete, so it's an ideal time to develop the life of the spirit.

Of course, we're living longer now, so many of us are still quite young at sixty and continue our earlier responsibilities. But now that I'm in my seventies, I've consciously chosen to accept my elderhood. I'm beginning a new life in which I'm free to make spiritual growth my top priority. I consider it to be the most valuable stage of life. Sure, I have plenty of aches and pains and other physical nuisances, but in prayer and meditation I sometimes glimpse a reality that is so vast and so glorious that those minor physical ailments shrink into insignificance.

So today this elder with the graying hair and thinning bones would like to leave two thoughts with you. If you're in the earlier life stages, think of each failure as a stepping-stone to wisdom. And if, like me, you're in your autumn years, you have fully lived your wisdom and your foolishness. It's now time to harvest the spiritual wonder of your life.

Awaken my spirit, Holy One. As my body weakens,
may my spirit grow stronger in You.
—MARILYN MORGAN KING

FEBRUARY 29

Certainly this is the day we looked for; we have found, we have seen it.
—LAMENTATIONS 2:16 (KJV)

Too often, when my "to do" pile threatens to topple, I excuse my inefficiency with "I could get caught up on all these tasks if I just had an extra day!"

Well, today is that day—a whole extra twenty-four hours to spend as I please! It's one of those every-four-year days inserted in our calendar to compensate for the quarter-day difference between man-made years and astronomical ones.

I must confess that as a senior citizen, I've had more complementary extra days than those who haven't reached my age. In fact, I've even had a few freebies that can't be attributed to leap year but instead to crossing the international date line. On one of those trips, I even had two birthdays when one February 17 came back-to-back with another. But that gained day was "lost" on the return a week later when February 23 jumped to 25, so I can't really count that as an extra.

So what will I do with today's gift of twenty-four hours? I wonder if, by midnight tonight, I'll tell myself, *I got my "to do" list done!* Or will it be, *I can't believe I wasted all that time!*

Thank goodness, Lord, for the time You give me that I can spend just with You.
—ISABEL WOLSELEY

March

MARCH 1

For you have been born again...through the living and enduring word of God.
—1 PETER 1:23

*O*nce a week, I stop by Mom's house for a cup of coffee and "Grann Hour," when we read the letters my great-grandmother wrote to he family in the early twentieth century.

At first, I wasn't really eager to spend an hour reading yellowed letters in difficult handwriting. I'd already heard stories about my colorful great-granny that was enough. Besides, I had other things to do. But I went for Mom's sake so we could pare down her closet clutter and save only the important things.

As we read the letters to each other, I began to appreciate my great grandmother's humor, struggles, shortcomings, wisdom, creativity, and faith as she labored through some of life's most difficult circumstances. The storie I'd heard really hadn't told me much about her. Yet by reading her letters, he words to her children, she became real to me.

I find that my Granny Hour has reinforced something I know in my hear but often fail to practice: I can hear stories about God, and I can read devotion and books about Him. But until I get into His Word, His letters written to us, Hi children, I can't really know Him.

Father, as I read Your Word, reveal Yourself to me,
so I can know You better and love You more.
—MARJORIE PARKER

I pray for them...for they are thine.
—JOHN 17:9 (KJV)

I stood and stared out of the kitchen window. The telephone was ringing, but I didn't move. I was overwhelmed by the news I'd received earlier that day. Colonel Palmertree, the ROTC commander at the high school where I teach, had told me he had a serious health problem, and I was devastated. We had begun teaching across the hall from each other ten years before, and we'd quickly become friends, sharing a firm belief in duty to our country and a love for the 104-year-old American flag that hangs in my classroom.

"Mom," my son called out, "Mimi's on the phone."

Mimi is my husband Roy's mother. I was pleased she had called. Her concern for others and her strong faith in the Lord had always been an inspiration to me. After I finished giving her the latest news about the children, I told her about Colonel Palmertree.

"I wish there were something I could do," I lamented. "I feel pretty helpless."

"Why don't we put him on the prayer line?" Mimi asked.

"What a great idea!" I replied. Over the years I had always found the prayer line to be a source of comfort. One phone call with Mimi, and my prayer request was sent to a vast network of people who took time to pray for all the concerns they received.

The next morning when I walked into the teacher's lounge at school, the colonel was sitting on the sofa. As I walked by I heard him say, "If I felt any better today, I don't think I could stand it!"

I listened to his laughter and said my own prayer of thanks.

Thank You, God, for a wise and experienced mentor
who knows where the answers lie.
—MELODY BONNETTE

MARCH 3

I remember thee upon my bed, and meditate on thee in the night watches.
—PSALM 63:6 (KJV)

When I was a child, I said my bedtime prayers out loud every day. Well, almost every day. Sometimes, when we got home from church especially late, or when we'd been in the hay fields all day, or when company stayed way past bedtime, Mother would tuck us in and say, "Pray yourself to sleep." And I always did. There, in the security of my room, bundled in handmade quilts, I would pray until I drifted off to dreams.

Several years ago, Mother had a stroke. By the time I could get to her, her powers of speech were gone. When I walked into her hospital room, she folded her hands and pointed her thumbs back toward herself. "Yes, Mother!" I assured her. "Many people are praying for you!"

I sat with her for six days, watching her slip further and further away. What was she thinking? Could she hear me? Was she in pain? I wrapped my prayer around her as I sat curled in a hospital chair near the foot of her bed. And when, on a cold March morning, Mother slipped easily into death, I was sure that—for the last time—she had prayed herself to sleep.

Whether we wake or sleep, You, O Lord, are God!
—MARY LOU CARNEY

MARCH 4

O Lord my God, in thee do I put my trust.
—PSALM 7:1 (KJV)

'm sitting in the El Paso County, Colorado, juror waiting room, hoping with all my heart that my number won't be called. I've never served 1 a jury and under other circumstances I'd be glad to do so. I think the :perience would be interesting and educational. But not now. My children and :andchildren (some of whom I haven't seen for nearly a year) will be arriving morrow, and I've been looking forward to their visit. The last thing I want is to e tied up with jury duty while they're here.

But I've learned in my seventy-two years that when I turn my concerns over God, things really do tend to work out for the best, regardless of whether I t my way.

So right now, this moment, I'm letting go of hoping my number won't be illed, knowing that whichever way it goes, God's higher purpose is at work. s I release my desire to control the outcome, my neck muscles loosen and an voluntary sigh escapes my lips. And for the first time since arriving here, I find yself noticing the gorgeous view of Pike's Peak with the American flag on the urthouse roof superimposed on its face, framed by the window I had ignored a my self-concern.

In this and all things may Your will be done, Omniscient One.
—MARILYN MORGAN KING

I am in pain and distress; may your salvation, O God, protect me.
—PSALM 69:29

I'd been feeling sorry for myself. It was two months after I'd moved from Hartford, Connecticut, where I had lived for twenty years and made close friends, to a smaller town on the shore. I had moved around Christmas, so I understood why people failed to keep in touch. After all, it was the season people couldn't keep up with their own schedules, never mind mine.

But then it was Ash Wednesday, the start of Lent, the darkest season of the year. I'd relied on my friends to get me through those short midwinter days. That year, no one called. And I was miserable.

I brooded. I cried. I shouted at the phone. I whined to my mother. But I didn't call the friends whose voices I so longed to hear. That just wasn't an option. After all, I'd supported them during their trials and tragedies. They had to know this move would be difficult. Where were they when I needed to talk, when I needed a little support?

I arrived home from church, marked with ashes, to a message from one of the offending friends on my answering machine. Mary had just returned from the hospital, where she'd waited alone while her husband was in surgery. Listening to her forlorn, aching voice, I knew that two months ago I would have waited with her at the hospital. I also knew that she still needed me.

Then I remembered something my mother had suggested—and I had immediately rejected—when I complained about my unfaithful friends. She said they were giving me room to make a new life before trying to fit themselves into it.

I picked up the phone.

Jesus, when I feel abandoned because no one seems to be reaching out, help me remember how You reached out and forgave those who truly abandoned You.
—MARCI ALBORGHETTI

MARCH 6

All the congregation are holy, every one of them, and the Lord is among them.
—NUMBERS 16:3 (KJV)

This was not one of our better Sunday mornings. Maria, just four, was fidgety. She tried coloring but kept dropping her crayons on the floor. She repeatedly wandered to the end of our row of empty chairs, and I pulled her back as if she were a wayward dog on a too-long leash.

"She should be in Sunday school," the woman behind me scolded. My face burned with embarrassment, then anger. Maria had been in Sunday school the previous hour; I had taken her into the service to see her daddy sing. Is that so bad? I hastily gathered up our things and moved to the back row. *What nerve!* I thought. Then I glanced at the picture Maria had been coloring. It showed Jesus talking with several children. The caption read, "The disciples thought Jesus wouldn't want to be bothered by children. They soon learned Jesus loves children."

See there! I thought. *Jesus invited everyone to follow him, even fidgety four-year-olds.* I felt more than a little smug until I remembered the previous week. I'd been critical of the teenager sitting in front of us in her short dress and spaghetti straps. Wouldn't Jesus have welcomed her, too? And I was annoyed by the man a few rows back who sang so loudly and off-key. I'm sure Jesus would have loved his enthusiasm.

I've been guilty of trying to impose my standards on other people's worship, whether it's a dress code or a judgment about their worship style. But my way of praising God certainly isn't the only way that pleases Him. Whether it's fidgety little ones, the dressed-down, or the shaky singers—all of us unique souls who fill God's house every week—He sees past the packaging to what's inside. Now I try to do the same.

> *Each Sunday, Lord, help me to join with—and not judge—*
> *those around me praising You.*
> —GINA BRIDGEMAN

"I have set before you an open door, and no one can shut it...."
—REVELATION 3:8 (NKJV)

I grew up in Yakima, Washington, with a large extended family. We cousins were as close as brothers and sisters; we lived in the same neighborhood, attended the same church and school, and often vacationed together.

After I married Wayne and moved to Kent, just a few miles south of Seattle, my cousin David, who was closest to me in age, developed leukemia. His doctor sent him to Seattle's Fred Hutchinson Cancer Research Center. Although I didn't often venture into the big city, I was determined to visit David.

Somehow I ended up at Swedish Hospital, which is connected to Fred Hutchinson by a sky bridge. Lost and confused, I wandered down a number of corridors without finding the bridge. Finally, I stopped a doctor and asked if he could give me directions.

"It's simple," he assured me. "All you need to do is walk down this hallway, take the first right, and walk through the door marked ABSOLUTELY NO ADMITTANCE." Those directions did more than show me the way to my cousin.

Somehow, that experience has given me the courage to walk through other doors: my dyslexia that I feared would keep me from working or my terror of speaking in front of people. God has met me at the door marked ABSOLUTELY NO ADMITTANCE and held it open for me.

Father God, thank You for the obstacles You send into my life that have taught
me to rely only on You.
—DEBBIE MACOMBER

MARCH 8

Choose the good.
—ISAIAH 7:15 (KJV)

I wish I had beautiful fingernails like you," I remember saying to Irene Solomon as I snuggled near her on the living room couch. Mrs. Solomon was a family friend who had come to stay with my brother Davey and me, so that my mother could go on a trip with my father. As far as I was concerned, everything about Mrs. Solomon, from her lovely red nails on, was perfectly wonderful.

Holding my seven-year-old hand in hers, she said, "Well, we can do something about that."

Soon Mrs. Solomon was patiently painting my scraggly fingernails that came bright red. "You know, Pamela," she said, "your fingernails are either being bitten off or they are growing long like mine. You can choose which way you want them to be."

I don't think I ever bit my fingernails again. And that's not all I learned from Mrs. Solomon. In the mornings, she put bright red cherries in the middle of our grapefruit; she let me wear my Sunday shoes to school; and at night she made us cola floats in my mother's crystal goblets. Later, on my eighth birthday, when everyone else was giving me useful things, she gave me an evening bag made of woven silver.

Though Mrs. Solomon worked well past retirement age in downtown Chattanooga, Tennessee, rode back and forth to work on a city bus, and lived in a tiny house in a modest neighborhood, she never stopped eating her cereal out of china bowls, painting her fingernails red, or (even in her late nineties) giving outlandish birthday presents to her friends.

The truth is, a cherry makes a grapefruit sweeter, china and crystal are made to be used, presents don't need to be practical, and you and I are either making life nicer or we're not. The choice is ours. Mrs. Solomon taught me that.

Father, in every moment of every day, a choice waits. Help us to choose the good.
—PAM KIDD

MARCH 9

The heartfelt counsel of a friend is as sweet as perfume and incense.
—PROVERBS 27:9 (NLT)

I'd always been a stay-at-home mom, working as time allowed, but when my children were grown, my goal was to get out of the house and become part of the business community. After ten years of working hard from home, I proudly signed my name to a lease for my own office and found myself facing hard decisions in a world completely foreign to me.

I knew I needed help, but where was I going to get it? As a first step, I contacted some successful businesswomen in our town—Lillian, a lawyer; Betty, a bank vice president; Diana, a social worker; Stephanie, a business owner; and Janelle, a real estate broker. I invited them to tea and asked their advice. We had such a good time together that we decided to meet every Thursday for breakfast.

That was eight years ago, and we still meet every Thursday to encourage and support one another. We bring our pains and our triumphs to breakfast; seek advice and share our troubles freely. We wept together when Stephanie developed cancer and died within five short months, and celebrated when Betty, a widow, met a wonderful man and remarried. We laugh together and cry together—often at the same time.

The years have seen many changes in our lives, but what started out as an easy way for me to learn more about being a good businesswoman has evolved into something far more powerful: friendship and a blessing from God.

Thank You, Lord, for the special friends You've brought into my life.
May we always continue to be close to You and to one another.

—DEBBIE MACOMBER

March 10

For God is not the author of confusion, but of peace.
—1 Corinthians 14:33 (kjv)

*S*ome folks eat chocolate when they're under stress. Some people bite their nails. My reaction to stress is more unusual: I lose things.

My TV remote control somehow finds its way into my laundry. My economics books migrate under my bed. My keys, purse, trombone oil, student ID, and floppy disks all disappear, though you wouldn't think I could lose much in a ten-by-ten dorm room. To make matters worse, in a frantic search for my homework, I'll ransack the room, burying my hole-punch, my journal, and a disgruntled cat.

My keys are the best at hiding. I've tried everything to keep from losing them. The "key receptacle" by my door worked until the cats discovered the keys made good prey and could be reliably hunted near the dish. I tried a key chain attached to my wallet, which attached to my purse, which attached to my backpack, and was always getting tangled. I've considered building a homing device for my key chain, but I haven't yet invested the time. Anyway, if I did, I'd lose the homing end just after I lost my keys.

Though I would like to be more organized, my current system does have its advantages. My busy student's schedule doesn't have enough time in it to get everything done, and often one of the first things I pass over is prayer. Soon enough, though, I lose something critical, and when I can't find it anywhere, I have no alternative to sitting down to pray. Usually, with God's helping hand and some careful excavation, I find what I'm looking for, be it my stapler, that book of stamps, or even some time to pray.

Jesus, no matter how much I have to get done, help me pencil in some time for prayer today.
—Kjerstin Easton

MARCH 11

"God my maker...gives songs in the night."
—JOB 35:10 (NASB)

*A*fter experiencing an irregularity in my heartbeat, I was admitted to the emergency room in a big-city hospital for observation.

Hooked up to a heart monitor, I lay awake most of the night, unable to sleep because of the unfamiliar surroundings. Hospital attendants were kind and conscientious, but I longed for morning to come, when the doctor would be in to assess my situation.

Around two in the morning a nurse came to make her rounds, pulling back the curtains at the foot of my bed, "Just so we can keep an eye on you." I could now keep an eye on the big round clock that hung across the hall: 2:15 a.m. 2:30 a.m. Snores were emanating from behind the curtains on either side of my bed, but sleep still eluded me. I could hear the nurses rustling papers, making reports, comparing notes. And then someone at the nursing station began to whistle softly bits and pieces of a song.

"I wish I could do that!" a voice remarked.

"You mean you don't know how to whistle?"

"Nope, never could get the hang of it."

For the next hour or so I was privy to a lesson given by a skilled whistler to a group of novices. Little did they know that the patient in bed four was listening—but I didn't want them to know. I just lay there with my eyes closed, listening to the clear, sweet notes of the teacher leading her eager pupils note by squeaky note. In the morning each of the nurses cheerfully began her rounds with "Whistle While You Work."

Remind me often, Lord, that an upbeat attitude encourages everyone's heart.
Thank You that my own heart is functioning just fine.

—ALMA BARKMAN

He who loves money shall never have enough. The foolishness
of thinking that wealth brings happiness!
—ECCLESIASTES 5:10 (TLB)

After I quit my job at the radio station in 1992 to work at home full-time as a freelance writer, a number of people suggested that I get a real job when times got tough financially for me.

"You should be a salesperson. You've got the personality for it. And think of the money you could make!" one friend suggested. "Why don't you consider teaching? Or, at the very least, you could be a substitute teacher. They make good money," another offered.

All good suggestions, but I've learned that the paycheck isn't nearly as important as the satisfaction I get from doing my work and living my life. My daily commute takes me approximately twenty seconds, from my bedroom to my office downstairs. No traffic to fight. No stress. If I feel like going for a bike ride at eleven o'clock in the morning, I go. If a friend stops by for tea, I'm thrilled with the company, knowing I can catch up on my work later. If I feel like sitting on the deck for an hour in the middle of the day with a good book, I do it. If I want to spend an extra twenty minutes pondering a perplexing Proverb, nobody's there to insist I "get back to work."

I'll probably never make enough money to be called rich. But I hope to have had a happy, content, and fulfilling life with plenty of time for the important stuff.

Tea, anyone?

Lord, thank You for this simple life of great abundance. A plethora of friends,
time to enjoy them, no stress, and a career I love. Help me
to hang on to this simple, happy lifestyle.
—PATRICIA LORENZ

"Then you will know the truth, and the truth will set you free."
—John 8:32

*I*f mama ain't happy, ain't nobody happy."

This popular ditty lived on a magnet on our refrigerator for years. At first, I liked the message because it affirmed the positive influence I have in our family. But over time, it began to weigh me down. Was I really in charge of everybody's moods? Yikes! What an exhausting responsibility. And what a guilt-producing message for a mom who already had a tendency to accept responsibility for all sorts of things she's not responsible for.

I learned in a parenting class that when I accept responsibilities that aren't mine—when I assume it's up to me to find lost shoes or be sure my children all have their stuff before they go out the door in the morning—I keep others from accepting theirs. And if I'm responsible for keeping my children happy, they won't learn that their choice of mood is up to them.

By the same logic, my mood is my responsibility, and I need to deal with it. Maybe the words on that magnet need to be changed to something like, "If Mama ain't happy, she might need a time-out." So far, nobody's asked me to edit refrigerator magnet messages. I guess that's not my responsibility.

Father, help me to learn what I'm responsible for and what I'm not, which is a truth that will set me free.
—Carol Kuykendall

March 14

As each has received a gift, employ it for one another,
as good stewards of God's varied grace.
—1 Peter 4:10 (RSV)

When class was over, the six- to nine-year-olds I was teaching in Sunday school all scrambled for the door at once. I was alarmed by their unruly stampede, but I didn't know what to do about it.

Then one Sunday I was surprised to learn that they all really liked one of the things I used in my lesson. It was a punch-out that folded into a small box with a different picture on each of its six surfaces. When I pitched the box to a child, he or she made up a story to fit the illustration. Because they seemed to like it so much, I said, "I'm going to give this box to one of you to take home. But you have to do something to earn it. When class is over, whoever remains quietly in his or her seat will get the box." I was certain they'd forget and dash out as usual.

When our time was up, I said matter-of-factly, "Class is over." No one moved. "You may leave now," I said. Again, they sat stock-still. "Okay," I said, laughing, "I'll think of a number and hold up that many fingers under the table. The one who guesses correctly gets the box." They thought that was fair.

As I was about to put my hands under the table, I noticed that Avie, a little girl sitting in front of me, had briefly bowed her head and folded her hands. When she opened her eyes, I whispered, "Were you praying?"

She nodded, smiling slightly.

"Would you like to tell me what you were praying about?"

She leaned over and whispered, "That I'd win the box!"

Amazingly, her guess was correct, and an enormous smile lit up her face as I handed the box to her. Still beaming, she gave it to the girl sitting next to her, along with a big hug. "I want you to have it, Bethany," Avie said. "I love you. You're my best friend!"

Lord, I'm beginning to see why You wanted me to meet these children.
—Marion Bond West

MARCH 15

"And we have heard his voice from the fire...."
—DEUTERONOMY 5:24

*M*y sister Susan and I stood at the checkout counter at a discou[n]t store in a neighboring town behind two carts overflowing wit[h] lamps, pillows, and other household necessities. It was hard to believe th[at] Susan's home had burned down just days before, and that she had frantical[ly] pushed Dad in his wheelchair out of the burning house in the middle of th[e] night right before the roof caved in.

I stared at the things in the cart. It was hard to see God's hand at work in th[e] face of such a sudden and terrible loss.

When Susan mentioned to the cashier that her house had burned dow[n,] a white-haired lady in line behind us asked, "Are you Bob Brown's daughter?"

Susan nodded, and the lady went on. "I'm a volunteer over at the hospit[al] where your dad used to help out." The woman pulled an envelope out of h[er] purse and handed it to Susan. It had Dad's name and address on it, and ha[d] already been stamped.

When we got home, Dad opened the envelope and found a card [of] encouragement with a hundred-dollar bill folded inside. Suddenly I wa[s] overcome with a feeling of God's continuing presence. Though the card ha[d] been intended for the mailbox, God had decided that it would mean much mo[re] for it to be sent special delivery through a chance meeting at a checkout counte[r.] And the wonder of it all helped remind me that God was indeed at work, eve[n] in the midst of overwhelming loss.

God, thank You for seeking me out with Your comforting presence.
—KAREN BARBER

MARCH 16

For I know the thoughts that I think toward you, says the Lord...
to give you a future and a hope.
—JEREMIAH 29:11 (NKJV)

The windshield wipers scraped aside the morning sleet. Miles of red glowing taillights lined Route 50 leading into Washington, DC. This was part of my daily routine: each day I woke up, inched through traffic, worked eight hours, sat in more traffic, walked my German shepherd, Kai, and went to bed. I was single and twenty-two years old. The year before, I'd dropped out of college. *God,* I prayed, *isn't there more to life than this?*

I'd grown up in a small Minnesota town. But I'd fled the miles of cornfields by transferring to a college in the DC area. After a year in the city, I didn't know what to do with my life or where to live.

That weekend Kai and I walked along a leaf-littered trail. The breeze caressed my cheeks and the sun warmed my back. Kai bounded ahead and splashed into the creek. All he wanted was to be with me, playing outdoors. I ached for my life to be that simple. I sat on a boulder, and Kai paddled over with a gift, a rock. I tossed it into the water. He dove after it, expecting adventure. *Adventure—that's what I need,* I thought. *So why am I living here?*

My dream had always been to work outside, preferably on horseback. I thought of my brother Chuck, who lived in Montana. Peace overwhelmed me when I remembered horses grazing under ponderosa pines on Rocky Mountain slopes. It was almost as if God's still, small voice was urging me to plunge into a new adventure.

That evening I phoned Chuck. "I'll be moving to Montana on April first," I told him. "Can I crash on your floor until I get a job?"

Lord, teach me to listen to Your still, small voice.
—REBECCA ONDOV

MARCH 17

But when you give to the needy, do not let your left hand know what your right hand is doing, so that your giving may be in secret. Then your Father, who sees what is done in secret, will reward you.

—MATTHEW 6:3–4

*D*espite my Irish heritage, St. Patrick's Day was always just a day to wear green and decorate the wreath on our front door with shamrocks. But that changed when my beloved uncle Pat died suddenly of a heart attack. It was then that I learned about the life of my uncle's patron saint, who introduced the people of Ireland to Christianity.

As friends paid tribute to my uncle, they pointed out a parallel between the lives of these two men who shared the same name. Though separated by nearly fifteen centuries in time, both were examples of caring, Christlike service.

Stories of Uncle Pat's secret acts of kindness—many bestowed on people who couldn't do anything for him in return—surfaced for the first time. I noticed, too, that the small, gentle gestures to which he never gave a second thought were remembered with great clarity by those whose lives he touched. The lady who wrapped his meat at the butcher shop recalled fondly how he always took time to inquire about her family. The glasses of ice water on hot summer days were remembered by the mail carrier.

The clerk at the local deli, her gray hair coiled tightly in a bun, was the first of many who shared the same wistful memory. "He bought me chocolates," she confided. Uncle Pat's trademark chocolates, I discovered, were a gift that elevated many a hardworking gas station attendant or stock boy to a position of prominence.

Today, as I don green and celebrate my Irish ancestry, I'm reminded anew of the legacies of St. Patrick and Uncle Pat. People are most attracted to Christianity by the love that drives our deeds.

Help me, Lord, to serve You in secret, loving ways.

—ROBERTA MESSNER

Do not forget the things your eyes have seen or let them fade from your heart as long as you live. Teach them to your children.
—DEUTERONOMY 4:9

One of the oldest Carmelite monasteries in America is not far from our former home in Maryland. A couple of years ago, the local paper ran a photo of a life-sized statue the nuns had designed and sculpted for the monastery garden. It depicts Joseph sitting on a bench in his carpenter's apron. In his right hand he grasps a tool, holding it in his lap about eye level for a very young Jesus. Joseph's left arm encircles the child, who is tucked up against his earthly father's side, learning.

The photo crystallized a moment from the week before. As our house was being restored that spring, our contractor Sid Marcus brought along his teenage son Russell and let him handle some of the tasks. With four boys in our family, whenever we had a question or request, we hollered! Not so with Sid and Russell. One morning I became aware of the quiet rumble of male voices. Instead of shouting for him, Russell had left his job and hunted up his father for help. In an even, gentle tone, Sid was telling Russell what was okay and what he needed to tear up and do again. There was no rancor, only quiet encouragement.

Holding the newspaper clipping and recalling that morning, for a moment, across the centuries, I heard the murmur of another father teaching his son.

Lord, I thank You for Joseph, who taught and nurtured Jesus so wonderfully. Thank You for those who still gently mentor others today. Help me to become a wise and kind teacher of the next generation.
—ROBERTA ROGERS

March 19

To all perfection I see a limit; but your commands are boundless.
—Psalm 119:96

As I got older, I realized my thighs weren't what they used to be. N only had they mysteriously become broader (translation: fatte and less firm, they were now noticeably mottled with what doctors told r were "spider veins," a purple and red filigree of capillaries close to the surfa of my pale skin. The spider veins were medically nonthreatening, probab hereditary, but as I one day surveyed the feathery patterns of magenta on r legs, it occurred to me, *Maybe this doesn't look so great to other people.* Many of r athletic relatives and friends, when in bathing suits and hiking shorts, had le that were tanned and firm. Not me. Flickers of self-consciousness set in.

One weekend I went for a sleepover with my goddaughter Linnea, who w around five at the time. Still in our nightshirts, we sat on the bed and color with felt-tipped pens. Our markers squeaked along on the pages of colorit books; we produced original compositions. Then Linnea stopped. "Wha that?" she asked. She pointed at the patterns on my legs.

"Some people get them when they're older," I said. "Little veins just benea your skin." I was about to add, "I know it's not very pretty," but Linnea attention had turned to choosing different colored markers.

I resumed my squeaky coloring, but Linnea's pens took on a softer sound looked over to see her drawing lines on the skin of her own legs. Concentratir and serious, she drew squiggles of purple, burnt orange, brick red. "Linne what are you doing?"

"I want marks like you have. I like them."

> *Dear God, help me to disregard my vanity and see my*
> *"imperfections" in a new way.*
> —Mary Ann O'Roark

Moses was an hundred and twenty years old when he died:
his eye was not dim, nor his natural force abated.
—DEUTERONOMY 34:7 (KJV)

Her old, elegant hands reach for the grand piano's polished keys. Fingers find familiar patterns. Love songs to God, love notes for her husband—gone these fifteen years—ripple and eddy around her petite body. Lustrous white hair forms a feathery halo in the lamplight.

Deep-set eyes—blue behind closed lids—are submerged in reverie. She is in conversation with her music, communing with her past. There is her "precious Al," the handsome tennis player she still can't believe fell in love with her; her mother Nanny, who saved her minister-husband's meager wedding and funeral earnings to give her oldest daughter a start at college; her friends in China, with whom she weathered perilous World War II years on the mission field; her three accomplished children—and maybe, too, the infant daughter she buried on foreign soil.

"I don't feel old when I play my piano," she tells me. "It's like I have a friend who talks to me and I talk back." She needs this friend who won't leave her, who keeps her secrets, harbors her sorrows, and releases her joys.

She is my aunt, Elizabeth Blackstone. And she is one hundred years and two months old. As I watch her fingers swirl across the piano keys, I know why I traveled 2,500 miles to Monte Vista Grove in Pasadena, California, to be her caregiver.

Her hands grow tired, and the music slows. Her eyes open. "The Lord's been good to me," she says, rising gracefully from the piano seat.

Silently, I thank her real Caregiver for inviting me to join Him.

As I grow older, Lord, may I continue to pound life's keys with passion.
—CAROL KNAPP

MARCH 21

In the beginning was the Word, and the Word was with God,
and the Word was God.

—JOHN 1:1 (KJV)

*H*ow well I remember my childhood church. It stood stiff and tall
Orange and Concord streets in Lancaster, Pennsylvania. A pair
broad steps led to the impossibly heavy wooden doors. Inside, twelve mo
steps, which I counted each week, took me to the sanctuary, cool and da
smelling of dust and old wood.

We children sat in the front pew with instructions not to kick under t
seat or bang the hymnals. The minister loomed high in the pulpit above us.
the sermon zinged over my head, I craned my neck and my eyes traveled to
ornate iron plaque bolted to the wall. It said, "The word of our God shall sta
forever. Isaiah 40:8." Over and over I read it, week by week, year by year. A
week by week and year by year, that Scripture grew with me and in me.

Today, whenever I feel myself sinking in the quagmire of a broken promi
or whirled about by a sudden, jarring change, those words come back to n
as truth that can't be bent, broken, or shaken. The Word of our God sh
stand forever.

Lord, in all the changes and chances of my life,
You and Your Word are solid rock.

—SHARI SMYTH

"Then his body will become as healthy as a child's."
—JOB 33:25 (TLB)

*I*n April 2001, my mammogram showed two spots of invasive cancer in my left breast, and I was referred to a surgeon. He verified the findings and ordered a biopsy. I was then advised that the entire breast would have to be removed.

Because my daughter and grandchildren insisted on a second opinion, I went to another surgeon. In the examination room, the nurse prepared me, then left to bring in the doctor. Before the two of them returned, I prayed, "If it is in Your will, Father, let this be just a misreading of the mammogram. But if cancer is there and the operation must be done, I know You will be with me through it all."

A deep, warm feeling of quiet submission swept over me as the second surgeon confirmed the original diagnosis. I told him to schedule the surgery, which went fine, but an infection made it necessary for me to stay in the hospital for eight days.

My daughter stayed with me as long as she could be away from her job. She hated to leave me alone, but I assured her I would not be alone. "God and I are going through this together," I told her and everyone else who questioned my staying at home alone. A dear young nurse living across the street from me came twice daily to check on me and change the infection drains I had to wear. Friends and church members took turns bringing me meals and driving me to the doctor for follow-up appointments. I was then referred to an oncologist who ordered a CAT scan of my chest and abdominal area and a bone scan of my entire body.

I was surrounded with prayer on the day the tests were performed. And when the wonderful report came: My cancer had not spread. There was no sign of cancer in my body at all. I cannot thank God enough for the blessing of this healing.

Dear loving God, help me to use this experience to help others who are facing frightening times to trust You and Your healing power. Amen.
—DRUE DUKE

Where is the way where light dwelleth? and as for darkness,
where is the place thereof?

—JOB 38:19 (KJV)

For years my father was an alcoholic. It was not until I was eighteen years old that he finally discovered a way to loosen the grip of the addiction that controlled him.

Things had gotten so bad that my mother had him committed to a mental hospital in Goldsboro, North Carolina. While he was there, he and all the others in the alcoholic unit were bused to town once a week to attend Alcoholics Anonymous at a local church.

Daddy had no interest in AA. He was biding his time until he could find a way to escape the hospital and make his way back home to Richlands. There our family, church, and friends were all praying for him.

Later, Daddy told us his story: "I remember stepping off the bus at the church in downtown Goldsboro and looking into the darkness around me. It was a powerful darkness. Blacker than the shades of any night that had ever enveloped me. I hesitated for a moment, strangely drawn to the only light that kept the terrible darkness at bay—the soft glow at the door of the church. Suddenly, the very voice of the universe seemed to speak, giving notice that this was my final chance. At that critical moment, before the door closed leaving me forever in the darkness, I made my decision. I followed my fellow inmates through the bright opening and into the light of the church."

That night marked the first day of thirty years of sobriety for Daddy, and his decision changed the lives of our entire family.

Today, when I have a tough decision to make, I think of the light that led Daddy and I know that it will do the same for me.

Father, how thankful I am for Your holy light
that dispels all the darkness around me.

—LIBBIE ADAMS

*But he was pierced for our transgressions, he was crushed for our iniquities;
the punishment that brought us peace was on him.*
—Isaiah 53:5

One Saturday morning, my husband Whitney breezed into the kitchen, holding out a hymnal. "I forget how this song goes, and in an hour I'm supposed to lead it at the men's Bible study. Will you sing it with me?" he asked, looking at his watch.

I frowned. I'd rather eat that hymnal than sing right now is what I wanted to say. Last night I'd relived a wrong done to me a few years earlier. I'd stumbled out of bed dragging resentment like a ball-and-chain. But Whitney didn't seem to notice my pain. And of all the songs....

"Please...if you just get me started I know I'll remember the tune," Whitney said.

"Okay," I mumbled. He sat next to me, and I led in a cracked, unhappy voice.

> *Beneath the cross of Jesus I fain would take my stand,*
> *The shadow of a mighty Rock within a weary land.*

The powerful old hymn pulled at my resentment. I pulled back. But I was wronged.

"I got it," Whitney said, launching into the last verse:

> *Upon that cross of Jesus mine eyes at times can see*
> *The very dying form of One Who suffered there for me.*

Those words I'd sung all my life drew across my resentment the picture of Jesus hanging on the Cross, looking at me with redeeming love. I began to cry.

"Is something wrong?" Whitney asked, closing the hymnal. My tears turned to laughter. In his obtuseness, my wonderful husband had inadvertently led me to the one place of peace. Surrender at the foot of the Cross. I bowed my head and prayed:

> *Lord Jesus Christ, Lamb of God, have mercy on me.*
> —Shari Smyth

MARCH 25

Impress them on your children.
—DEUTERONOMY 6:7

At 3:00 a.m. in the bedroom of my father's house in the mountains, a crash of thunder shook me awake. In a voice nearly drowned by the sound of heavy rain drumming on the roof, my ten-year-old son John said, "Why did Grandpa just drive away?"

Alarmed, I jumped from bed and searched the empty house until I found a note on the dining room table: "Gone to the emergency room."

Dad had been suffering from a severe virus. Now my heart pounded thinking of him driving off alone into a violent thunderstorm. John and I hastily dressed and ran through the soaking rain to our car.

When we arrived at the emergency room, I was relieved to find Dad's white car parked safely in the lot. He was in the examination room, being fixed up with a prescription. As we were leaving, Dad ran into a friend of his whose husband was suffering from a serious lung infection. As Dad introduced us, I recognized the worried look in the woman's eyes as the same call to prayer that I had felt in the thunderstorm.

It was a simple exchange. I asked the woman if I might pray with her. She nodded. I put my hand on her shoulder and said a short, quiet prayer for her husband's successful treatment.

Several days later, while we were driving back home, John asked, "Why did you pray with that woman from the hospital?"

"Well, John," I answered, "she needed it, just like all of us."

In the midst of the thunderstorm and in the emergency room, I had nearly forgotten that John was with me, watching what I did. During those pre-dawn hours, my son had been observing, remembering, and evaluating my prayer habits. How many times had he been watching when I slogged my way through an emergency without stopping to pray? How many worried people had he seen me pass without offering a hand to grab on to in prayer?

Dear Father, today make my prayer habits ones that will invite others into closer communion with You.
—KAREN BARBER

March 26

O Lord my God, I cried unto thee, and thou hast healed me.
—Psalm 30:2 (kjv)

Like most animals, my dog Tara does not enjoy going to the veterinarian. So there we were in the waiting room, Tara shaking while I tried to reassure her. "It's going to be okay," I told her, holding her close to me. "It's just a simple blood test."

Easy for me to say. I knew what a blood test involved. But Tara had no idea what was going to happen.

I was worried, too. An earlier X-ray of Tara's heart showed some suspicious dark areas that might have indicated heartworm disease, a serious condition that is often fatal. I always had her inoculated against heartworm disease, but I didn't know what had gone on in her life before I adopted her. The disease was capable of hiding out in the body for years.

"This won't take long," said Penny, the vet tech, as she reached for Tara's leash and took her to one of the examining rooms. A few minutes later, the door opened and Penny beckoned to me. "I think Tara will be calmer if you're with her," she said. "I have to draw some blood, and she won't hold her leg still."

Tara was standing on the floor, trembling. I crouched down alongside of her and put my arm around her. "It's okay, honey. I'm right here," I said.

I could feel her calming down, and I told her to sit. When Penny lifted her left front leg up and deftly inserted the needle into a vein, Tara didn't pull back. I kept talking to her and the trembling stopped. When it was all over, I gave her a big hug.

Tara's blood test revealed traces of an early presence of heartworm disease. The shadowy areas in the X-ray were like scar tissue; they meant that she had survived the attack. The good news was that there was no threat to her any longer.

Lord, I thank You that whenever I have to go through something strange and scary, I have a loving Father by my side. Amen.
—Phyllis Hobe

Thy testimonies are very sure: holiness becometh thine house, O Lord, for ever.
—PSALM 93:5 (KJV)

The tears rolled quietly but steadily down her face and dripped onto her blouse, making a dark mark. We were standing around the Communion table at an early morning service, and I didn't know if her tears came from sorrow or from the wonder of worship. I had never seen her before. Big-city churches welcome many strangers.

I am both reserved and shy—foolish at this stage in my life, but a fact. So it surprised, almost shocked me to see my hand stretch out and take hers. The serene voices of the choir continued to sing:

Here I am, Lord.
Is it I, Lord?
I have heard You calling in the night.

And the weeping stranger and I held hands. The hymn ended. The congregation greeted one another. She squeezed my hand, said "thank you" almost in a whisper, and walked out of my life.

Afterward, I thought about those few moments. I wondered what gave me the confidence to reach out and take her hand. I just never do things like that; I never ask questions at lectures or offer my opinion unsolicited.

The explanation is so simple that it took awhile for me to realize it: I was in God's house, and when you're in someone's house, you follow His rules.

Lord, let me listen always for Your voice and do what You ask of me.
—BRIGITTE WEEKS

March 28

The memory of the righteous is a blessing.
—Proverbs 10:7 (RSV)

The sun was warm, but the wind had a sharp edge to it as I lifted the sap bucket off the maple tree. The bucket was full, and I focused my attention on the task of removing it from the small hook that held it securely to the tree.

When the ground thawed, the sap was drawn upward toward the branches to give the tree new life. This was the liquid that we would boil down to make maple syrup.

I lowered my eyes to the gathering pail on the ground and carefully poured the gallons of clear liquid into it. As the last drop fell, my eyes moved from the bucket to the granite marker that sat beneath the maple tree. It had been resting there for more than eleven years. On the stone were engraved the names of four family members who had passed away. Just looking at their names brought a rush of fond memories.

I paused for a moment and retreated from the labor at hand to remember my dad, my aunt, my cousin, and my mom, and the impact each had on my life. The memory of their love flowed into my soul just as the sap flowed from the maple tree into the bucket. God felt very close on that warm spring day as I gathered maple sap by the old rock wall.

Thank You, Lord, for allowing me to remember all those who were
Your hands and heart here on earth, those who shaped my life
and helped to make me who I am today.
—Patricia Pusey

MARCH 29

Why art thou cast down, O my soul? and why art thou disquieted in me?
—PSALM 42:5 (KJV)

I was feeling sorry for myself. Lethargic and blue, I trudged along. The weather had been rainy and cold for days. The spring that all New Englanders yearn for seemed perpetually out of reach, and Lent seemed to be dragging on forever. Everything was gray, tedious, and miserable as I wrestled with the umbrella that had become a seemingly permanent part of my walking garb.

Suddenly a flatbed truck came careering around the corner. Just as it passed me, the tractor it carried came loose and flew toward the sidewalk. My guardian angel must have been with me, because I somehow managed to drop my umbrella and roll onto the soft wet grass, barely out of the path of the crashing tractor.

The truck came to a screeching halt, and the driver came running back, all apologies. I was fine but trembling violently. No one had been hurt, and the young man couldn't reload his equipment and get out of there fast enough.

After he left, I sat in the wet grass and looked around. Everything was different. The grass was the soft, luminescent green of early spring. As I looked hard at the grass, I could see some tiny crocuses poking up. The magnolia across the street appeared to have tight, tiny buds. And the sky definitely looked ready to clear. Easter was still a couple of weeks away, but I'd already gotten a chance at a new life, and I wasn't about to waste it.

Father, help me to remember each day what a magnificent gift You've given me.
—MARCI ALBORGHETTI

All the days ordained for me were written in your book
before one of them came to be.

—PSALM 139:16

"Mom, I'd like to celebrate my twentieth anniversary of being diagnosed a diabetic by climbing a 'fourteener,'" Derek said in a phone call from his home in Oregon to ours in Colorado. "And I'd like to invite some friends to join me."

His words triggered a memory so vivid it might have happened yesterday: a nine-year-old boy in a droopy hospital gown bravely learning to give himself daily insulin shots and finger-prick blood tests. As I watched him take on this responsibility that would be part of his life forever, I prayed that diabetes would never hold him back or change his choices in life.

"We'd love to help plan a celebration," I told him. Yet as I hung up, I wondered if he knew that the "fourteener" (a mountain at least fourteen thousand feet high) would still be covered with snow in March.

Over the next few weeks, Derek made plans. He invited his buddies from college, who had stood by him during some tough physical challenges. He asked his two sisters to come from California and called a few close friends from Colorado. Amazingly, they all showed up! And so it was that Derek and his wife Alexandra and the rest of us stood together at the base of a huge mountain on a bright blue-sky morning in March, ready to strap on our snowshoes and tackle the challenge.

Several hours later, Derek and his macho buddies made it to the top of the windswept mountain. (Some of us turned back at the halfway point.) Later that evening, we hosted a celebration dinner, and as we stood in a circle, holding hands to pray before eating, with sunburned faces and tired bodies, I thanked God that a little boy had grown into a young man who has not let diabetes hold him back from achieving his dreams.

Thank You, Lord, for using life's difficult challenges to shape us
into the people You've created us to be.

—CAROL KUYKENDALL

MARCH 31

But the Comforter...shall teach you all things, and bring all things to your remembrance, whatsoever I have said unto you.
—JOHN 14:26 (KJV)

One snowy March day I got a call from my dad, who was being treated for cancer. "Honey," he said, "my good sweater has a hole in the elbow, and I was wondering if you could help me find another one like it." I knew the sweater well. It was a V-necked cardigan, the color of pine needles, and just about as prickly. "It has to have pockets," he reminded me.

The local department stores had already switched over to their spring merchandise, so I telephoned a mail-order company. I told the clerk that my dad needed a nice sweater to wear to his radiation treatments. Later that afternoon she called me back. "We've struck gold, Mrs. Messner," she said. "I can get you one in forest green, red, navy, chestnut brown, yellow, or camel. Why don't I send them all out to you, so your dad can choose the one he likes best?"

My mind quickly began to calculate the cost of all that return postage when something I learned in nursing school came back to me. When you're old and ill, you don't get many choices.

When the sweaters arrived, Dad tried on the entire shipment, his eyes dancing as he fingered the soft wool and checked out the pockets. "This brown is my favorite.... No, I like the red best.... No, I'll take this yellow one. Wait until those nurses see me in it!"

Marveling over the sweaters' bargain-basement prices, I recalled Dad's stories about the hardships of his childhood and how embarrassed he'd been by the threadbare hand-me-downs he'd worn to school. I sensed another nudge and this time I didn't waste a moment. "I have a solution, Dad. It's high time you had that back-to-school wardrobe."

Thank You, Lord, for the pure magic in store for me when I follow Your nudges.
—ROBERTA MESSNER

April

Your adversary the devil, as a roaring lion, walketh about, seeking whom he may devour: whom resist stedfast in the faith.

—1 PETER 5:8–9 (KJV)

I'd gone back to walking four miles a day after years of telling myself that I didn't have the energy. At first, my imagination was getting as much of a workout as my legs. *What should I do if I meet an unfriendly dog?* I wondered. A variety of scenarios played themselves out in my mind.

Then one April morning I left home when the sun was barely up. Birds greeted each other as I walked quickly down the street. At the bottom of the hill, a strange dog charged out of the woods, headed straight for me. My heart thumped as the big fellow, who weighed about a hundred pounds, continued to charge, snarling, teeth showing, muscles straining.

Lord Jesus, help me!

I sensed His answer: *rebuke him now.*

Somehow I managed to stomp my foot as though I had power and authority and screamed, "Nooooo!"

He froze, then dropped his head as though he suddenly sniffed something very interesting. With his nose glued to the pavement, he made a quick exit back into the woods and disappeared. I felt the fear again and relief. *Thank You, Lord.*

I sensed a silent message: *you can call on Me this way every time the enemy tries to attack you with troubling thoughts, memories, or what-ifs.*

Now, I wouldn't necessarily recommend that you try this method with a threatening dog, but I've found that where dangerous spiritual critters are concerned, it works wonders.

Father God, when the enemy comes like a roaring lion to attack my thoughts, help me remember to call on Your name.

—MARION BOND WEST

APRIL 2

Let us examine our ways and test them, and let us return to the Lord.
—LAMENTATIONS 3:40

*F*igure skater Michelle Kwan, elegant and graceful, was favored to win the gold medal in the women's figure skating competition at the 1998 Winter Olympics, but a little dynamo named Tara Lipinski exploded onto the ice in a brilliant performance that gave her the gold.

A TV reporter later asked Michelle, "How did it feel to lose the Olympics?"

Michelle looked at her in astonishment and said, "I didn't lose. I won the silver."

Way to go, Michelle! I thought, applauding her positive attitude.

Then I remembered something an elderly neighbor said to me long ago when, as a child, I cried over having lost a declamation contest that had been sponsored by our church. "Honey, you memorized your piece and you did your best. Just getting up there took a lot of nerve, but you tried your hardest and that makes you a winner even if you didn't get a ribbon. The real losers in this world are the ones who don't even try."

My neighbor's wise words have inspired me ever since to try to do my best in whatever I attempt and to respect an honest effort—from myself or anyone else—even if that effort doesn't include a prize.

Lord, please give me the words today to encourage someone
who is facing a challenge. Amen.
—MADGE HARRAH

"You will call your walls Salvation and your gates Praise."
—ISAIAH 60:18

I had recently moved from our country home of twenty-seven years to a condominium. It had been a gut-wrenching decision. Not only was leaving a place where every nook and cranny had a precious memory of our happy family of seven, and where almost every bush and tree was one I had planted and nurtured to its blazing glory; the move from our family home also signaled the painful end of a marriage. I desperately needed a new beginning.

My care group from church wanted to give me a housewarming. "Could you make that a house blessing?" I asked. "Instead of gifts, each person can write out a personal blessing."

On that special night sixteen people crowded into my small condominium, their arms laden with food, their faces beaming goodwill. Here are some of the blessings they read to me:

> *"Even the sparrow has found a home, and the swallow a nest for herself... place near your altar, O Lord Almighty" (Psalm 84:3).*
> *"The crown of the home is godliness/The beauty of the home is order;*
> *The glory of the home is hospitality/The blessing of the home is contentment*
> *A good laugh is sunshine in a house/We wish you all of these in your new home.*
> *"Trust in the Lord and do good. Live in this house and enjoy its safety."*

Now, whenever the problems of my new life threaten to overwhelm me, I take out the carefully written blessings of my friends. As I reread them, I'm keenly aware that the God of blessing, who delights to bless His children, is with me in this new venture.

Father, thank You for Your promise to watch over my comings and goings,
both now and forevermore.
—HELEN GRACE LESCHEID

APRIL 4

Sing psalms, hymns and spiritual songs with gratitude in your hearts to God.
—COLOSSIANS 3:16

The scratchiness in my throat was growing worse as we rehearsed Easter anthems at Wednesday-night choir practice. By the time it was my turn to launch into the triumphant "Alleluia," the solo I looked forward to singing all year, I could barely whisper. Laryngitis had silenced me.

It wasn't fair! Just last Christmas another severe head cold and bout with laryngitis had prevented me from singing with the eighty-voice Community Christmas Chorale. Since I had no family for two thousand miles and worked outside of town, singing with the church and community choirs helped me to feel that I belonged somewhere. Yet here I was, sidelined again.

Easter morning seemed unusually serene without the frantic rush to church for early vocal warm-ups, sleepy children in tow. In fact, our family enjoyed a leisurely breakfast and a chance to savor my braided Easter bread—and each other. I didn't know Sunday morning could be so calm.

Even with the overflow Easter congregation, we sat in our regular pew. My children, who usually sat with friends when I sang, basked in the unaccustomed coziness. When did we last sit together as a family at Easter?

Since I had rehearsed for several weeks before the laryngitis hit, I found myself lip-synching all the anthems. The substitute soloist motioned for us to stand as she began the joyous "Alleluia." Despite my regret at not leading it, I found myself singing with gusto—soundlessly. Lip-synch "Alleluia"? Why not? The joy begins in my heart, not in my mouth. Singing only makes it louder!

Now I noticed for the first time the sweet, tentative voices of the worshippers around me: the elderly couple, the bashful widow, the teenager. I quickly resolved to sing more softly in the future; I'd probably been drowning them out for years.

Heavenly Father, thank You for the praise that fills my heart
even when my voice is still.
—GAIL THORELL SCHILLING

The Lord has anointed me...to give them a garland instead of ashes....
—ISAIAH 61:1, 3 (RSV)

*T*wo tall silver vases stand behind the altar in our church. During Lent the hold only dark green leaves—no flowers—to represent the "wilderness season of penance and preparation. We take this tradition seriously. A fe years back, when St. Patrick's Day fell on Sunday, someone asked the pastor permission to add a dozen kelly-green carnations to the leafy altar bouquet "We'd better not," the pastor said, "but they'd look great in the parish hall."

Easter morning we celebrate with banks of regal white lilies delivered to th church by a florist. But that's not all. Everyone brings fresh-cut flowers to th service, and we "flower the Cross." Blossoms in hand—azaleas, daffodils, tulip carnations (some kelly green)—we process down to the front of the church an fill up a chicken-wire frame about three-feet high. Last year I brought purpl grape hyacinth stems, enough to share with others who had forgotten their ow colorful contributions. The result? A lush visual reminder of abundant an everlasting life.

Lord, prepare my heart for Your Easter blessing.
—EVELYN BENCE

The Lord passed before him, and proclaimed,
"The Lord, the Lord, a God merciful and gracious, slow to anger,
and abounding in steadfast love and faithfulness."
—EXODUS 34:6 (RSV)

For years, I had longed to go to the Church of the Holy Sepulchre in Jerusalem, which for more than sixteen hundred years Christians have believed marks the very place where Jesus died and was buried.

The church itself is a huge, cavernous building, a combination of several churches built over the centuries. Even though hundreds of tourists were wandering through when we first entered, I experienced a hushed reverence. In various corners of the church, people were worshipping or quietly kneeling to pray. But as we climbed the narrow steps to the section built over Golgotha, the atmosphere changed completely.

The area was packed with people and tour guides chattering in many languages. People pushed and shoved to reach the front to light a candle and kiss the floor under the altar where Jesus' cross had stood. I stared in amazement as a young woman tried to put a big stuffed teddy bear on the altar and pose next to it. Instead of scolding her, the monk tending the candles gently told her it wasn't appropriate to put her stuffed animal on the altar. He suggested she hold it for the photo and asked people to stand back for her to do so.

I continued to watch him handle the crowd. He quietly yet firmly reminded people to wait their turn and give others a chance to kneel or pray a few moments. He answered questions, patted the children's heads, and gave them leftover candles to "take home for your prayers." His gentle firmness diffused the tension and frustration of the crowd; his patience brought peace.

He was a reminder: Jesus died for all of us different people, whether reverent or rude. He welcomes each of us as we are and lovingly helps us change.

Lord Jesus, in all my dealings with people today, help me to love as You love—
with patience, kindness, and forbearance.
—MARY BROWN

APRIL 7

When Jesus therefore had received the vinegar, he said, It is finished:
and he bowed his head, and gave up the ghost.

—JOHN 19:30 (KJV)

*A*t our Easter Sunday service, my friend was intrigued with the large wooden cross covered in red squares of paper standing beside the altar. I explained that on Good Friday our pastor had spoken about Jesus' last words from the Cross: "It is finished."

"What did Jesus finish for you?" he had asked the congregation. "On the red square inside your bulletin, write out what Jesus finished for you personally, then come to the front and pin your paper here," he said, pointing to a rough wooden cross lying across the altar steps.

"What did you write?" my friend asked.

"Condemnation."

She looked puzzled.

"For most of my life, I've felt that no matter how hard I try, I'm not measuring up," I said. "I think it had something to do with being the oldest in the family."

"And did it help—going to the front?"

I nodded. "It was like driving a truth home to me," I said. "The fact that 'there is therefore now no condemnation to them which are in Christ Jesus' [Romans 8:1]."

My friend was silent for a moment. Then she shared a personal need with me. "That's what I would have written on the paper and pinned to the Cross," she said.

"You can still do it," I said. "Do you want to?"

She nodded.

Later, as we gazed at the Cross covered with red squares, hers included, I marveled at the power of the Cross of Jesus. One cry—"It is finished"—covered all our needs.

Dear Lord Jesus, thank You that the debt we owe is paid in full.

—HELEN GRACE LESCHEID

Sarah said, God hath made me to laugh,
so that all that hear will laugh with me.
—GENESIS 21:6 (KJV)

A special cake for a special day," I reminded grandsons Ryan, nine, David, six, and Mark, three, as we carefully poured cake batter into the lamb mold on Holy Saturday night. "After it's baked and cooled, you can decorate it." The cake, symbolizing Jesus the Lamb of God, was an Easter tradition. Sharing it as a family always brought us a solemn and special awareness of Christ's sacrificial love.

Perhaps I shouldn't have let small boys decorate unsupervised. The finished cake was Pepto-Bismol pink, except where the blue-gumdrop eyes had combined with the frosting to create purple blotches. The lamb's head wobbled precariously. And someone had put black jelly beans in the coconut "grass" to symbolize...well, you get the picture.

There wasn't time to make another dessert. I touched up the eyes, secured the head with a dozen toothpicks, and picked out the jelly beans. After Easter dinner, I carried the cake to the table, repeating the words from John 1:29 (RSV): "Behold, the Lamb of God, who takes away the sins of the world." But when I set down the cake, the lamb's head toppled off, spraying us with coconut before it came to rest upside down on the tablecloth. The kids burst into peals of laughter; so did their parents.

The moment was ruined. Or was it? As I cleaned up the mess and passed round slices of cake, I remembered that while Jesus was indeed the Lamb of God, He was also part of the everyday world. He helped with refreshments at the wedding in Cana, got Zaccheus out of a tree, and ate and drank with common people. He not only blessed little children but used them as an example of the kingdom of heaven—a kingdom that surely includes laughter.

Lord Jesus, thank You for showing the heavenly and the holy
in the laughter of Your little children.
—PENNEY SCHWAB

APRIL 9

"I am the Good Shepherd and know my own sheep, and they know me."
—JOHN 10:14 (TLB)

Our children's church is always lively. A small group of kids run to the front of the sanctuary and sit on the steps leading to the altar for a short sermon and prayer time. Recently, Pastor Warren's topic was "The Good Shepherd." "Sheep obey the shepherd because they know the shepherd will feed them, give them water, and keep them safe," he said. "They trust the shepherd and follow him without question, don't they?"

Makayla, who has had experience with her friend Danielle's sheep, thought for a moment, then said, "Well...except for the sheep that have an attitude!"

We all laughed. In our rural community almost everyone is familiar with the traits of farm animals.

"Sheep do have an attitude," Pastor Warren told Makayla. "They can be stubborn, some wander off from the flock, and some butt you away when you try to help them."

Makayla's observation and Pastor Warren's response hit a sensitive spot in my heart. Just like those sheep, I often "have an attitude" that keeps me from listening to God. I make plans, then expect God to bless them instead of waiting for the Shepherd to walk ahead and reveal His will. I let other voices crowd out His gentle words. I forget that the Shepherd has other sheep not of my fold. He loves them and expects me to do the same.

How thankful I am that Jesus loves all His sheep...even those of us who sometimes have an attitude!

Good Shepherd, let me hear Your voice and follow
Your lead every day, in every way.
—PENNEY SCHWAB

I have planted...but God gave the increase.
—1 CORINTHIANS 3:6 (KJV)

*E*very spring, I steal a bouquet of lilacs.

Okay, maybe *steal* is too strong a word. But the lilac bush isn't mine. Still, I load my arms with the fragrant purple blossoms.

The flowers bloom just barely in sight of the highway. I park my car on the shoulder of the road and wade through neglected grasses, past the foundation of a long-gone house, and through a small patch of cactus to the purple wonder, bent and splendid, offering itself to me in polite submission. I gather the blossoms in my arms and walk back to my car.

I'd like to think that whoever planted my secret lilac bush would be pleased that I seek out this annual bouquet. Perhaps she watched it grow from her kitchen window. Maybe, long before the highway was here, her mother planted a small, gangly twig. And with sun and rain and time it became a lilac bush of extraordinary beauty.

Later, as I inhale the heady scent of my bouquet, I'm reminded that good things take time. And that, in ways we can't begin to imagine, the seeds we plant today will produce fruit. And maybe a few lilacs.

*Oh, Master Gardener, thank You for the miracle of growth and the role
I'm called to play in it. And thank You for lilacs!*
—MARY LOU CARNEY

APRIL 11

And ye shall serve the Lord your God, and he shall
bless thy bread, and thy water.
—EXODUS 23:25 (KJV)

I*t was April 1950, and my husband John and I were returning from Europe for the birth of our first child. Because the harbor at Cherbourg was still war-damaged, the *Queen Elizabeth* was anchored offshore. As we walked down the ramp to the launch that would ferry us out, not a ripple showed on the placid surface of the sea. But the instant my foot touched the deck, my stomach rose into my throat.

"It will be better on the big boat," John said.

It wasn't better. John helped me down several stairways and onto the lower bunk in our cabin. And there I remained for the five-and-a-half day crossing. Eating was out of the question: I couldn't bear even to hear John's enthusiastic reports from the dining room. What I remember most from that nightmare trip is the thirst. Water was all I could think of. Unable to hold down more than a teaspoon's worth, I fantasized about gulping it down by the tumbler, the gallon.

Dehydration finally brought on a kind of delirium. In the refrigerator of my childhood home there had always been a jar of ice water. I saw it now, suspended from the upper bunk just above me—a tall narrow bottle with a red cap. Again and again I reached for it, felt the cold moistness of the glass, unscrewed the cap....

All of it came back this morning. They're working on the water main in our part of town, and when I turned on the faucet this morning, nothing happened. I stared at that dry kitchen faucet. How generously water has always come from it! Water so abundant, so readily available in our part of the world that I've forgotten what a blessing it is simply to pour a glass and drink.

I'm learning, this year, to thank God for overlooked daily gifts. But, oh, let me not forget the everyday provision on which life itself depends!

Come to me today, Lord, as Living Water.
—ELIZABETH SHERRILL

For ye have need of patience, that, after ye have done
the will of God, ye might receive the promise.
—HEBREWS 10:36 (KJV)

The help wanted ads leered at me. I'd sent out hordes of résumés to no avail. Still, every morning I prayed: "God, help me find a job that will make me smile."

I saw a job I never would have had the guts to apply for if I hadn't been desperate. "Ordinary people wanted for a two-day fashion show in the shopping mall." *Hmm, I sure fill the bill on that one*, I thought.

By the time I got there, I was quite hopeful. "The manager will see you right away," the receptionist told me.

After that warm welcome, I was astonished when the man gave me a three-second glance and brusquely waved me away. "No," he said, "you won't do." His head was already down reading his magazine.

Feeling sure I'd been led to answer his ad, I boldly asked, "Sir, may I ask why?" At his startled look, I plodded on, "Your ad did say you were looking for ordinary people."

"Oh," he exclaimed, "you got it wrong! We're not looking for ordinary people. We're looking for models who *look* like ordinary people!"

He went back to reading his magazine. And I? Well, I managed to stifle my laughter at the absurdity of the situation until I left his office. And on my way home I passed a bookstore, went in, filled out an application, and have been happily employed there ever since!

When I'm down in the dumps, God, remind me that even there
You can give me something to smile about.
—LINDA NEUKRUG

April 13

*Blessed is the man who trusts in the Lord.... He is like a tree planted along a
riverbank, with its roots reaching deep into the water.*

—Jeremiah 17:7–8 (TLB)

Our California oaks are becoming endangered. Years of drought and mo[...]
of all the spreading urban sprawl that is creeping into our open spac[...]
and up our hills are taking their toll. It is heartbreaking to see so many of tho[...]
beautiful trees, some three or four hundred years old, come crashing down.

We live under a canopy of four large oaks. Having lost one several years a[...]
to beastly borer bugs, we guard them fiercely. When wildfires blaze across o[...]
hills, we aim our hoses at the oaks. A house can be rebuilt in a hurry; it wou[...]
take three hundred years to regrow one of these oaks.

I've sat in the hollow separating the four main trunks of an oak up on o[...]
terrace and, held in the comfort of that embrace, I've watered it with my tear[...]
I've traced my fingers along its rough bark and poured out my soul, knowin[...]
whatever confidences I've shared would never be betrayed. I've laughed wit[...]
the ripple of its leaves as rosy-cheeked children swung high on the simp[...]
plank hung from the massive girth of one huge branch. I have spent a lifetim[...]
sharing my joys and sorrows and pulling on the strength of that old oak—an[...]
I've wondered about those in generations before me who, too, have soug[...]
its sanctuary.

With their feet on the ground and their heads in the sky, trees are much lik[...]
us: arms lifted up in prayer, deep roots watered by the Word of God. That's wha[...]
grounds us in the faith and steadies us in the stormy seasons of our life.

*Lord, what awesome wisdom You've given us in Your creation!
Give me the heart of an oak: strong, steady, and with the will to endure.*

—Fay Angus

April 14

And Ruth said, Intreat me not to leave thee,
or to return from following after thee: for whither thou goest, I will go.
—Ruth 1:16 (KJV)

The cavernous Union Depot in St. Paul, Minnesota, was the first scheduled stop for the traveling *Titanic* exhibit. I waited patiently in line for the chance to see what haunting mysteries the sea had yielded after more than eighty years. Wandering by each display case, I felt one poignant stab after another as I gazed at a child's marbles, some of them cracked in two; a broken clarinet, corroded an eerie green; a man's safety razor and blades, laid out ready to use; the backs of a woman's mirror and brush set; a deck of playing cards, fully restored by freeze-drying them; and a jar of fat olives, meant for the dining room.

As if this weren't enough, every so often a recording of the *Titanic*'s magnificent whistles blew through the crowded, subdued room. It was easy to imagine how that sound must have thrilled the passengers leaning over the rails. The whistles could be heard for eleven miles.

But the most impressive discovery for me was the account of the matronly, gray-haired Ida Straus. According to the story, she stepped back out of the lifeboat about to carry her to safety, allowing her maid to take her place, and calmly told her husband, "We have been living together for many years and where you go, I go." Together they went down with the ship.

Ruth's statement to her mother-in-law Naomi, "Where thou goest, I will go," has been repeated by brides and grooms in many modern-day weddings. But I never truly understood it until I stepped on board the *Titanic* eighty-seven years after it sank, and overheard Mrs. Straus.

Timeless Lord, thank You for great examples from the past that help me
to live my present more fully for You.
—Carol Knapp

APRIL 15

"Never again will I make you an object of scorn."
—JOEL 2:19

My cousin Bunny was born in the 1930s, profoundly deaf. Our family decided that no allowances would be made for that, and Bunny learned to lip-read at a very early age. With training, he learned to speak so well that many people had no idea he couldn't hear, which helped him escape some of the teasing other children directed at him when they learned about his condition. When Bunny began to look for work after high school, I could see that my parents were really worried about his future, even though they didn't say anything in front of me.

At Passover the next year, Bunny came to our seder, bursting with news that he had gotten a job in the office at an oil refinery. We asked him to tell us how it happened. Bunny said, "They tried to tell me that they couldn't hire me because I wouldn't be able to hear the alarm if it went off, but I told them that there was nothing at all wrong with my eyesight. I said, 'If I see everybody running for the doors, I'll run, too, and you can tell me about the alarm later.'"

God had given Bunny all the strength he needed to cope with whatever came his way, and over the years that followed, I've discovered that even if there are areas in which I, too, fall short, God has done the same for me.

Thank You, Lord, for Your gifts to us, despite our flaws.
—RHODA BLECKER

APRIL 16

I will praise thee; for I am fearfully and wonderfully made.
—PSALM 139:14 (KJV)

One of my favorite memories of my mother is the celebration of her last birthday. Her worsening emphysema, the result of a childhood lung infection, had mostly confined her to bed by the age of sixty-five. But on this glorious spring day, we surprised her by having a horse-drawn hayrack pull into her driveway, loaded with all of her children and grandchildren carrying balloons and singing "Happy Birthday." We bundled her up, put her on a lawn chair, along with her oxygen tank, and off we went for a ride on country roads at sunset. She'd always loved horses, sunsets, and family celebrations.

In our family, birthdays have always mattered. When our kids were little, we started with balloons at breakfast and candles in the doughnuts on the red-and-white "This Is Your Special Day" plate.

The kids are grown and on their own now, but we're still a birthday family. Though I can't find any Scripture that exactly says this, I believe that God, who gave us our birth dates, intends our annual birthdays to be a time to consider the unique gift of His personal creation of each of us. It's a great time to think about who He created us to be, and where we are in the process of becoming that person. Though we grow up, we never outgrow the opportunity to celebrate that life-shaping gift. That's why birthdays matter.

Lord, may I use my birthday to celebrate the person You created me to be.
—CAROL KUYKENDALL

April 17

We are the temple of the living God.
—2 Corinthians 6:16 (nasb)

One Sunday in spring I walked into our little church earlier than usual and noticed something different. Dusty footprints covered the foyer rug. Crumpled bulletins lay scattered under the sanctuary pews. Hymnbooks sat askew in their racks. A deaconess who was hastily tidying up stopped to apologize. "I'm afraid there was a mix-up in the volunteer schedule, and as a result the church didn't get cleaned this past week."

"Let me help," I said as I removed my coat. Whisking our way through the sanctuary, we straightened hymnals, and I wondered, *When was the last time I spontaneously made a joyful noise unto the Lord?* We picked up stray bulletins, and I recalled how I'd often neglected to have my quiet times lately.

Moving downstairs to the Sunday school rooms, we erased blackboards as I prayed, *Lord, I'm having a hard time wiping away a past hurt.*

We picked up scraps of paper and crayons, and I asked forgiveness for picturing a certain person in a bad light when she was only trying to do her job. We straightened chairs. *Haven't I shoved aside a good intention recently?*

Coming back upstairs, we agreed that the dusty footprints on the foyer rug would have to stay for now…like that belated apology I still owe a friend.

Tidying the church had made me aware of the clutter that had accumulated in my own inner sanctum. I had tried to dismiss each scrap of guilt with "Oh, it's nothing much." Perhaps it seemed like nothing much when taken separately, but collectively it became quite noticeable. I couldn't blame it on a mix-up in the volunteer schedule either.

More than forty years ago, I promised God I would try to keep my spiritual house in order so that nothing in my life would distract others from worshipping Him. Now it was time to ask His forgiveness for becoming a spiritual litterbug.

Lord, thank You for the privilege of worshipping in a neat, clean sanctuary that challenges me each week to tidy up my own personal walk with You.

—Alma Barkman

*Make sure that nobody pays back wrong for wrong, but always try
to be kind to each other and to everyone else.*
—1 THESSALONIANS 5:15

On my desk sits one of my all-time favorite pictures of me with my older sister and two younger brothers. There we are, four adults in midlife, with our arms around one another, each wearing an expression that reflects our childhood personalities. The picture is proof that we're still comfortable enough to be ourselves when we're together.

It also reminds me that family matters. "You can argue all you want here at home," Mom used to tell us, "but when you go out in the world, you stick together." After she died, I wondered if that legacy of loyalty would last without her at the hub of our wheel, connecting us and keeping our circle intact.

I recently heard a woman complain that visiting family is just too much trouble, what with all the packing, all the travel, all the emotional baggage and hassles. "So we stopped doing it," she said simply. My picture represents the opposite choice. In spite of the hassles, in spite of the distance or our differences or the missing hub, my siblings and I haven't given up our bond. We make the effort to get together. At the bottom of the picture, I've taped this quote by Kurt Vonnegut:

"Be nice to your siblings. They're your best link to your past and the people most likely to stick with you in the future."

The picture on my desk reminds me that family matters, and in each other, we not only have a common history, but a hopeful future.

Lord, thank You for my unique circle called family.
—CAROL KUYKENDALL

APRIL 19

There is a time for everything...a time to be born and a time to die.
—ECCLESIASTES 3:1–2

*T*watch out the car window as the scenery zips by: fields of corn and beans, freshly painted red barns, and herds of grazing Holsteins. I've made this trip to the small town where I grew up hundreds of times. But I realize, as I look at my son-in-law driving and my daughter sitting beside him, I've never before made it sitting in the backseat. Always I was the one driving—each mile bringing me closer to my mother and my sister, closer to the warm familiarity of going home. But now my sister has retired to Florida, and Mother is buried in the small cemetery down the road from where she lived.

Small feet kick against the car seat, and the sound of a rattle breaks into my thoughts. I turn to look at my six-month-old grandson Drake. He smiles and bangs the rattle against his leg. I reach for his hand and begin singing silly rhymes.

Later, I stand at Mother's grave, shaded by the branches of a giant tree. The only sounds are the calls of birds high overhead. With Drake in my arms, I kneel to place a bouquet of purple roses (Mother's favorite color) at the base of her headstone. "She would have loved you so very much," I whisper into Drake's soft baby neck. Suddenly, the baby leans forward, and his tiny hand pats the warm granite.

And maybe, just maybe, somewhere in the halls of heaven, Mother smiles at the touch of her great-grandson's hand on her shoulder.

Comfort us, Father, with the continuing blessing of Your love—in this life and in the one beyond. Let us teach it to our children and our children's children.
—MARY LOU CARNEY

The beasts of the field shall be at peace with thee.
—Job 5:23 (kjv)

Taking down the plaster walls of our house was like peeling back time: first a layer of paneling, then sheets of floral wallpaper, and then the plaster and lathe. Behind the lathe the south side of the house was one large mouse and squirrel nest, tucked with newspaper and cloth—even a teddy bear.

Most of the squirrels had been frightened away by our banging, but one headstrong little red squirrel was unwilling to give up its home. While we worked, it stood outside the house, stamping its feet, batting its tail, and chattering incessantly. When we left, it would find a way back inside and make a new nest—usually with scraps it stole from my husband's newspaper.

As autumn neared, black walnuts from the tree in the front yard appeared on the now-visible rafters, evidence of our little squirrel's hard work. As I took them down, I thought about the squirrel carrying one nut at a time, running over the ground, up the side of the house, and then back again. We had a lot in common: each of us was trying to get our house ready for winter.

By then, my husband and I had moved in and the little squirrel had disappeared. On frigid nights when the wind whipped against the house, I prayed that the little creature was safe and warm. Closing my eyes, I imagined scraps of my husband's half-finished crossword puzzle tucked beneath the squirrel in a neighbor's attic.

I had almost forgotten about the squirrel when I spotted it early that spring in a nearby apple tree. It was thinner and its expression had changed from anger to surprise. I imagine it saw the same expression on my face—surprise, mingled with relief that each of us had survived the winter.

*Lord, thank You for hard work and a warm house
and a no-longer-angry new friend.*
—Sabra Ciancanelli

He retaineth not his anger for ever, because he delighteth in mercy.
—MICAH 7:18 (KJV)

inda, if beating yourself up were an Olympic sport, you'd win gold medal!"

Annabel, my close friend, stunned me with that blunt observation after I told her how I had mishandled a situation with a student in a third-grade class whe I was substituting. "I should never have let him go to the boy's room withou pass! It was my fault he got into trouble with the hall monitor! I'm so stupid!"

My friend burst out laughing, and then made her "Olympic" comment. Aft a brief period of reflection I had to admit that she was right. I did put mys down an awful lot. Why, just during the previous day I had called myself "a slo for having some papers spread out on my desk, "ugly" when I left the hou without makeup, and "an idiot" when I left the house for an emergency substitu job without my emergency lesson plan.

In a more reflective tone, Annabel said, "I once took a workshop at chur where the woman in charge had us list all the mean things we say about ourselve

"How many did you have on your list?" I asked.

"Fifteen," she confessed. "But then the teacher said, 'Now turn to the pers next to you and say all the items on your list as if you were speaking to th person!'"

My jaw dropped. "What did you do?"

"Nothing. Nobody did. We all just sat there, until I said, 'I could never s these things to anyone else!'

"And our teacher replied, 'Well, if you can't say them to anyone else, th don't ever say them to yourself!'"

My friend had a point. I would never insult a child of God—and I'm Go child, too!

God, today let me be as kind to myself as I would be to another of Your childre
—LINDA NEUKRUG

In my Father's house are many mansions.
—JOHN 14:2 (KJV)

*M*y dear friend and coworker Sylvia Gardner retired from the Veterans Affairs Medical Center in Huntington, West Virginia, this past year, and her leaving reminded me of a time when she was my treasured God-find. It was a chilly day in April, the day we buried my mother.

What made the day even more difficult was the fact that my dad was in the hospital and unable to attend Mother's service because of the stroke he had suffered the day Mother died. As we five siblings and five grandchildren huddled around the casket at the gravesite, I imagined Dad in his hospital room grieving all alone. *Why didn't you think to have someone stay with him?* I berated myself. But it was too late to change things.

What I hadn't counted on was Sylvia, a Yankee nurse practitioner who had relocated to the hills of Appalachia in the 1970s and quickly claimed the mountain people as her own. Instead of attending Mother's service, Sylvia had gone to the sixth floor of St. Mary's Hospital. Along with a hospital chaplain she'd met on the elevator, she headed to Dad's room in hopes of conducting a makeshift funeral service. Once there, Sylvia, always a nurse with a hearing heart, gave Dad the greatest gift of all by simply listening. Dad, nearly blind, his speech slurred from his stroke, recited words he had long ago committed to memory for such a time as this:

"Let not your heart be troubled: ye believe in God, believe also in me. In my Father's house are many mansions: if it were not so, I would have told you. I go to prepare a place for you. And if I go and prepare a place for you, I will come again, and receive you unto myself; that where I am, there ye may be also" (John 14:1–3 KJV).

Thank You, Lord, for Your promise of life eternal.
—ROBERTA MESSNER

First go and be reconciled with your brother; then come and offer your gift.
—MATTHEW 5:24

At a church potluck awhile ago, older parishioners were asked to sha childhood memories to help us younger parents strengthen o families. An elderly Greek lady, Helen, told us that every Saturday evening h family had prayed special prayers ending the week and starting the new on Most importantly, they asked forgiveness of each other and their Father. "On then did I feel ready to go to church the next day," Helen said.

Their Saturday ritual seemed only an interesting old custom until a fe weeks later, when our family attended the Liturgy at a Romanian Orthod monastery in southern Michigan. During the Liturgy, the clergy embrace an ask forgiveness of each other, then bow to the congregation, asking the peop to forgive them. When they had finished doing this, the woman in front of m turned to the lady next to her and whispered, "Forgive me, Mom." Her mo asked her for forgiveness in turn, and they hugged each other. Then, befo receiving Holy Communion, I noticed each nun go to the abbess, bow and as forgiveness, then turn and bow to all the other nuns.

Looking at my husband Alex across the heads of our children, I mouthed th words, "Forgive me."

"I do. Forgive me, too," he whispered. We reached behind the kids and gav each other's hand a squeeze.

Now, before our family receives Communion each Sunday, we ask eac other's forgiveness. Sometimes we think of specifics, such as "Forgive me fo losing my temper and shouting at you," or "Forgive me for not doing wha you asked right away." At other times, nothing definite comes to mind, b we ask pardon for any ways we've wronged or failed each other, knowingl or unknowingly, and seal our reconciliation with a big hug. Cleansed of th past week's failures or irritations, we are renewed to start fresh another wee "fighting the good fight of the faith."

Father, before I worship You today, help me be at peace with everyone.
—MARY BROWN

APRIL 24

Strait is the gate, and narrow is the way, which leadeth unto life.
—MATTHEW 7:14 (KJV)

I hurried across the plaza at Rockefeller Center. I was late, late enough not to notice the beautiful weather. As I ran up the steps at the side of the famous skating rink, I stopped dead in my tracks.

Above me was a slender silver column reaching up to the sky at a seventy-five-degree angle to the earth. It glittered in the sunlight. And walking up the steep silver slope were seven life-sized figures.

For a minute I was confused. The figures weren't a troupe of acrobats; they were part of a daring and eye-catching sculpture. *Who are they?* I wondered. *Where are they going? Who created this amazing sight?*

"Excuse me," I said to a security guard leaning against the wall, "but could you tell me what that is?" I pointed to the sculpture.

"Yes," he said. "That's 'Walking to the Sky.' Put up just the other day."

"What is it doing there?" I asked.

"I dunno. Sometimes they put things up here," he replied.

What "they" had put up there was a hundred-foot-tall sculpture, the work of Jonathan Borofsky, an artist from Maine, on temporary display in the plaza as part of a public arts program.

One of the life-sized figures was a woman wearing a red skirt that looked as if it were blowing in the wind. She and her six companions seemed to be climbing that mysterious path upward to heaven itself. The sun was shining, and I wanted to be climbing with them.

> *Lord, we are all making life's climb together.*
> *Help us to keep our feet on the narrow beam.*
> —BRIGITTE WEEKS

And God saw that the light was good; and God separated the light from the darkness. God called the light Day, and the darkness he called Night. And there was evening and there was morning, one day.
—GENESIS 1:4–5 (RSV)

This afternoon the house across the street from mine has golden windows. They're not always so. In the early morning, they're a soft, warm gray, and any time the rains come, the panes gather tiny drops and turn them into sparkling diamonds. But they're never more beautiful than now, when I've washed my supper dishes and stepped out onto my front porch. How blessed I am that God shares His heavenly beauty with me in this way, just before night comes and the windows disappear in darkness.

I've often seen my life reflected in those windows. How golden were the early years! But then came heavy clouds of trouble, bringing worry, illness, and grief, and blotting out the radiance I once knew. How brightly the diamonds of my tears shone until the time of sadness passed, and the soft glow of a new day flooded me with warmth and made me know that the golden days would come again—in God's own good time.

Father, when my days become dark, let my trust in You never weaken.
—DRUE DUKE

APRIL 26

The earth is the Lord's, and everything in it, the world, and all who live in it.
—PSALM 24:1

As I sit on my porch, the world according to the morning paper lying heavy on my lap, grim news fills me with a sense of doom. The world, I think, is spinning out of control. *Lord, where is the hope?*

Across my long porch, a male finch perches on the edge of a hanging fern, warbling his heart out. His tune, I think, also carries news. Grabbing my binoculars, I look inside the fern at the tiny nest cradling three pale blue eggs. The eggs have somehow survived cat-stalking, storms, and at least one bird of prey. My newspaper slips to the floor. Through my lenses, I watch the plain brown female pecking at the eggs. They're hatching!

I wait awhile, then I creep closer, climb on a railing, and angle the binoculars to peek inside. The hatchlings are twined together, the size of a nickel, naked, helpless, and mud brown. They cannot feed themselves and, left alone, their shallow, exuberant breathing would soon cease. But their parents are hovering nearby to nurture their brood, so they can grow up and fly and sing their song and propagate their species all over again.

Here, in this little backyard miracle, I see the hand that holds the world. An event too small, too ordinary to make the morning paper. But, light as a feather, soft as a whisper, its good news lands in my soul. God is in control.

Creator God, thank You for the works of Your hand
that cry out the awesome truth of Your care for me.
—SHARI SMYTH

April 27

Now the Lord God had planted a garden in the east, in Eden.
—Genesis 2:8

*I*t was a beautiful spring morning as I walked out to get the paper from the driveway. Mary, my next-door neighbor, was already working in her garden; flats of bright yellow marigolds lay nearby ready to be planted.

A twinge of longing ran through me. *Oh, how I wish I was planting flowers,* I thought. But I had decided against it. My husband and I, newly married, were planning to buy a home. In the meantime we were renting a small duplex that was landscaped with a few evergreen shrubs.

"Your flowers are beautiful!" I called out as I walked over to get a closer look.

"Thanks," she said as she picked up another flat of marigolds. "I bought these over at the high school. The horticulture students are selling them. You might want to pick some up. You can't beat the price."

"Thanks," I said, "but we'll be moving at some point, so it would really be a waste of time. But I've been planning the flower gardens I'll have when we buy our own home—camellias, wisteria, azaleas, and lots of zinnias—so I can have fresh-cut flowers inside."

"Sounds wonderful," Mary said as she dug a hole for the next flower. "It's great to have plans for the future, but don't forget about today. What a waste it would be to miss it."

Mary was right. I was so busy planning tomorrow that I wasn't fully living today. Later, while running errands, I stopped by the high school and bought a flat of marigolds. It was time for me—and a few spring flowers—to bloom where we were planted.

Keep me present, Lord, to appreciate and participate in Your daily gifts.
—Melody Bonnette

APRIL 28

Then will...the mute tongue shout for joy.
—ISAIAH 35:6

When my mother moved into a nursing home, I said a pleasant, "Hello. How are you today?" to Mom's new roommate Jeanie, but I got no response. I turned my back and moved on to my visit with Mom.

Over lunch Dad told me, "Jeanie had a stroke and can't talk, but she understands clearly enough."

Feeling a bit ashamed of how I had ignored Jeanie, I decided to make a better effort at conversing with her. As I nervously entered the room, my eyes caught three or four small statues of dachshunds on the bed table. "Did you have a dachshund?" I asked.

Jeanie slowly nodded her head.

"Was it this big?" I asked, holding my hands apart.

She shook her head and pushed my hands closer together. "Oh, she was a miniature!" I said.

We went on with our yes/no guessing-game conversation, and I discovered that she had a daughter and several grandchildren.

Before my next visit, I found a small dachshund kitchen magnet to take to Jeanie. When she pulled the little gift out of the bag, a small miracle happened. She opened her mouth, and exactly one enthusiastic word came out quite distinctly. "Baby!"

That was all she said, but it was gift enough for both of us. I squeezed her drooping shoulder. "Oh, Jeanie," I said, "how wonderful! I heard you say 'baby' loud and clear."

One of the miracles that always sent shock waves of praise and amazement through the crowds that followed Jesus was when He caused the dumb to speak. You, too, can hear a miracle happen if you listen hard enough to the silences beyond the words.

Lord, today, help me to offer my own silences wisely to bring out
a word from someone who is struggling to be heard.
—KAREN BARBER

APRIL 29

*"The hope of the godless man shall perish. His confidence
breaks in sunder, and his trust is a spider's web."*
—JOB 8:13–14 (RSV)

*L*ast summer I lost my Social Security disability status. My fragile finances toppled, and I found myself feeling hopeless and depressed. With nothing else to do, I headed back down to the Social Security office to file an appeal, took my number, and waited in line. Beside me sat a tall, wiry man with an interesting sort of hound-dog face. He wore a faded baseball cap, and a long pencil-thin gray ponytail hung down his back. We got to talking. He lived on Lummi Island, near Bellingham, Washington, he told me, in a blue school bus he called "Recess."

I smiled and told him a little of my troubles. He sat listening with his long, lean frame hunched over, legs crossed, an elbow resting on one thigh, his chin propped up by his thumb. "You ever think about praying?" he suddenly asked, peeking at me from under his cap and waggling his index finger in my direction, thumb still holding up his chin.

"God doesn't seem to be answering these days."

"Maybe you've got to pray more."

"Yeah?" Another smile.

"You believe in God, don't you?" he demanded.

"Sure, I believe in God!"

"Tell me then," he suddenly whispered, leaning in close and briefly glancing at the bored clerks on the other side of the room. His long finger swept clear down the line like a pointer. "Who'd you rather trust?" he whispered, pointing his finger back up the line. "God? Or these folks?"

I burst out laughing.

He thrust his big hand at me. "Name's Briggs. What's yours?"

I told him.

"Well, Brenda. Nice to meet you."

*Thanks, dear Lord, for introducing me to Mr. Briggs and
for reminding me that for real security I can depend on You.*
—BRENDA WILBEE

*In the shadow of his hand he hid me; he made me
into a polished arrow and concealed me in his quiver.*
—ISAIAH 49:2

*M*y kitchen window is a mess. It's over a garden, and the water from the sprinkler hits it at regular intervals, leaving unsightly water stains that resist my best efforts to remove them. Recently, when we were having dinner with some friends, I mentioned my frustration with those water-stained windows.

"Oh, I have just the thing," our hostess said. "It's great, but be careful. If you don't follow the directions, you'll ruin your windows."

I picked up the miracle window-cleaning cream the next day and carefully read the instructions: "Charlie Puka Pau's Diamond Magic contains finely ground diamond dust that will scratch surfaces if applied with too much pressure. Use only two to four pounds of pressure when cleaning glass surfaces." Armed with a soft cloth, limited pressure, and lots of elbow grease, I went after those nasty water spots.

As I was carefully trying not to apply "too much pressure," a thought occurred to me: Sometimes God's work in my life is a lot like Diamond Magic. I can vividly recall getting angry with a colleague, saying some things in a sarcastic tone, and then feeling the pressure of guilt on my drive home. I didn't find relief until I sat down and wrote a note of apology and then hand-delivered it the next day. Then there was the time I enthusiastically took over a project at church and stepped on a few toes before I felt the pressure of discontent on my committee and had to do some fence-mending. Without those gentle pressures, what might have happened?

With a final swipe, I stepped back to admire my crystal-clear windows. Thanks to Charlie Puka Pau, I was able to see my garden—and my life— more clearly.

*Thank You, Father, for knowing how much pressure I can bear and for loving me
enough to polish me gently so that one day I can reflect Your love with purity.*
—PAMELA KENNEDY

May

May 1

*Yea, the sparrow hath found an house, and the swallow
a nest for herself, where she may lay her young.*
—Psalm 84:3 (KJV)

I've been sitting front row center for a miracle this month—a robin built a nest in my second-story office window. There, two Wedgwood-blue eggs nestled safe from the rain. The mother sat on them for days, her tail feathers pushed up against my screen. She got used to the *tat-a-tat* of my keyboard, the *rring-ring-ring* of my phone.

When the babies hatched, they were the size of my thumbnail, with pinkish skin, tiny wisps of white down, and huge eyes. Almost at once the mother began to feed them, flying down into the front yard and procuring a range of delicacies: worms and bugs and silky-winged insects.

Now, after a few short weeks, the birds are dark and fully-feathered. Their chests are the pale red of diluted cranberry juice. They flutter their wings and stretch their legs. I become concerned that they might not fly. What if they fail and crash onto my concrete porch below?

I came into my office yesterday and the nest was empty. (Yes, I did check the front porch.) Looking out from my desk, I saw one tiny bird still perched on the window ledge. I needed to open the window, but I was afraid I'd frighten the little thing, throwing off its first attempt to fly. Cautiously, I opened the window a crack. The bird looked at me with a familiar eye. Then I lifted the window to its full height. With a single screech, the reluctant robin threw itself off the ledge and soared to the top of a pine tree fifty yards away.

*You care for all Your creatures, Lord. Sustain me with Your love and truth.
And nudge me when I linger too long on the window ledges of life!*
—Mary Lou Carney

May 2

The Lord will perfect that which concerneth me.
—Psalm 138:8 (KJV)

I sat at my computer this morning to write an important letter, a task th*
I'd been procrastinating. But the words didn't come easily, so I decid*
to clean my keyboard instead (another procrastination technique). I got so*
cotton swabs from the bathroom and cleaning solution from the kitchen. The
I went to work wiping off each key.

That's when I noticed that the question mark key was much dirtier than t*
exclamation mark key. Had I been doing more questioning than exclaiming late*
How about since I woke up this morning? I easily remembered several questio*

Why did I eat two muffins? Why is my friend experiencing more than h*
fair share of difficult circumstances? Why do I still worry about our childre*
even though they're grown and gone? What do I really want to be when I gro*
up? What should I say in this letter? Why do I procrastinate so much?

How about exclamations? Had I uttered any words of conviction? My mi*
went totally blank. But then I spotted some, right there above my desk; a bun*
of God's promises that I'd taken from the Bible and written on sticky notes
they would permeate my mind when I sat there.

"I can do all things in Him who strengthens me" (Philippians 4:13 RSV).

"For nothing is impossible with God" (Luke 1:37).

"The joy of the Lord is my strength" (Nehemiah 8:10).

"God is with me always" (Matthew 28:20).

"God knows the plans He has for me...to give me hope and a futur*
(Jeremiah 29:11).

Amazing how these one-line promises could become exclamation answe*
to most of my questions.

I looked down at my clean keyboard. *The question mark and exclamation po*
are at opposite ends,* I thought, *but for today, at least, I've connected them. No*
back to that letter!

Father, may every question today lead me to an exclamation of Your promises
—Carol Kuykendall

May 3

He that hath a bountiful eye shall be blessed.
—Proverbs 22:9 (KJV)

Often, on our early morning walks, I pray for a man I never met. He died long before I was born, and I know only two things about him: his name was Percy Warner, and because of his dedication and his family's generosity, more than two thousand acres inside the Nashville city limits were set aside in 1927 to be used as a park. Mr. Warner's park lies just beyond our neighborhood, giving my husband David and me a perfect place to refresh our spirits when things get hectic.

Percy Warner Park offers hills and valleys, clover-strewn meadows and deep woods. Today as I walk down a narrow road that cuts through the woods, the sunlight filters through the trees and finds a single dandelion. I stop and wonder as a sunbeam transforms it into a silver globe. Just being here in the midst of all this amazing beauty energizes me for the work that waits at home.

Better yet, anytime I come here, no matter what the season, I find myself chatting quite naturally with God. And today, as the birds call out and the last of the jasmine and honeysuckle bloom, the air is heavy with His presence. No wonder I'm often moved to offer yet another prayer of thanksgiving for Mr. Warner's bounty.

Father, open my heart and my hands so that I may also be Your bountiful child.
—Pam Kidd

MAY 4

God made the wild animals according to their kinds, the livestock according to their kinds, and all the creatures that move along the ground according to their kinds. And God saw that it was good.
—GENESIS 1:25

The small waiting room at the veterinarian's office was crowded with animals and their humans, including me and my two big dogs, Rosc and Chaucer. They were getting their nails clipped. The woman next to me he a Schnauzer on her lap. "Routine shots," she said. A balding man with a bea stroked his black mitten-foot cat. "Infected chigger bites," he said. One woma was silent, gently patting the top of a small animal crate, her foot swingi nervously. Finally, the balding man asked, "Is it a cat in there?"

"Yes, she's having kittens," the woman answered. "She's had two, but th third one won't come. She's been in labor all night. She was a stray. She arriv on my doorstep one night, pregnant. I named her Buffy. She's a calico. I'll ha her spayed after this, but I'm keeping the kittens."

The room was now silent; all heads turned to the dark interior of the cra that hid Buffy. "She's so sweet and such a good mother to the two already born The woman stopped and bent her face to the cage door. "Oh, she's had it! Loo here it is!" Carefully opening the door, she held up a wet, mewling little thin the size of a hair ball, its mouth making sucking motions. We clapped, cheere and beamed at each other. I felt tears on my cheeks.

Why all this emotion? I wondered. *Is it for the woman who took in a homele feline? For the triumph of the mother cat?* Yes and yes. But a deeper awarene showed itself on each face and in me. Awe. No matter how small the creatur birth is a miracle. As God ordained it so long ago.

Creator God, thank You for the daily miracles
through which You renew Your creation.
—SHARI SMYTH

MAY 5

Confess your faults one to another...that ye may be healed.
—JAMES 5:16 (KJV)

*I*t was a street of new homes and raw brown yards—except for the place next to ours. Most of our neighbors were young parents like ourselves; but this was a retired couple, passionate gardeners whose lawn was a green carpet on our barren street. That spring I'd watch them train rosebushes on the side of the garage and weed the stately row of red tulips on either side of their front walk.

I was ironing one afternoon, one eye on three-year-old Scotty in the backyard, when a row of brilliant red spots in the bare earth caught my attention. I went to the window, willing them to be Scotty's trucks.

They were tulips. Fourteen of them.

I went out and to Scotty's wails gathered the fragile cups from the little mounds of dirt he'd patted around one-inch stems. For a tempting moment I thought of putting them in the trash—who would know we were the guilty ones? But that older couple, ever after, would believe it was an act of hostility by some unknown neighbor.

And so, Scotty beside me, I carried the poor cropped heads next door, down the walk where fourteen empty stems pointed skyward like accusing fingers, and rang the bell. For a second, when the woman saw the tulips, she grew pale. I don't remember what I said and I doubt she heard it. She took the flowers from me, nodded speechlessly, and shut the door.

My husband had come home and put Scotty to bed, with a lecture about flowers you pick and flowers you don't, when about 8:30 p.m. the doorbell rang. It was our neighbors. She held a pot of geraniums, he carried a tray of begonias.

"These are easy to grow," the man said. "If you like, we'll show your little boy how."

Bestower of blessing, grant me, too, the grace to respond to hurt with the transforming power of forgiveness.
—ELIZABETH SHERRILL

MAY 6

They have cheered me greatly and have been a wonderful encouragement to me.
—1 Corinthians 16:18 (TLB)

One evening after a stressful day, when I still had six things left on my to-do list, I collapsed in the big green chair in my family room and picked up the photo album I'd started in sixth grade. It brought back a flood of memories of the fourteen years I was taught by the Sisters of Loretto.

I remembered the nuns going for rides in my dad's airboat with their long black habits tied down to keep them out of the propeller. In the winter, Dad bolted water skis on the bottom of the airboat and took them out on the frozen Rock River. Bundled up, the nuns rode sleds, saucers, and toboggans behind the boat, screaming with delight. Once, when a freak storm left the entire school playground covered with smooth ice, the sisters let us bring our skates to school and extended our normal recess time so we could skate.

I remembered the sisters holding the ends of our long jump ropes so we could do Double Dutch, or letting us beat them in dodgeball. Of course, they also had us read books, write stories, learn science, and memorize our times tables and the Baltimore Catechism. But it was the fun we had with those nuns that stayed with me. They must have had dozens of things on their to-do lists, but they knew how to relax.

I closed the album, determined to take a page from their book. Now, for at least an hour every day, I take an adult recess: I bike or walk along the shore of Lake Michigan, enjoy my favorite hobby of painting jars, treat myself to the $1.99 breakfast special at my favorite restaurant, read a book for pleasure, or simply take sidewalk chalk and draw flowers on the driveway.

Thanks, Lord, for a world where fun is so easy to come by.
—Patricia Lorenz

May 7

Our Father.... deliver us from evil.
—Matthew 6:9, 13 (kjv)

The impression was so sharp I actually pulled the car to the side of the road. My husband John, on a business trip to California, needed prayer! I looked at my watch: 4:30 p.m. here in New York, 1:30 in Los Angeles.

Though I had no idea what the emergency was, I'd had too much experience with these nudges to prayer to ignore them. Like the time I'd "known" our granddaughter Sarah was in danger; at the very moment I prayed, I learned later, she'd fallen from the top of a jungle gym—and walked away with only a chipped tooth. Or the letter that came from my elderly friend Barbara Nelson saying she'd prayed for me for hours one day. Barbara had no way of knowing it was the day of my cancer surgery.

So I sat in the car, praying for John's safety. After about forty-five minutes, the urgency left me and I felt a tremendous peace. All evening I wondered what story of averted calamity he would have to tell.

When John phoned around 10:00 p.m., my time, however, it was to report an uneventful day. Where had he been at 1:30? Circling the farmers' market, looking for a place to park. No, no particular problems.

I hadn't told John over the phone about my overheated imagination. But when he got home, I mentioned the foolish episode. "I'm glad I was wrong about your being in trouble!"

John shook his head. "I'm not sure you were wrong," he said. "That no calamity happened doesn't mean your prayer was wasted. It means it was answered."

I stared at him in silence. I was thinking about the tens of thousands of miles we drive safely each year, the illnesses we haven't had, the plane that doesn't crash. The disasters that don't happen to John and me, our family, our friends, people everywhere. I thought of the millions of voices joining each day in the Lord's Prayer. *Deliver us from evil.* And I thanked Jesus again for teaching us to pray.

Our Father, keep me obedient to Your prompting,
whether I see all or only a fragment of Your providence.
—Elizabeth Sherrill

MAY 8

Their soul shall be as a watered garden;
and they shall not sorrow any more at all.
—JEREMIAH 31:12 (KJV)

I am romancing the earth, cultivating, planting, and coaxing from it the greening of this plot of land we call home. Running my fingers through the soil is a therapeutic balm on my heart, hurting from looking around and not finding the lanky bent-over figure of my husband weeding the beds or stretching tall to snip shaggy whiskers from the hedges round about.

Raised on the fertile plains of Canada, John knew how to woo the earth into a good harvest. Tomatoes, picked warm from the sun and sliced right into a lunchtime sandwich; peaches, persimmons, and bunches of grapes, which he would preserve into jams and jellies and present as a love gift to me, his city-bred girl, who didn't know one end of a canning jar from the other. His memory lingers in the garden and is as strong and firm as each rock he laboriously moved to form the steps I tread on every day while he rejoices with his Lord in heaven. But this is a new adventure for me.

I probe and twist my tools around to yank up endless roots of crabgrass that together with the ants, I am convinced, are inheriting the earth, at least in my backyard. I find nutrients carefully stacked in the garage: bone meal, citrus, avocado, and camellia food. All the good stuff that makes things grow. I toss it around with the thought, *What's nourishing my soul today?*

Now I am planting a bed of flowers. Soft colors, gentle on the eye. Lavender, pink, and creamy white, named yesterday, today, and tomorrow.

How grateful I am for all my yesterdays. I will take pleasure
in the moments of today and, blessed Lord, I rejoice in the hope
of whatever is Your perfect plan for each of my tomorrows.
—FAY ANGUS

In thy presence is fulness of joy.
—PSALM 16:11 (KJV)

"I have to work late." I could hear the stress in my daughter's voice. "Can you pick up Drake and let him spend a few hours with you?"

I was always glad to spend time with my grandson. "Of course. I'll go straight from work."

When I pulled into the driveway of the sitter's house, I heard Drake before I saw him. He was giggling, peeking through the railing on the porch steps. "Hey, buddy!" I said. With that, he ran down the sidewalk and threw himself into my arms.

Drake had no idea what I had planned for us to do—whether it was sort laundry or take a trip to the park, whether we would eat at his favorite fast-food restaurant or have grilled cheese at my house. It didn't matter to him. His joy was in being with me, basking in the presence of his nana.

I thought about that later when I began my evening prayers. Did I run to God with a list of "give-me's" and "help-me's," or did I approach Him filled with joy at simply being with Him?

I didn't say much to God that night. I just drew near to Him and waited. Whatever He had planned for our time together was just fine with me.

Joy, joy, joy, Father! I fling myself into Your arms...and trust.
—MARY LOU CARNEY

*We are the children of God: and if children,
then heirs; heirs of God and joint-heirs with Christ.*
—ROMANS 8:16–17 (KJV)

I am an honorary auntie to several small girls, and when one of the
has a birthday, we share afternoon tea in a quaint little shop
our neighborhood.

For me, the best part is the food: hot scones with jam and clotted crea
finger sandwiches and shortbread cookies. For the children, the best part
getting to dress up in feather boas and frou-frou hats, all pulled out of an o
humpbacked trunk in the front of the shop. The birthday girl gets a rhinesto
tiara to play the role of Anna, the seventh Duchess of Bedford, who invent
afternoon tea when she felt hungry between lunch and dinner. The othe
each get a title to put before their names, such as "the Lady Kathleen," and a
expected to behave well and converse as if they were to the manor born. For o
bright shining moment, we are all dress-up royalty.

After tea the costumes go back into the trunk, and we shed the trappin
of our party. As we hug good-bye, I remind the children that we never shed o
identities as real princes and princesses of the King of kings.

The glorious fact is that here and now and for an eternal forever, we are joi
heirs with Jesus of the greatest kingdom of them all.

*What an awesome legacy You have given us, blessed Jesus!
At those moments when my self-esteem sags, help me to remember that I am
a child of the King of kings and Lord of lords—the ultimate nobility!*
—FAY ANGUS

We have this treasure in earthen vessels,
to show that the transcendent power belongs to God.
—2 CORINTHIANS 4:7 (RSV)

We recently had an open house for our neighbors in the small mountain village of Green Mountain, Colorado. A couple from across the road brought their grown son Sid, who was visiting his parents. As I and I stood on the deck overlooking the untouched property in front of our house, he said, "Did you find my buried treasure?" Then he explained that he and his brother used to play here when it was a vacant lot full of pines. When he was about eight, he'd buried a coffee can full of toy soldiers, marbles, and golf balls under a tree where our house now stands. Sadly, I had to tell him that the excavator hadn't mentioned a coffee can when he used his backhoe to dig the hole for the foundation.

"Oh, that's okay," Sid said, holding his hand to his heart. "It's still in here."

I have a buried treasure in my heart, too. It's my childhood memory of singing under the wisteria arbor in our backyard, trusting that, for that moment, the colorful tulips, the soft blue sky, and the singing birds were all that mattered. I think it was my first glimpse of God's presence living in me and in all things. It's a treasure the backhoe of advancing years can never touch.

What buried treasure lies in your heart?

Help me, Beloved One, to hold sacred the hidden treasures of my heart.
—MARILYN MORGAN KING

MAY 12

[God] will be our guide.
—PSALM 48:14 (KJV)

*D*uring a vacation to St. Charles, Missouri, the quaint town that in 18[ ] was the launching point for Meriwether Lewis and William Clar[ ] history-making expedition west of the Mississippi River, I became fascinat[ ] with the courage of these adventurous men. Knowing little about what th[ ] might find, the Corps of Discovery was thrilled to head off into unchart[ ] land, land so mysterious that even President Thomas Jefferson believed that t[ ] woolly mammoth might still have inhabited the area.

I was feeling a little like Lewis and Clark at the time, only a bit overwhelm[ ] by another kind of uncharted territory ahead of me: special work projects; t[ ] presidency of an organization I belonged to; becoming leader of my son Ros[ ] Cub Scout den; leading a Bible study for the first time. I wondered how Lew[ ] and Clark were able to bridge the gap between the known and the unknown. [ ] I learned more, the answer seemed to lie in their great faith—faith in themselv[ ] and in each other, unfailing trust in their own skills and judgment.

That's the kind of faith God wants me to have in Him, I thought. I must tru[ ] in His limitless abilities, His leadership, and His judgment to know what's rig[ ] for me. He created these wonderful opportunities for me: to lead an organizati[ ] I care about; to spend time with my son in learning and fun; to express myse[ ] creatively in work and church. When I feel I'm in over my head, I need to tu[ ] to God in prayer, asking His guidance and direction. I can count on His infini[ ] skill to lead me through the wilderness He sets before me.

Creator of all, guide me with Your strength and Spirit,
so I may confidently explore the world You make new each day.
—GINA BRIDGEMAN

MAY 13

"Let the beloved of the Lord rest secure in him, for he shields him all day long."
—DEUTERONOMY 33:12

Alone. Sad. Tired. And now lost. I gritted my teeth as the empty trailer banged along behind my van and I strained to read the next street sign.

I hadn't wanted my daughter and grandbaby to move in the first place. Last week I had boxed up much of their apartment, yesterday I had loaded the trailer, and early this morning I had driven 150 miles and unloaded much of the cargo. Now I had wasted an entire hour driving around Casper, Wyoming, trying to find the drop-off point for the rented trailer.

I pulled into a convenience store lot to ask directions. Before I reached the door, I noticed an elderly rancher wearing a white cowboy hat and a denim jacket. The silver badge he wore suggested he worked as a night watchman. The slow smile spreading under his white mustache prompted me to ask for directions.

"You're only two blocks from the street you need and about seven blocks from the drop-off," he said. Following his blue pickup truck, I edged into traffic and turned left as he had directed. He seemed to be going the same way.

Within a few moments, I found the trailer place. My newfound navigator pulled in ahead of me, hopped out of his vehicle to direct me as I backed in the trailer, then quickly unhitched it and set it down.

"Now, if you want to follow me, I'll get you on your highway home." I thanked him over and over. He merely tilted his hat brim. Then, with his dog's long ears flapping out of his pickup's cab window, he piloted me to Route 26, waved vigorously, and disappeared. I felt so relaxed that I sang all the way home.

Later that night I awoke and smiled, recalling lettering on his silver badge: S-E-C-U-R-I-T-Y.

Lord of comfort, thank You for caring for us through the kindness of strangers.
—GAIL THORELL SCHILLING

MAY 14

*A woman giving birth to a child has pain because her time
has come; but when her baby is born she forgets the anguish
because of her joy that a child is born into the world.*

—JOHN 16:21

*M*other's Day arrives at a great time for Louisianans. It's not too hot, the gardenias are blooming, and it's crawfish season. It's no surprise that many mothers here are honored on this day with a crawfish boil and, if they're lucky, plump Ponchatoula strawberries for dessert.

It's a ritual around these parts to boil the crawfish yourself. That's part of the fun. The crawfish are sorted and rinsed while the fifteen-gallon pot of water heats up. Garlic and seasonings are thrown in, and when the water comes to a full, roiling boil, the crawfish, small red potatoes, and corn on the cob are added. Before long, hot, steamy crawfish are dumped onto newspaper-covered picnic tables, and everyone gathers around to peel and enjoy them.

My sons Christopher and Kevin were working hard, keeping their promise that I would not have to lift a finger for my Mother's Day meal. I got up from my chair on the patio and walked into the kitchen to refill my lemonade.

"Kev, don't worry about peeling the garlic," Christopher instructed. "They go in just as they are. And the bell peppers, hold them like this when you slice them and they'll be the perfect size for boiling."

Kevin looked on, nodding in agreement. "Okay," he said, "thanks."

There were my sons, twenty-three and twenty, joking and laughing together. As a young mother I'd wondered if such a scene would ever happen. I walked in, hugged them both, popped a strawberry into my mouth, and relished not only the sweetness of a perfectly ripe fruit but the gift of motherhood.

*Patient Father, thank You for Your reminder that many
of the gifts we receive take time to ripen.*

—MELODY BONNETTE

MAY 15

Continue in prayer.
—COLOSSIANS 4:2 (KJV)

Several years ago, I developed a yen to make cinnamon rolls. I chose a cookbook, gathered ingredients, sifted, stirred, rolled, and baked according to instructions. The rolls smelled good baking, but…"We could use these to pave the driveway," my husband David said with a laugh.

Oblivious to humiliation, I located a second recipe, and soon the smell of cinnamon rolls curled through the house again. "Uh, Mama…a little doughy. Are you baked them long enough?" Keri commented.

Stubborn me went on to make cinnamon rolls too sweet and then not sweet enough. Finally, though, I got it right.

Over the next four months, my family and I are going to commit ourselves to the four points that Dr. William R. Parker considers "inherent in successful prayer." The first point—as you've probably guessed—is to make prayer a regular activity. Practice makes perfect, and though this is obvious, it is also imperative. Don't fail to set aside a regular prayer time.

Without practice, I never would have known that moment when my family gathered around the breakfast table awed by my perfect cinnamon rolls. If you commit yourself—if every time you fail but get up the next morning and try again—you will at last find yourself in communion with God.

Practice praying at a set time. Develop the habit of praying the last thing at night; pray the first thing in the morning. You will forget. You will lose your train of thought. You will think nobody's listening. You will fall into superficial dialogue. But after a while, Dr. Parker promises, your prayers will become "the practice of the presence of God."

Set aside a special prayer time—for me, it's an early morning walk. Go to sleep with a prayer on your lips. Say a prayer the moment you wake up. Pray, pray, and keep on praying.

Make every moment of my waking and sleeping a prayer to You, my Father!
—PAM KIDD

"Do not destroy it, for there is a blessing in it."
—ISAIAH 65:8 (RSV)

I spilled some coffee on the kitchen counter this morning. I grabbed the sponge to wipe it up, then looked closer. The stain was shaped like a sassafras leaf! I stood for a moment, enjoying the pattern—and remembering an art exhibit.

I've always admired the work of the sculptor Henry Moore, whose giant creations enhance public spaces around the world. So I was lucky to be in Texas two years ago when the Dallas Museum of Art held a Moore retrospective. Room after room, his genius unfolded—huge, sensual, curving shapes, compelling and memorable.

Leaving the exhibit, I noticed a glass display case holding what looked like an array of rubbish awaiting the dustbin. Pebbles, broken shells, splinters of wood, bits of bone, scraps of rusting metal. Why in the world would an art museum put such worthless stuff on view?

I bent down and read the label. The objects in the case, it stated, came from Moore's studio, where they had been for him "a constant source of inspiration." All his life, the label continued, Moore had picked up random debris, drawing from the shape and texture of the smallest, most insignificant objects ideas for his monumental sculptures.

Worthless stuff? Not to the discerning eye of the artist. I thought of Leonardo da Vinci's famous remark that he could be inspired by "the mottled stains on an old wall." I'll never have the perception of a Moore or a da Vinci, but since that visit to Dallas I've often been aware of pattern, color, and surprise harmonies in the untidiness of daily life.

Spilled coffee—a small mess or a small blessing?

Give me an artist's eye, Lord, to see in the
accidental a display case for Your wonders.
—ELIZABETH SHERRILL

While he was blessing them, he left them and was taken up into heaven.
Then they worshiped him and returned to Jerusalem with great joy.
—LUKE 24:51–52

W hen our family lived in Germany, we were surprised that Ascension Thursday was a national holiday. Glad to have a break from our workday routine, we packed a picnic lunch and headed through the wald (the forest) to a park. There, to celebrate Himmelfahrt (heaven-going), a kite-flying festival was under way.

Brightly colored kites filled the sky like floating jewels, fluttering, dipping, soaring. As we strolled through the park, we found our gaze constantly turning upward. What a perfect way to celebrate the Ascension—the sky that had received Jesus was now adorned with banners of victory!

I had never thought much about the Ascension before, but I began pondering what the disciples experienced that day. How could they possibly have "returned to Jerusalem with great joy"? I think I would have felt devastated to see Jesus leave.

They must have believed His promise to be with them always and give them the power of the Holy Spirit. Perhaps the sight of Him ascending gave them a glimpse of their heavenly home with Him. Maybe they thought, *This earthly life is not all there is. Someday we will be with Him again!*

So they went to Jerusalem with joyful expectation. And God gave them His Spirit as He promised. Those who formerly had huddled full of fear in a locked room boldly proclaimed the gospel "to the ends of the earth." Through all that assailed them, He was with them. No matter what they endured, wherever they went, they were on a journey home to be with Him.

Here in the United States, Ascension Thursday is a normal workday. Yet for me, it can be a reminder to seek renewal in the Holy Spirit and, like the disciples, find courage for my own journey.

I'll be submerged in work today, Lord, but please help me focus
on You and remember that You are with me always.
—MARY BROWN

And God saw every thing that he had made, and, behold, it was very good.
—GENESIS 1:31 (KJV)

I had an overgrown shrub bed and got some help from a ve[ry] knowledgeable man named Bob Chandler. As he was finishing up, h[e] pointed to the telephone lines that run along the east edge of my propert[y] adjoining a county bird sanctuary. "You've got bluebirds!" he said. I looke[d] up and saw mourning doves, pigeons, and two small chubby birds I didn[t] recognize. At that moment, the two little ones took off and I saw how they g[ot] their name. In flight their color is a brilliant, deep blue.

Bluebirds have returned to many areas, but Bob explained that developme[nt] had made bluebirds rare in our neighborhood because they can't find places t[o] build their nests. So he and several other neighbors were setting up bluebir[d] houses on their properties—little boxlike wooden houses on tall poles set i[n] the ground. "They like to nest near the fields," Bob said. "That's where they g[et] their food."

The next day Bob surprised me with a bluebird house and a long pole, whic[h] he set up along my driveway, looking out on the fields. One morning when I too[k] out my dogs, I saw a bluebird sitting on top of the house, looking as if it owned i[t].

A few times I saw a bluebird with a twig in its beak entering the small ho[le] in the front, and I assumed it was building a nest. Then one morning as I wa[s] passing by, I heard the sound of chirping inside the house. Little ones! And [a] few days later I looked up at the telephone wire and saw not one, not two, bu[t] four bluebirds. I was so excited that I called Bob to tell him the good news.

"That's great!" he said. "You see, all they needed was a little help."

He's right. So many of God's creatures are having a hard time these day[s] because they have to fit in with our way of life. But the story doesn't have to hav[e] a sad ending. As Bob says, all they need is a little help.

Thank You, Jesus, for the gift of Your many wonderful creatures.
Surely, we can share our space with them. Amen.
—PHYLLIS HOBE

For what is seen is temporary, but what is unseen is eternal.
—2 Corinthians 4:18

I used to see her in the morning, walking purposefully with her dog. She moved fast and pumped her arms hard, always looking straight ahead. Sometimes I'd wave and smile, but the woman never made eye contact. She never waved back.

Her dog was brown, a medium-sized mixed breed, and she carried his red leash, folded, in her hand. She'd let the dog run loose in the tall grass on either side of the road. He never strayed far. If a car came along, the woman called the dog to her and snapped the leash onto his collar, but only temporarily. They understood each other.

One day I was at my window as the woman passed. I didn't see her dog. The woman was carrying the leash in her hand, so I assumed the dog was hidden in the tall grass. But he did not appear, and a feeling of dread came over me. But why the leash?

A few days later I was halfway down my driveway when I saw the woman approaching. As usual, she looked straight ahead, but there was no sign of her dog. When she got closer, I called out to her. "Hi," I said. "Where's your dog?"

She stopped and looked at me, then at the leash in her hand. "I had to have him put to sleep," she said. "He was very sick."

"Oh, I'm so sorry!" I wondered where the woman got the strength to continue their daily routine.

The woman took a few steps forward and stopped again. She held up the red leash. "He still walks with me," she said. "Always will." Then the woman moved ahead, quickening her pace.

Dearest Lord Jesus, thank You for understanding
how painful it is to be separated from those we love.
—Phyllis Hobe

MAY 20

Consider the lilies how they grow.
—LUKE 12:27 (KJV)

I often see bird-watchers in my neighborhood because I live next to a bird sanctuary where there are miles of fields surrounding a big reservoir. But the woman I began to see almost every morning wasn't your typical bird-watcher. Most of them stand still, peering through binoculars. This woman had binoculars hanging by a cord around her neck, but she didn't always use them. What made her different was that she would stop and peer intently at the ground, or up at the trees on the ridge. Sometimes she just stared at the sky. She must have liked what she saw, because she was always smiling.

Since we passed each other so often, we nodded. Then we said "hi," and finally she asked if she could say hello to my dog. My curiosity got the better of me, and I asked her what she was looking for.

"I'm interested in everything," she said. "The different grasses, the birds, the deer peeking out from the bushes." I felt a little embarrassed because I've lived here fourteen years and I've seen the same things, but they didn't stop me in my tracks. I think the woman must have read my expression because she told me she had recently moved from the city to live with her son and his wife. "It's so beautiful here!" she said, looking around.

"Didn't you like the city?" I asked.

"I loved it!" she said. "I used to walk around, just as I do here, looking in store windows and at the fronts of houses, even little alleyways, marveling at it all." She stopped to look at some geese flying toward the reservoir. Then she smiled and said, "I feel as if each day is a gift, and I get to open it."

Dear Lord Jesus, thank You for the gift of this day. Amen.
—PHYLLIS HOBE

MAY 21

*The love of God has been poured out within our hearts
through the Holy Spirit who was given to us.*
—ROMANS 5:5 (NASB)

As I sat in the hospital room with my ninety-two-year-old mother, I longed to be comforted. She was so very sick and weak that I knew without being told the prognosis wasn't good. I'd done everything I could think to comfort her.

The nurses shut the door each time they left our room. I felt closed in and alone, and I longed for someone—anyone—to come through the door.

I was staring at the door when it opened and a tiny, well-dressed, young woman came in. She smiled and offered her hand. "Hi, I'm Brenda," she said.

Reluctantly, I shook her hand. "Can I do anything for you?" she asked.

"No, thank you," I said, eyeing her neat little "chaplain" pin.

"May I pray with you?"

I looked into her eyes. "How will you pray?" I asked bluntly. I didn't want a canned prayer or a memorized one. I didn't want this efficient young thing just to mumble something and then check us off on her list.

She looked at me silently for a moment. Her face glowed. "I'll pray as the Holy Spirit leads—unless you'd rather I didn't."

Suddenly, I knew there were four of us in the room. "Oh, please do pray. Thank you, Brenda," I managed.

Brenda prayed powerfully, concluding with Romans 8:38–39: "For I am persuaded, that neither death, nor life, nor angels, nor principalities, nor powers, nor things present, nor things to come, nor height, nor depth, nor any other creature, shall be able to separate us from the love of God, which is in Christ Jesus our Lord."

She couldn't have known it was my mother's favorite Scripture.

*Holy Spirit, the way You suddenly bind believers
together remains a marvelous mystery!*
—MARION BOND WEST

MAY 22

And this is my prayer...that you may be able to discern what is best and may be pure and blameless until the day of Christ.

—Philippians 1:9–10

When I have a decision to make, I say a prayer that a friend shared with me years ago: "God, either shut the door real tight or open the door real wide. That way the answer will be clear." God's answer has never been so clear as it was one spring night not long ago.

I'd had a tiring day at school. The senior play was that night, and I'd promised my students I'd go. I arrived at the gym just in time to squeeze into my seat in the second row. The curtain opened. As tired as I was, I couldn't help but smile. My students were singing and performing as I'd never seen.

The lights came on at intermission. Suppressing a yawn, I looked at my watch. If I left now I could be home and in bed in an hour. "Lord," I prayed silently, "I really want to leave. Please open the door real wide or shut it real tight, so I'll know what to do."

I got up, walked to the side door that led to the parking lot, and pushed the handle. The door wouldn't open. I tried again. It wouldn't budge. I reached my seat again and sat down. *Guess I found my answer,* I thought.

The play ended, and within minutes I heard my name called. My students hurried over, all talking at once.

"I knew you'd be waiting!"

"I saw you right when I got onstage!"

"Miss B, my mom couldn't make it. I knew you'd be here to take her place!"

I gathered them in my arms, scratchy costumes, sweaty bodies, and all. "I can't think of any place I'd rather be!"

Thank You, Lord, for the wisdom of locked doors.

—Melody Bonnette

"Let me inherit a double portion of your spirit," Elisha replied.
—2 KINGS 2:9

We were at a school picnic when my dad began watching an Arizona Diamondbacks baseball game on his tiny three-inch television. My nephew Christopher peered over his shoulder and with the double-edged sword of innocence and boldness typical of an eight-year-old said, "Papa, can I have it when you die?" My dad had to laugh at his honesty.

I thought of that story recently when I ran across Elisha's reply to Elijah in the Old Testament. Before God takes Elijah to heaven in a fiery chariot, Elijah asks Elisha what he might do for him. Elisha longs not for material wealth but for an inheritance of the great prophet's spirit. My first thought was, *Now that's what I'd like to inherit from my dad, a large measure of the indomitable spirit that keeps him working tirelessly for the causes he believes in.*

But then came the question: what kind of spirit might my children inherit from me? I remembered the promises my husband Paul and I made when our children were baptized, and I wondered how faithful I've been to those promises and what spirit I convey. I have taught them the Lord's Prayer—do I show a spirit of forgiveness? I bring them to church—do I show a spirit of community? I've placed the Scriptures in their hands—do I show the spirit of compassion Jesus taught?

Every day I have the opportunity to pass on so much more to my children—and to everyone I encounter—than a few material gifts. And going through the motions of worship and church life isn't enough. I need to show the gift of God's Spirit as it lives and works in me. That's a priceless inheritance.

*Great God, give me as large a portion of Your Spirit as You think
I can handle, and help me share it with everyone I meet.*

—GINA BRIDGEMAN

*"Haven't you read," he replied, "that at the beginning the Creator
'made them male and female,' and said, 'For this reason a man will leave
his father and mother and be united to his wife, and the two
will become one flesh?' So they are no longer two, but one."*

—MATTHEW 19:4–6

There are no two ways about it: my husband Wayne and I are about
different as any two people can be. He's introspective and quiet; I thr
on being around people. When we met, it was just he and his mother, where
I came from a large extended family with lots of cousins. He's a night owl, a
I'm a morning person.

For the past thirty-seven years, for the most part, we've managed to love a
accept each other's strengths and weaknesses. There are times, however, whe
can't help being frustrated with him.

Last week I wanted to go to a movie, but he didn't. We stayed home. I want
to invite friends over for dinner; the two of us ended up watching televisic
An exhibit on the September 11, 2001, terrorist attacks had come to Tacom
I wanted to go, Wayne didn't. Frustrated, I went without him, grumbling t
entire way.

I wasn't quite done being upset when I was dressing for church the followi
morning. After the singing—I sang, Wayne didn't—the pastor began h
sermon.

I don't remember the topic—in fact, I don't think I can even tell you
which Bible passage he was preaching. But at one point he said, "The grass isr
greener on the other side of the fence. It's greener where it's watered."

Wayne looked at me, and I looked at him. He smiled and so did I. I offere
my husband my hand, and we scooted just a bit closer to each other. We'd bot
heard something we needed to hear.

Lord, thank You for my husband, for his quiet strength and his love.

—DEBBIE MACOMBER

He gathereth together the outcasts.... He healeth
the broken in heart, and bindeth up their wounds.
—Psalm 147:2–3 (KJV)

I was nine years old, being hustled out of our farm home and into my grandparents' car just as a stern-looking official drove up, sprang out of his Model A, quickly nailed a quarantine sign reading SCARLET FEVER in bold, black letters on a yellow background to our front door, and then, just as quickly, jumped back into his car and roared off.

Of course I felt sorry that my little sister had this contagious disease. I felt sorry Mom was quarantined, too, to take care of her. I was sorry my father was relegated to being the go-between—leaving food, medicine, and other necessities on the porch, bunking in the barn because he couldn't go in and out of the house either, lest he risk contaminating others with whom he came in contact. And I felt sorry for myself. I hated being shunted to Grandma and Grandpa's place. They baked cookies and tried to make me happy, but they were Methuselah-old to my eyes.

Worst of all, everyone had heard about the quarantine sign on our door, so my school classmates avoided me. "My folks said to keep away from you. We might catch it." I was in fourth grade, and this was my first experience of being shunned. Even my teacher said, "Sit in this special chair up here by me." At recess I stayed in a corner of the playground, watching other kids having a good time, until Pearl came and shyly asked, "Want to play jacks?"

Pearl was the class outcast. All the rest of us girls had short, permed hair; Pearl's was straight and long in a waist-length braid. Pearl was just...different, and, well, it simply wasn't cool to be associated with "Pigtail Pearl." But during the six weeks that elapsed before the quarantine sign was removed from the door and our family was free to come and go again, Pearl and I became best friends.

Thank You, Father, for the experiences that teach us compassion.
—Isabel Wolseley

"Then will I purify the lips of the peoples, that all of them may call on the name of the Lord and serve him shoulder to shoulder."

—Zephaniah 3:9

I had just finished speaking to a Christian Women's Club in William Lake, Canada, and was saying good-bye to the women at the door, when my host came into the room clearly agitated.

"Your son was on the phone. He and his wife are passing through town, and he wants to know if you'll meet them for lunch at the White Spot."

I was stunned. My son, who hadn't wanted to talk to me in three years, who would visit in our hometown and not let me know that he was there, now wanted to see me. "Where did he call from?" I asked. "When am I to meet them?"

"I don't know." I left the meeting room in a hurry and waited by the telephone hoping my son would call again to give me the particulars. He did, and we had a wonderful reunion. Not much was said, but both of us sensed that we had begun the healing of a strained relationship.

In my talks with women, I find that many a mother's heart has been broken because a son or a daughter is avoiding her. I pass on to them what has helped me during this difficult time. Often an estrangement develops during a traumatic time such as a death or a divorce. Raw emotions take time to process. We need to give our children time and space to sort them out. No amount of talking will help the situation. In fact, too much talking makes it worse. It's like egg whites: the more you beat them, the bigger they get. We can't hurry the healing process in ourselves or in others.

In the meantime, though, we can be grace-givers. Grace lets another person be, gives him or her the freedom to grow, to make decisions, to fail, and to mature at his or her own rate. We can pray for our children and wait expectantly for Jesus, the great Reconciler, to bring us together again. And when He does, we can be there with a warm embrace.

Jesus, my children and I are Your people, the sheep of Your pasture.
Help me to trust You with them.

—Helen Grace Lescheid

And they were all filled with the Holy Spirit.
—ACTS 2:4 (RSV)

*I*t's Pentecost Sunday. Our Sunday-school children, from first through sixth grades, are having a birthday party for the church. There are red streamers, balloons, tablecloths, and, of course, a cake with as many candles we can get on it. We sing "Happy birthday, Christian church." The children pull names out of a hat to see who gets to blow out the candles. There is great excitement, much laughter and noise. Meanwhile, standing in the back of the room, I'm trying to relax and enjoy the party I've worked so hard to put together. But I can't. I was up until the wee hours of the morning getting everything ready, and now I'm worn out and cranky.

One of the teachers holds up her hands for quiet. When the room is still, she begins the story: "A long time ago, in the upper room, one hundred and twenty people waited and prayed for more than a week. Finally, it happened. A mighty, rushing wind swept through the whole place, and what looked like tongues of fire sat on each one of them. They began to speak in different languages. It was the Holy Spirit, who had come to fill them with a power that would change their lives."

As I listen to this familiar story, my heart is pierced. I've spent so much time working and so little waiting and praying as the disciples did so long ago. No wonder I'm burnt out and anxious. Closing my eyes, I pray:

Lord, my body is tired and my heart is empty.
Fill me with Your Spirit and make me new.
—SHARI SMYTH

Forever, O Lord, your Word stands firm in heaven.
Your faithfulness extends to every generation.
—PSALM 119:89–90 (TLB)

*I*f ever you need a shot of spiritual adrenaline to give you confiden
in the enduring promise of America, visit the Library of Congress
Washington, DC. Completed in 1897, its breathtaking sculptures, murals, an
paintings trace our cultural heritage and represent every aspect of civilized li
and thought. It is the official repository for copyrights; its shelves hold what
claimed to be "approximately the entire current product of the American press
its research resources are among the best in the world. The Latin inscriptions
the family corridor of the main entrance capture its essence: *Litera scripta man*
(The written word endures); *Liber dilectatio animae* (Books, the delight of th
soul); *Efficiunt clarum studio* (Study, the watchword of fame); and *In tenebris l*
(In darkness, light).

For me, visiting the library was a pilgrimage. Most inspirational were th
quotations lettered above the symbolic sculptures in the west gallery of th
Rotunda. Religion, holding a flower in her hand representing God reveale
in nature, has the inscription: "What doth the Lord require of thee, but to d
justly, and to love mercy, and to walk humbly with thy God?" (Micah 6:8 KJV
History, holding a mirror turned backward to reflect the past: "One God, one la
one element. And one far-off divine event, to which the whole creation move
(Tennyson). And most remarkable, Science, holding a globe of the Earth in her le
hand, and in her right a mirror, held forward so all may look into her images
truth. Hard-nosed Science, with her traditional demand, "Prove it to me before
will believe," has above her statue Psalm 19:1 (KJV): "The heavens declare the glo
of God; and the firmament sheweth his handiwork." Proof enough!

With tears in my eyes I paused and reflected, thanking God for the endurin
faith of our forefathers, indelibly inscribed in the halls of the Library of Congres

Almighty and all-merciful God, through the witness of those who have gone before u
and with prayers for those who will come long after us, continue to bless America.
—FAY ANGUS

As the earth bringeth forth her bud, and as the garden causeth
the things that are sown in it to spring forth.
—ISAIAH 61:11 (KJV)

This is the twelfth year of our planting pansies in honor of my mother, who dearly loved them. "Look," she would tell the children, "this is the ly flower with an angel on its petals. See—two wings, two flares for a skirt, d there, in the center, a small golden head, or halo, if you like!"

Before she died, she asked if we'd "please keep angels" in her garden. It sn't much of a garden, a small patch of green that led to the porch of a tiny ttage, but enough for her to putter in. That she did, with a green thumb that axed enormous blooms from the smallest seeds, scattered helter-skelter in the ative disorder that was her English style: larkspur, hollyhocks, tiger lilies, and ips in season. Against the fence, she planted beds of roses.

No disorder for the roses; they were carefully spaced and cultivated, each th a formal border of pansies, her angel flower. These the children learned press in waxed paper, between the pages of a 1943 edition of Webster's cyclopedic Dictionary, the thickest, heaviest volume on our shelf. Fittingly, its ntispiece shows an angel holding high the crown of knowledge over a family ading books.

Look for angels all around you. You'll find some in the pansies in your garden.

There are angel blessings round about us, a promise of Your constant care.
Help me, dear Lord, to look and find them, Your love revealed everywhere.
—FAY ANGUS

MAY 30

Yea, they may forget, yet will I not forget thee.
—ISAIAH 49:15 (KJV)

he lilacs were especially abundant that year, so I encouraged my eleve
year-old daughter Trina and her friend Rachel to clip extras. Now w
would make our Memorial Day journey to decorate the graves of several frienc
Since I had grown up in New Hampshire but relocated to Wyoming twen
years ago, I had no relatives to honor here; however, I wanted my children
understand the eloquent ritual of remembering and blessing loved ones wi
spring flowers.

The ride to Mount Hope Cemetery took only a few minutes. Many othe
were there ahead of us. They spoke in hushed voices as they arranged a va
or spray, straightened a flag or simply stood shoulder to shoulder gazing at
headstone. We delivered jars of dewy lilacs to the resting places of those we ha
known for all too short a time: Mick, the sheep shearer; Roy the chicken ranche
Loraine and Emmett, godparents of my son Tom.

When we had finished, I walked back toward the van reminiscing, whi
Trina and her friend lagged behind carrying the leftover lilacs.

"Gee, this one says 'BORN OCTOBER 31, 1903, DIED MARCH 29, 1904.'" Trin
squinted, calculating. "She was only a baby! Look, Mom." I retraced my steps
the bleached stone, topped with a lamb.

"And nobody even brought her any flowers," said Rachel disconsolately.

"Well, let's give her some!" said Trina.

"Are there any more babies?" Rachel wondered. Both girls scanned th
flowerless plaques, some bearing sentiments like "Budded on earth to bloom i
heaven" or "God needs angels, too." The girls continued to put flowers on th
babies' graves until the lilacs were gone.

I shouldn't have worried about carrying on the tradition far from home. Ot
Memorial Day recollection is in compassionate hands.

Dear God, thank You for the gift of children who reflect Your compassion.
—GAIL THORELL SCHILLING

MAY 31

A gift is as a precious stone.
—PROVERBS 17:8 (KJV)

The thought popped into my head out of nowhere: *Why, that was a gift!*

I was thinking back to a party my husband and I had attended a ▢ nights earlier. The bandleader announced, "We have a request from David ▢ld," and David led me out to the floor to dance to "our song."

How had I missed something so obvious? I couldn't count the number of ▢es I had complained to David after some party or celebration, "We didn't ▢nce a single dance!" Even though I like to dance, David doesn't. That special ▢nce had been a gift of love!

Later, after delivering a belated thank-you to David, who was working in his ▢dy, I began to wonder just how many other gifts I might have missed lately.

There was the prune cake with old-fashioned caramel icing that my mother ▢d just made for my birthday. Not just any cake, but my favorite cake—and she ▢esn't really like to bake! There was my son Brock's anxious call after I returned ▢m my doctor's appointment. "Mom, are you okay?" There was my daughter ▢ri's unexpected visit; she'd driven three hours just to help me prepare for a big ▢eeting at our house.

How many such gifts do you receive in a day? The paper brought up to your ▢rch by a kindly neighbor or the morning coffee brewed by an early-rising ▢ouse, a note of encouragement, an affectionate hug, a compliment, an article ▢pped from a magazine, an invitation to lunch—you can certainly make your ▢n list!

Think back to the last love-gift you received. Look at it in your mind's eye as ▢ough it were a rare jewel. Enjoy the intricacies of its beauty. Then say a prayer ▢ thanks for the giver. Isn't today a good day to give a gift in return?

Father, how rich my coffers become when I count each loving gesture extended to me as a jewel. Remind me daily, Father, to share my wealth.
—PAM KIDD

June

*Let's see if the whole collection of your idols can help you when you cry
to them to save you! They are so weak that the wind can carry them off!
But he who trusts in me shall possess the land.*
—ISAIAH 57:13 (TLB)

I lived in a six-bedroom brick house in Oak Creek, Wisconsin, for twenty-four years. I raised my four children there, mostly as a single parent. But years after my empty nest began, I decided to downsize and move to Florida, where the winters are more to my liking.

Imagine the stuff you collect over the years when you have a two-car garage, a big shed out back, and all those bedrooms. I only wanted to take about one-third of what I owned to Florida, so I gave prized possessions to my kids, begged them to take much of the other stuff, had two huge garage sales, and donated the rest. After I had settled into my small condo in Florida and rearranged my furniture and knickknacks at least a dozen times, I discovered that I didn't miss any of my old stuff.

Not long after that, I saw thirteen women on TV who had purchased a beautiful diamond necklace to share among themselves. Each woman gets the necklace for four weeks a year. The joy on their faces as they talked about how they share the necklace was inspiring. One woman said, "You aren't what you own, you're what you do."

Giving away my things now feels like a wonderful cleansing of sorts. And I have lots of "doing" down here. I entertain my children when they come for visits. I swim every day with my friend Jack. I ride my bike. I volunteer. I am what I do, not what I own. Amen to that!

Lord, help me always to be a doer, not a collector.
—PATRICIA LORENZ

June 2

Cease from anger, and forsake wrath.
—Psalm 37:8 (KJV)

"Can I open it?" my daughter asked. She was holding up a large cardboard box, red with yellow flowers, that she had found in the storage locker we were clearing out. I shook my head. "Oh please, Mom. I want to see what it's like."

In the box, unopened for thirty-seven years, was my wedding dress. My mother had made the dress, far away in the English village where I was born. It was beautiful—white silk-trimmed with lace and a long veil. She could sew better than anyone I've ever known. But my mother was not at my wedding to see me walk down the aisle in the dress she had made.

My parents had disapproved of my husband-to-be without even meeting him. He was American, of a different religious denomination, and, worst of all, he was of German heritage. My parents had lived through two horrific world wars.

Finally, I said, "Okay, sweetheart. Open it if you like."

There it lay, slightly yellowed, but otherwise just as it had been all those years ago. I touched the skirt. The silk was smooth and gentle. As I looked down at my fingers, I realized that even after my husband was accepted and the family happy again, I had never stopped being hurt and angry that my parents weren't there on the day that changed the rest of my life.

As my daughter held up the dress, saying, "Oh, Mom, it's beautiful!" I looked my hurt and anger in the eye and let it go forever.

Lord, let me remember that forgiveness is a divine gift
to the forgiver as well as to the forgiven.
—Brigitte Weeks

JUNE 3

Whatsoever things are lovely...think on these things.
—PHILIPPIANS 4:8 (KJV)

One of my favorite things to do is to climb partway up the mountain behind our home in this little valley village of eight hundred in Colorado, find a boulder with a flat surface to sit on, and just soak up the stunning beauty of amazing, living world God has created.

I walk up Falls Avenue and leave the road just between Pine Shadows and r Run Cottages to start my climb. The lavender wild asters nod to me in the eze as I pass. There are pinecones and ponderosa needles on the path and a ier large seashell! How in the world did it get here? I pick it up to bring home h me. The mountain is as generous as the Creator.

I hear a bird, but I can't see it. It seems to be singing, "Here, here, over here!" ybe it's calling me. This boulder will be a good place to sit and be silent.

As I listen to the sound of the falls in the distance and the creek running wn the mountain, bringing water to the thirsty land, I suddenly want to sing. in feel the wonder of this place and the glory of God's creation.

I feel sure there's a place of beauty near your home. Even in the midst of a stling city, there are art museums, parks, gardens, and old churches to feed beauty-hungry soul. Maybe today would be a good time for a visit.

Thank You, Great Creator, for loving me so much that
You provide sacred places to rest and refresh my soul.
—MARILYN MORGAN KING

JUNE 4

Let us fix our eyes on Jesus.
—HEBREWS 12:2

The weather was perfect as we drove through miles of green springtime, admiring the prosperous farms with their huge barns set on beautiful stone foundations, and gracious old brick farmhouses encircled by gardens bright with tulips. My husband Harry and I had gone to Michigan for experimental cancer vaccine therapy, and during the two weeks between my treatments we decided to explore some new territory. Just over the river and across the bridge was Canada, so we set out for the Bruce Peninsula in Ontario, that bit of land between Lake Huron and Georgian Bay.

We spent several days in the provincial parks, hiking well-kept trails through dense evergreen forests and rock-hopping our way along boulder-strewn beaches. We perched ourselves happily on the sunny high bluffs and cliffs of the Niagara Escarpment, overlooking the vast blue of one of the world's largest freshwater lakes.

Paradise...except for the black flies. Tiny little biting things, traveling in dark cloudlike swarms, they threatened to disrupt our idyllic vacation. Slapping and thrashing, we soon became preoccupied with the little beasts and oblivious to our beautiful surroundings.

Living with cancer is a lot like dealing with those black flies, we soon agreed; it all depends on where we focus our attention.

Gracious Creator, help me to keep my eyes on the beauty and joy that surround me rather than on the "black flies" in my life.
—MARY JANE CLARK

JUNE 5

"I will surely show you kindness.... and you will always eat at my table."
—2 SAMUEL 9:7

We hadn't known Erin and Peter very long when they invited us to their house for dinner. We were surprised to discover that they lived in [on]e of Nashville's grand old homes. Every room was impressive, but when Erin [ush]ered us into the dining room, I was astonished by the dazzling chandelier [tha]t set the entire room ablaze.

"Oh my goodness!" I gasped. "That's the most gorgeous thing I've ever seen!"

Erin looked at me, surprised. "You like the chandelier?"

"I love it!"

"Do you want it?"

I was struck mute.

"It's just not our style," Erin continued. "We've already bought a replacement. [W]e have an electrician coming next week to install it."

"Oh no," I answered, "I couldn't take it."

"I'd like to give it to you," she said. "Why don't you just think about it?"

As we drove home, I talked it over with David.

"Why don't you take it?" he said. "Erin is showing great kindness in offering [yo]u such a lavish gift. Are you being a little prideful?"

He had a point. Why did I feel embarrassed when Erin offered me the [ch]andelier? How would I feel if I offered someone a gift, no matter how big or [sm]all, and she refused to take it?

Finally, I found myself dialing Erin's number. Peter answered. I swallowed [ha]rd. "Peter, Erin offered me your chandelier. I would love to have it...if...you're [su]re..."

"Great!" Peter answered. "Erin will be so happy. We'll both be happy, Pam."

These days, one of my favorite things is to get up early, grab a cup of coffee, [an]d sit in my blue chair in the living room. From there I have a full view of the [din]ing room and the most beautiful chandelier I have ever laid eyes on.

Father, let me remember the great kindness not only of giving but of receiving.
—PAM KIDD

JUNE 6

"See how the lilies of the field grow. They do not labor or spin. Yet I tell you
that not even Solomon in all his splendor was dressed like one of these."
—MATTHEW 6:28–29

When I was a child, my family lived in a city, not a big one, but a c
nevertheless. Outdoors I played on concrete, and the only time I s
a tree was when we took a bus to a small park. Then we moved to a suburb wh
some of the roads weren't paved and trees were everywhere. I was thrilled!

Next door to our house was an empty overgrown lot just waiting fo
builder to come along. To me it was the most beautiful garden I had ever se
filled with bushes, grasses, and flowers of every color. I didn't know they w
weeds—"stinkweeds," the neighborhood kids called them. I thought they w
the kind of flowers people picked to give to someone they loved, and I pick
a huge bouquet for my mother. As I carried it home I heard some of the k
making fun of me, although I didn't know why.

My mother must have heard them because she met me at the door a
opened her arms wide to receive the bouquet. "What beautiful flowers!" s
said in a voice loud enough for the kids to hear. Then she hugged me. When s
closed the door, she said, "We must give them some water right away." She fou
a vase and arranged the weeds as if they were the rarest flowers in the world.

Eventually, I learned to tell the difference between a weed and a flower, b
to this day I have a deep affection for weeds. I got that from my mother, wl
cared more about the meaning than the price of things. To her, my wild bouqu
told her that I loved her, and that's what mattered.

Lord, help me to see Your love for this beautiful earth
in the wild things You have made.
—PHYLLIS HOBE

Everlasting joy shall be upon their heads;
they shall obtain joy and gladness.

—Isaiah 35:10 (RSV)

One day when my daughter Maria and I were playing on the bed, she suddenly pointed to the fine lines beside my eyes.

"What are these?" she asked.

"Wrinkles," I said, thinking, *Oh, great, now my two-year-old has to remind me that I'm not getting any younger.*

"Twinkles," she said, pleased with herself.

"No, wrin—" I stopped in mid-correction. "You know, that makes them sound like something good, Maria. 'Twinkles' they are."

That night as I looked in the mirror, I realized that my twinkles do come from smiling and laughing, forming a kind of road map of the great joy with which God has blessed my life. From parents who filled our house with laughter and taught us not to take ourselves too seriously, and brothers who are still two of the funniest people I know, I learned the value of a laugh a day. If there's one thing God has given me in abundance, it's joy, and I have the twinkles to prove it.

I'm turning forty in December, and while I haven't been particularly excited about it, or about those subtle lines or my one pesky gray hair that returns each time I snip it off, I'm ready to look at it all in a new way.

Mark Twain wrote, "Wrinkles should merely indicate where smiles have been." So, rejoice in the twinkles! They're a sign to the world that God has given me a lot to smile and laugh about.

Joyful Creator, in Your grace continue to fill my life
with laughter, joy, and an abundance of twinkles.

—Gina Bridgman

June 8

Six days you shall labor and do all your work, but the seventh day
is a Sabbath to the Lord your God.
—Exodus 20:9–10

Each day of the week has a unique personality. Monday is get-up-and-get-a-good-start day. Wednesday is halfway-there day. Friday is fun day. Saturday is sleep-later day. And Sunday—well, Sunday is different.

I grew up in a family where that wasn't so. In fact, Saturday and Sunday were nearly identical, even though I started going to church on my own in high school. For my husband Lynn, who grew up in a small town in Colorado, Sunday was very different. It meant coming home from church to the savory smell of a roast in the oven. Sunday was for church and family and friends and a big dinner at noon. I liked his descriptions. (Except for the noontime dinner part. For me, dinner's always been an end-of-the-day meal.) In our new marriage, we faced choices about Sundays.

We started out slowly. While Lynn was in the navy, we moved around, and our church attendance was sporadic. Church was something we did before getting on with our weekend life. But once we settled down in Colorado, things changed. We joined a church, had children, taught Sunday school, went to Bible studies, and grew in our faith—together.

"How was Sunday different in our house?" I recently asked my twenty-something daughter.

"That was the one day we all got up and went to the same place for the same reason," she said, "to worship God with our friends at church."

That sums it up for our family. Sunday's the day we become part of a larger family who worship and sing and praise God and pray together. (And sometimes we have dinner at noon.) What we do on Sunday makes the rest of the week different. And better. That's why Sunday matters.

Lord, You tell us to keep the Sabbath holy.
What a difference it makes. Thank You for Your Word.
—Carol Kuykendall

JUNE 9

And that these days should be remembered
and kept throughout every generation, every family.
—ESTHER 9:28 (KJV)

Next Saturday my husband Bob and I will attend the graduation of our granddaughter Christy as she receives her MBA degree.

We've shared all of Christy's and her brother Bob's school years. On the [firs]t morning of each term, we've telephoned them, wishing them happiness [an]d success. One morning when Bob was nine years old, the time drew near for [the]m to leave their house and start for school. Glancing at his watch, Bob said [dej]ectedly, "Our grandparents didn't call this morning." At that moment, the [tel]ephone rang, and he sprang to his feet shouting, "Yes, they did!"

We've been with them at every graduation, even kindergarten. Now, as we [lear]n the details of the arrangements Christy has made for us this time, my [he]art overflows with love and gratitude. She has borrowed a friend's sport utility [veh]icle so that my husband Bob, who is handicapped, can ride comfortably [fro]m our home in Sheffield, Alabama, to hers in Huntsville. She has provided a [wh]eelchair to assure him good seating during the program. And since we will be [sta]ying overnight with Christy and her family, she has outfitted a bed with the [sp]ecial equipment he will need.

What a joyful time we're expecting when we celebrate together!

Dear Father, thank You for the landmarks of life
that bind together the generations. Amen.
—DRUE DUKE

June 10

*"Let your hand be with me, and keep me from harm
so that I will be free from pain."*
—1 CHRONICLES 4:10

This year, my birthday fell on a regular workday, so I took the day off, just as I've done for the past several years. "Why?" asked a coworker who many years younger. "When you become an adult, isn't your birthday just like any other day?"

"Actually, I have this thing about birthdays," I told her. "I see them as God gift of a once-a-year day to celebrate the person He's created each of us be, and an opportunity to pause and consider where we are in the process becoming that person."

She rolled her eyes, so I continued to defend my birthday theory. "It's a day when you're supposed to have a private birthday party with God."

"How?" she asked.

"I like to find a nice quiet place outside. Sometimes it's at the table on ou back patio, or on top of a rock by a stream in the mountains, or on a bench the shade at a nearby park. I take a notebook and my Bible. I read and refle back and look forward and talk to God and listen to Him, asking Him where we are in my growing-up process. I always end by writing a birthday prayer, fille with 'thank-yous' for past blessings and 'pleases' for future ones. Then I tuck th prayer in my journal or Bible so I can read it several times during the year. Late in the day, I like to celebrate with my family and friends."

She gave me one more roll of her eyes before turning and walking away, as my birthday tradition sounded a bit odd to her. But when her birthday fell on regular workday a few weeks later, she took the day off, too.

*Father, thank You for my once-a-year birthday
and the opportunity to celebrate with You.*
—CAROL KUYKENDALL

JUNE 11

How good and pleasant it is when brothers live together in unity!
—PSALM 133:1

As the airborne school graduation ceremony began at Fort Benning, Georgia, patriotic music blared over the loudspeaker and a camouflage-clad column of three hundred men and women from all branches of the armed forces began marching past. I strained my eyes trying to pick out our son Chris somewhere within the ranks, about to be presented with the wings that signified he was qualified to parachute. Unfortunately, as I peered intently under the brims of hundreds of hats pulled squarely down on sweaty foreheads, I failed to find Chris.

When the time came for family members to participate in the presentation of the insignia, we left the stands still not knowing where Chris was. It was only when we heard a familiar voice call our name that we finally found him.

As I stood in the sea of identically dressed men and women, I found I could easily distinguish them by their accents, their faces, and the names printed on their nameplates. Suddenly, I felt as if I were standing in the middle of a living map of America. Of course, I thought, that's why the word "United" is first in the name of our country. When we look at each other up close, we see individuals of different ethnic groups, denominations, and ages. But when we step back and see the larger picture, all we see are our fellow Americans.

Dear Lord, today we pray that we will see beyond our country's many differences and be united by bonds of faith, love, and brotherhood.
—KAREN BARBER

JUNE 12

Open his eyes, that he may see.
—2 KINGS 6:17 (KJV)

For hours I'd watched eight-year-old Alanzo wait patiently outside our makeshift clinic, an abandoned church with its interior divided by brightly colored sheets.

Every day that week, he had made the two-mile trek across the Belize countryside in hopes of finding relief from his headaches. Every day, he sat quietly while the doctors explained that the eyeglasses they had ordered for him had been delayed at customs and might not arrive until the next day.

On the final day of our two-week clinic the glasses arrived. Alanzo, always at the front of the line, eagerly waited as I fished out his prescription and quickly fitted him with a pair of too-large frames that he would eventually grow into. He looked up at me through the lenses, his dark eyes magnified by the prescription. His face lit up and he began pointing. "I see you!" he shouted. Running around the churchyard, he exclaimed, "I see you, rock! I see you, tree!" He turned, pointing to me, "I see you, lady!"

Laughing, I called him back over, holding up a mirror so he could examine himself. Looking into the glass, he drew in a slow breath and whispered, "I see me." That day he went home happy, calling out the names of sticks, buildings, and friends as he passed.

I'm a long way from Belize now, but Alanzo's message has remained in my heart. There's a world of beauty all around me, if only I have eyes to see.

Lord, open my eyes to see Your glory in every flower and every face.
—ASHLEY JOHNSON

JUNE 13

The one thing I want from God, the thing I seek most of all, is the privilege of meditating in his Temple, living in his presence every day of my life.
—PSALMS 27:4 (TLB)

n 1999 my brother Joe and sister-in-law Linda invited me to join them on their trip to Japan. One day, after visiting a breathtakingly beautiful mple and seeing some of Japan's amazing parks and gardens, we stopped a sit-on-the-floor lunch at a small restaurant nestled among the shops on a ding, busy street in the small town of Narita.

As we finished our meal, we heard drums pounding and music playing in the eet. We looked up to see rows and rows of women dancing in perfect unison, wearing festive black and white kimonos with different colored sashes.

We quickly paid our bill and stepped out onto the street to catch what figured would be the tail-end of a short parade. But instead, the happy ocession continued. Row after row of women of all ages, arms and legs oving in unison to the music, danced past us. The magnificent parade went for at least thirty minutes.

"Where are they going?" I asked a shopkeeper.

"They're going to the temple. Once a year all the women in the town process the temple in this way."

As I watched the women, joy on their faces and a bounce to their perfectly oreographed steps, I started to feel a little guilty. I've never ever felt that happy my way to church back in Wisconsin.

When the parade of women was over, we walked through the market shops ere Linda and I each purchased a lovely cotton kimono. Now, whenever I see it nging in my closet or slip it on over my shoulders, I try to pursue everything I that day with a little more energy, a little more excitement, and a little more joy. t like the thousand dancing women of Narita, Japan, on their way to the temple.

Lord, help me to be joyful as I make my way to Your house each Sunday and to keep the joy I find there in my heart all week.
—PATRICIA LORENZ

JUNE 14

His banner over me is love.
—SONG OF SOLOMON 2:4

For my husband Bill and me, as for so many Americans, every day I become Flag Day. Our flag, a bit tattered from wild mountain winds, fl day and night at the edge of the garage. It has a special poignancy: Our young son David is in the army, just back from a year in South Korea. After that, may be sent elsewhere to fight. Our son Peter has been called from his civili job for up to two years of active duty with the air force as part of Operati Enduring Freedom. He has already been to Afghanistan, and he may be se elsewhere to fight. My mother-heart vacillates between fear and faith.

Yet in the midst of these changes and concerns, I think of another flag in r life, one flying in a refrain my boys sang as tots:

> Joy is the flag
> flung high
> from the castle of my heart...
> when the King
> is in residence there!

This chorus comes alive at Christmas when I change the small WELCON garden flag along our front walk to a red, green, and gold one with the wo Joy emblazoned on it. It reminds me of the kingdom yet to come, the kingdo of God, whose flag flies invisibly above my life every day and night. No matt what trials I face, no matter what troubles threaten, I am safe wrapped in the fl of my Father because "His banner over me is love."

Lord, thank You for the flag of our nation, which strives to be "under God."
Thank You, too, for symbols like flags that are sweet shadows of truth.
May Your love become the banner over us all.
—ROBERTA ROGERS

JUNE 15

I thank my God every time I remember you.
—Philippians 1:3

When I arrived at my desk at work that third Friday in June, there was a large envelope addressed to me in bold calligraphy. *It's not my birthday and I'm not sick,* I thought.

I opened the envelope to find a periwinkle blue card with a picture of a bouquet of forget-me-nots tied with a dainty blue ribbon. The front of the card said: "Father's Day is now a day for remembering. A day for smiles and tears. A day to honor what can never be forgotten." Of course! Father's Day is this coming Sunday.

The inside of the card continued: "May this Father's Day be special to you for the memories you hold dear in your heart. Thinking of you, Joyce."

It was my first Father's Day without my dad, and someone had remembered. Joyce Boggs, a secretary in the department across the hall, had made the card especially for me on her home computer. A card that communicated some of the most powerful words of friendship: "When you hurt, I notice."

We are most like You, Father, when we stand with people in their pain.
Help me to feel others' hurt in my heart and take action.
—Roberta Messner

JUNE 16

And your Father, who sees what is done in secret, will reward you.
—MATTHEW 6:18

*D*uring the last year of my mother's life, she only left the house to go the doctor or to get her hair done. My dad had always loved Mothe hair, and he couldn't wait for her to return from the hairdresser so he co award her hairdo his seal of approval. I'd no sooner help her into the house th he'd kiss her on the cheek, stroke her shiny gray hair, get a faraway look in eyes and say, "That hairdresser fixes my Bunnie Pie up as pretty as the first ti I laid eyes, on her."

But I didn't learn the full story of Mother's shimmering hair until right af she died. As a special gift, her hairdresser, Linda Sue, had gone to the fune home to fix Mother's hair, and now, just before the funeral, she was doing mi We were reminiscing about Mother when Linda Sue pointed to a white squee bottle and asked, "Okay if I use this on you? It always made your mother's h so pretty and shiny."

"I thought that was Mother Nature," I answered, smiling for the first ti in days. "And wait a minute, she never paid you for any extra treatments. Ev when your price went up, you wouldn't take a penny more."

"I snuck some of that rinse on your mother's hair when it first came o just to see what it would do," she said. "Then I got such a kick when she told about your dad that I couldn't stop. She'd look into the mirror and say, 'My h does have a sheen to it, doesn't it?' It became my little secret, and I never enjoy anything more."

Only your hairdresser—and God—knows for sure. Oh, the power of a sec gift to soothe the saddest of days!

Thank You, Lord, for those who conspire with You in secret to give from the hea
—ROBERTA MESSNER

JUNE 17

Whoever sows sparingly will also reap sparingly,
and whoever sows generously will also reap generously.
—2 CORINTHIANS 9:6

The Father's Day fax from London arrived late in the day. My husband Whitney, who'd feared that Wendy, his eldest, living away from home for first time, had forgotten his day, took it eagerly and read:

Dear Dad,

It's raining here in London. What else is new?

On days like this I think of sun and beach. On this day I'm thinking of a special ...ch the summer I was eight. It was nearing the end of the day. We were all exhausted ...m volleyball, football, and building sand castles. You and I had just finished ...owing a tennis ball (you know how we used to throw them into the waves), and ...d decided we'd had enough for the day. So we had a last toss and then you said you ...nted to show me something.

"Sit down next to me in the sand," you said. We were standing in the water near ...ere the waves break and shoot toward the shore.

"What are you doing, Dad?" I asked, mystified.

"Just sit here and let the water wash over you, and you can feel your feet and hands ...ng buried in the sand."

So we sat there, not minding that we were getting lumps of sand in our bathing suits ...d that our skin was wrinkling like prunes. We sat there till after everyone else left. I ...n't know what we talked about. What I do know, what is still with me to this day, is ...t feeling of sitting next to you, with salt in our ears and noses and eyes, and idling ...ay the last of the daylight, knowing that you loved me enough to take the time to sit ...t to me in the water and watch the world go by.

Thanks for that and all the other great memories you've given me. They're with me ...erever I go.

Love, Wendy

Lord, thank You for loving fathers—an image of Your love for us.
—SHARI SMYTH

JUNE 18

"Each of you must respect his mother."
—LEVITICUS 19:3

On the anniversary of his mother's death, my husband Robert became aware that he had not fully completed the task of grieving for his parents. We'd learned in our hospice training that delayed grief is not unusual and needs to be faced, so Robert decided to honor his parents by making a trip through Kansas. He invited me to accompany him.

We visited the important places the family had lived throughout his life with them. At each home, he took pictures and shared memories with me. It seemed we were outside of time, as I imagined the young couple with their new baby, the birth of Robert's sister Carolyn, the children's growing-up years, and their move into a new home after the children were gone. At the end of a long Saturday, we went to the retirement home where Lola and Floyd spent their last years and came to the end of their lives.

The next morning we visited the cemetery. Robert had potted some of the flowers he'd grown in our Colorado garden, which he placed by his parents' headstones. Then the two of us knelt and said prayers of thanksgiving for their lives and for the many tangible and intangible gifts they had given him. We said a regretful good-bye and ended our time there with a long hug.

The trip was very healing for my husband, and it blessed me with a deeper sense of closeness to this tenderhearted man who has chosen to spend his remaining years with me.

Whether or not your parents are still living, perhaps you will consider honoring them in some concrete way. You will be blessed beyond measure.

Heavenly Parent of us all, may I think of some
loving way to honor my parents this day.

—MARILYN MORGAN KING

JUNE 19

But one thing is needful: and Mary hath chosen that good part,
which shall not be taken away from her.
—LUKE 10:42 (KJV)

My husband's business trip happened to take us near Mount Rushmore in South Dakota's Black Hills. Since we had heard all our lives about the four gigantic presidential faces chiseled in the mountain, we made a little side trip to see them for ourselves. Maybe it was the fact that it was nearing the Fourth of July, or that the day was all blue sky and sunshine, or that a youth choir had traveled a long way from home to sing patriotic songs in its shadow, but the magnificence of Mount Rushmore overwhelmed me.

George Washington, Thomas Jefferson, Abraham Lincoln, Theodore Roosevelt—each seemed to be staring straight at me from his lofty perspective. Especially Washington. Caught by his demanding "give it your best" gaze, I had no trouble picturing his soldiers following him anywhere.

Visiting Mount Rushmore that day, I learned something new about the carving of the mountain. Severe funding problems had threatened the project in 1930. The commissioners created a "school children's fund," asking each South Dakota grade-school child to contribute a dime and each high-school student a quarter. Imagine the disappointment when the campaign that year yielded only 1700 dollars toward the hoped-for 10,000 dollars. It seems there was a new fad sweeping the country just then, a gadget called a yo-yo. The basic model cost a dime; the larger, fancier one a quarter. For a child, the choice between inspiring faces set in stone and a bit of fun on a string was really no choice at all.

I wonder sometimes about my own choices in life. Am I reaching for the rock-solid things that will endure beyond the moment? Or do I too often grab for what's merely fashionable? I hardly ever see a yo-yo anymore, but I do know of an incredible mountain in South Dakota that draws thousands of admirers every year.

Jesus, may I always make my choices under Your steady gaze.
—CAROL KNAPP

JUNE 20

*Better is an handful with quietness, than both the hands full
with travail and vexation of spirit.*
—ECCLESIASTES 4:6 (KJV)

It's getting harder for me to read. I may soon have to go to large prin
My hearing is slowly fading, too. My body seems to be gradually closi
some of its windows to the outside world as I grow older.

But there's another side to that page of life. As my sensory input diminishe
I'm less easily distracted by external things and more inclined to turn to God
presence within me for nourishment and spiritual companionship. I now ha
more time to savor silence, to spend an hour sitting on the mountain or by th
stream, soaking up God's presence in nature, and to open myself to the life
the spirit in prayer and meditation.

Could it be that the dimming of our senses in age is made for this qui
turning inward? I have to admit that it's not an easy time in life. Body parts a
wearing out, endurance is diminishing, short-term memory has started to fa
Yet in their place has come the priceless gift of contemplation.

My husband Robert and I have decided that now is the best time of our live

*God of grace and mercy, may I stop dreading the losses of age, and accept
with thanksgiving the special gifts You have provided for this time in life.*
—MARILYN MORGAN KING

JUNE 21

When Jesus spoke again to the people, he said, "I am the light of the world."
—JOHN 8:12

When I was growing up on the Connecticut shore, summer was a golden time: long days at the beach, barbecues in our backyard, fireworks over the ocean on the Fourth of July, trips to the town library on cloudy days, and rides in our old blue Chevy to the local ice cream shop for double-dip cones. By mid-July, when some kids were already whining about being bored, I was just warming up. So why is the first day of summer always one of the saddest days of the year for me?

It's the last day of the long light. Immediately afterward, the minutes of daylight start to drop away and the darkness slowly encroaches.

My glorious childhood summers were edged with the sorrow of that waning light. Every day, I'd check the newspaper to see how much earlier the sun would set tomorrow than today, aware that the minutes were adding up to the day when the clocks would be set back and we'd lose yet another precious hour of daylight.

I still have a tough time figuring out how to feel good about the long nights of New England's cold, gray winters. But one June morning, as the sun poured through the window, making a prism of the bedroom mirror, I found something that helped—the words of Jesus in John's gospel: "I am the light of the world. Whoever follows me will never walk in darkness, but will have the light of life." No matter how dark the night may get, Jesus is there.

I still feel a twinge on the first day of summer. But now, when grief for summer's end pricks my eyes, I close them gently and see the Light of the World.

Lord, You are the Light of the world. Shine on me!
—MARCI ALBORGHETTI

JUNE 22

"That all of them may be one, Father, just as you are in me and I am in you."
—JOHN 17:21

I took the hymnal out of the pew rack at the 9:00 a.m. church service, found the first hymn, and attempted to pass the right side of the open hymnal over to my husband Gordon to hold. But our twelve-year-old son John was standing between us. His two-sizes-too-large brown dress shoes were spread wider than his boyish shoulders and his scowling face clearly communicated *Why'd you make me get up for church? I wish I were still in bed.*

"You'd better get your own hymnal," I whispered to Gordon. As he fished one from the pew rack and we began to sing, it occurred to me that as long as we've been married, Gordon and I have shared a hymnal. It doesn't matter that there are plenty of hymnbooks in the racks. And it doesn't matter that Gordon is nearsighted and that over the years I've become farsighted. It doesn't even matter that neither one of us can read music, or that we occasionally sing off key. Sunday after Sunday we stand up, each take a side of the open book, read from the same page, and sing along with the congregation.

We say that people are "on the same page" when they share a basic understanding. Earlier that morning, Gordon and I had been on the same page when John fussed about getting up for church. I'd known what Gordon would say and he'd known what I'd say, in part, perhaps, because of all of those years of holding the same book and singing hymns such as "Blest Be the Tie That Binds." How important such a seemingly inconsequential act of togetherness can be!

Dear Father, help me today to welcome the small opportunities
You send to build unity with those I love.
—KAREN BARBER

I will strengthen thee; yea, I will help thee.
—ISAIAH 41:10 (KJV)

*W*hen my dad came to live with me some years ago, along with some other possessions he brought an old toolbox. Dad was a man who wasn't the least bit handy. He knew it, too, yet he always tried to repair whatever was broken, just because he wanted to be helpful. He never succeeded.

After Dad passed away, I would come across his toolbox in the closet every now and then and wonder what I ought to do with it. But I left it where it was.

Recently, while the inside of my house was being painted, I asked the painter to install some new curtain rods in the living room. When he opened the package, he found that a screw was missing.

"Would you happen to have anything like this?" he asked, holding up a screw. And, of course, I didn't. But I knew where I might find one!

I went to the closet and pulled out Dad's toolbox. As I lifted up the top, Mr. Gehman, the painter, came to look at what was inside. We both were astonished. There were all kinds of screws and nails and tacks neatly stored in little containers, each one carefully labeled.

After finding what he needed, Mr. Gehman looked at the tools. "Look at this!" he said, pointing to a folding wooden rule. "What a fine rule—much better than you can get today," he said.

Suddenly I knew what to do. "Mr. Gehman, can you use a tool like this?" I asked.

"Sure could," he said.

I held it out to him. "Please, I'd like you to have it."

As I closed the toolbox and put it back in the closet, I had the comfortable feeling that Dad was pleased. He had finally helped to fix something that was broken.

Dear Lord Jesus, make me aware of those who need my help.
Even when I can't do what needs to be done, I can always be by their side.
—PHYLLIS HOBE

JUNE 24

And the earth brought forth grass, and herb yielding seed
after his kind, and the tree yielding fruit, whose seed was in itself,
after his kind: and God saw that it was good.
—GENESIS 1:12 (KJV)

I'm conducting a campaign to keep my lawn free of dandelions. Now this is not an easy task on my street, which could be renamed Dandelion Lane without anyone wondering why. Lawns across the street and on both sides of us are alternately speckled in yellow and then white and then yellow again, and the breeze carries seeds from their dandelions onto our thick green grass.

I haven't had time to root out every one, so my campaign is limited to picking every yellow flower and bud I can find on my way to the car in the morning or from the car in the afternoon. (I don't care about the backyard; it belongs to the dogs). I've been winning. Every yellow bloom that sticks its head up on my lawn or my next-door neighbor's driveway gets plucked and tossed away.

Recently, though, I've reached the conclusion that God wants me to have flowers on my lawn, even if they're not the all-pervasive dandelions. Down among the blades of green grass, nearly but not entirely hidden, are patches of other flowers, white and yellow, much tinier and less obtrusive than the dandelions, and also much less likely to be plucked out by someone with limited time, like me.

I'm starting to think they look kind of nice, splashes of color in the green. I'll admit that God knows best about that. But I still think dandelions look better on the other lawns.

Dear God, thank You for green lawns and for wildflowers
and even for weeds, dandelions included.
—RHODA BLECKER

I, even I, will sing unto...the Lord God of Israel.
—JUDGES 5:3 (KJV)

*Y*ears ago, I went on a mission trip to the Philippines. The heat, mosquitoes, hard work, and lack of sleep were intense. A handful of ministered to people who were desperately poor but wondrously receptive the gospel. Our leader, Ben Barredo, possessed a steady, persistent faith that en the most difficult circumstances couldn't shake.

One hot night we were with four or five hundred people in a public square ar Bacolod City. Families with small children had walked the dusty roads most the day to attend. Ben had finally acquired a film projector—he'd prayed for e for years—but just as he was about to show *Peace Child*, a drizzle began to l. Quickly, Ben took off his shirt and covered the projector. Then, looking ward heaven, he prayed, "Lord God, please move that cloud over." People ddled around the precious projector to keep it dry.

To my horror, Ben looked over to me and said, "Marion, you lead the crowd praise songs until the cloud moves."

"Ben," I answered, "I don't sing—not at all! I'm tone deaf. I can't."

"Marion," he said gently, "over here, we do whatever is necessary. God will lp you. Now sing."

Hesitantly, fearfully, I began: "Praise Him, praise Him, all ye little children...." e huge crowd joined in loudly. We sang for six long minutes—until the cloud oved. Hundreds of people knelt in the dirt that night to receive Jesus. And I me to a new level of trust in Him.

My Father, give me the voice to sing Your praises.
—MARION BOND WEST

JUNE 26

A man's pride will bring him low, but a humble spirit will obtain honor.
—PROVERBS 29:23 (NASB)

*M*y husband Rick is a man of many hobbies. Recently, he picked a new one that made no sense to me. In fact, it embarrassed m raising chickens in our suburban backyard.

Every week he'd come home with brochures on the various breeds chickens and how to raise them. He set up an incubator in the basement a sent away for eggs. Then he built a big box surrounded with heat lamps to ke the chicks warm until they were big enough to survive in wire cages.

"Don't you want to go outside with me and watch the chickens?" Rick ask one night as I washed the supper dishes, a folding chair under his arm and glass of iced tea in his hand. "I'll get you a chair."

"Watch chickens? Watch them do what?" I scrubbed at the stubborn scu stuck in the bottom of a pan. *Why can't you just play tennis,* I thought. *Or may get into gardening.*

"They do all kinds of neat things. Chickens are fun to watch."

"I don't think so."

The dishes done, I straightened up the kitchen. I guess I could just tiptoe o for a second and stand there.

I walked down the deck steps. Rick was squatting on the ground in fro of the cage, talking softly to the chickens. "How are my little girls today?" said. The chickens blinked and cocked their heads as though they understoo "Brenda Sue, you're looking mighty fine." Rick opened the cage and slow smoothed her feathers.

"Looks like they recognize you," I said.

"Of course. What'd you think?"

I knelt in the dirt beside him, feeling an unexpected admiration for this ma secure enough to talk to chickens, no matter what anyone thinks.

Father, forgive me for my pride.
And thank You for my husband—and his chickens.
—JULIE GARMON

I lie awake; I am like a lonely bird on the housetop.
—PSALM 102:7 (RSV)

tuck in "empty-nest syndrome," I've often wondered how to redefine my role in life now that the children are on their own. But this spring mother, who lives directly behind me, pulled my late grandfather's garden brella out of storage—and I turned a corner.

To Mum's dismay, mice had been busy chewing up Grandpa's umbrella ge. She dragged out her shop vac but didn't realize she'd forgotten to put in a uum bag and was now blowing mouse droppings and tassel all over the deck nd her. When I went to sweep my own deck a few days later, I discovered e of the tassels on my back step. The next day I found more. I thought it l: there had been no wind to carry the fringe from Mum's house to mine and heavy growth of wisteria sheltering my deck. When my father came over, I ntioned it to him. "Do you suppose it's the mice again?"

"No," he answered, "but maybe it's birds." We both looked up. There, in jungle of wisteria, was a robin's nest—with bits and pieces of Grandpa's brella fringe tucked into the twigs!

"How pleased he would be," exclaimed Dad, "to see the birds make use of fringe."

Growing up, I'd been proud to be my grandfather's granddaughter. He was a lly man, generous and kind to friends and strangers alike. It pleased me when ple patted my head and said, "Such a good man, your grandfather. And my, t don't you look just like him!" Looking up at his umbrella fringe, I suddenly lized I didn't need to redefine myself at all: I'd been a granddaughter long fore I was a mother. And how many things had Grandpa taught me about o I am? Two stand out most: I am precious. And Jesus loves me.

Summer ripened, the baby robins hatched, thrived, and flew away. But I'm t left behind feeling lonely. I have Grandpa's umbrella fringe: I am still his ecious granddaughter, and Jesus loves me.

Jesus loves me, this I know, for my Grandpa told me so.
—BRENDA WILBEE

I have written to you...encouraging you.
—1 Peter 5:12

I love e-mail! It's a casual, almost instantaneous way of communicatin especially with our children, some of who are currently living in Afri But I also miss the special pleasure of receiving "snail-mail"—noting the stam slitting open the envelope, unfolding and holding in my hand words put paper by someone who cares about me.

It seems like a lot more trouble to write a real letter—find the stamps, sel some stationery, find the address and a pen that works. But we have son friends who help me keep that "inconvenience" in perspective.

Several times a year we get letters from our Tanzanian friends, the Kimamb We've been in their home, and we know they don't have a drawer devoted varieties of note cards and letter paper, as we have in our study. Our last lett from them was written on two sheets of paper from different school table held together with a straight pin. And because they don't know English, th have to walk to a friend's house and dictate their letter to her in Swahili, whi she translates into English and writes down. Then it's off to the stationer's buy an envelope, and to the post office to buy a stamp and mail the letter. Th letters are a great gift to us, a source of encouragement and joy.

Isn't there someone in your life who would appreciate hearing from y today? Find some paper and a pen. Writing a letter is a wonderful way to t someone you care.

Lord of all things, may my words to a friend bring encouragement and love.
—Mary Jane Clark

Let your requests be made known unto God.
—PHILIPPIANS 4:6 (KJV)

*M*y husband Bob and I celebrated our golden wedding anniversary last June. For days our mailbox was filled with beautiful cards, ringing congratulations and words of love. I saved the cards for our scrapbook and cut their colorful envelopes into small pieces to fit face down in the notepaper holder on my desk.

Now when I need to make a shopping list or jot down a telephone number, I reach for one of these pretty slips. On the reverse of the one I choose, I find the return address of a friend, and at once my heart is warmed with special thoughts. I pause a moment to speak with God about that friend. Another friend has an afflicted child; another, an aged parent. I know of two who are facing financial burdens. Then there are the happy grandparents and the man who has been promoted in his job. Each one has a special need for my prayer, be it asking for aid or voicing thanksgiving.

From time to time all of us can use a nudge to pray for others. These little pieces of paper do the nudging for me!

*Heavenly Father, heed our prayers, especially
as we seek Your blessings for others. Amen.*
—DRUE DUKE

Our mouths were filled with laughter.
—PSALM 126:2

I was tired. It was the end of a long school day at the end of June, a teaching was getting me down. The kids were eager to begin summ vacation, and while I understood, it was my job to settle them down. I assign a composition. The topic, I announced, drawing one from thin air, was "My Peeve." Frankly, any topic would have done. I was merely trying to gain a lit peace and quiet. "My pet peeve," I commented in a serious tone, "is students w don't take their work seriously." I looked pointedly at Cliff, the class "wise gu Oh, he was genuinely funny and not malicious, but I felt that the classroom w not the place for any hijinks or jokes. "Remember, report card time is comin blah...blah...blah...." I droned on, boring even myself.

Of course, that night I had to pay for it by marking thirty-five pape I groaned, even more so when I discovered Cliff's essay on top. My forehe creased as I read his first line. Then I burst out laughing. "My pet, Peeve," he h written, "is a good pet. He has to be fed and watered three times a day. He li to be walked at a brisk pace...."

Laughing, I shoved the remainder of the papers back into my briefcase a the next day announced, "As a 'Here Comes Summer' gift, everyone gets an A that paper!" Then I silently thanked Cliff for teaching me an important lesso lighten up!

God, help me to stop taking my life—and myself—oh-so-seriously all the time And if there are people in my life with a sense of humor, may I learn from then
—LINDA NEUKRUG

July

JULY 1

Now the Lord God had planted a garden in the east in Eden.
—GENESIS 2:8

The Butchart Gardens of Victoria, British Columbia, enjoy a worldwi[de] reputation. Begun in 1904 in Mr. Butchart's abandoned stone qua[rry] north of the city, the gardens now contain fifty acres of year-round blossom a[nd] sculptured greenery.

I first visited the Butchart Gardens as a child. My grandfather knew M[r.] Shiner, the head gardener, and one summer day Grandpa took me to visit [his] old friend. Lest I get lost in the sea of people oohing and aahing and bendi[ng] over to sniff the endless varieties of flowers, Mr. Shiner took me by the han[d] traipsed alongside, mesmerized.

As we traveled the pathways, Mr. Shiner explained flower rotation, b[ug] infestation, and his ideas for irrigation along the high rockeries. He showed [me] the greenhouses, where spent flowers could rest and recuperate, and he sp[oke] of expansion plans. He pointed with pride to a new kind of rose he'd develop[ed.] Mr. Shiner knew every flower in the garden, and it was he who made sure th[ey] stayed healthy and beautiful and always growing. *What a privilege,* I thought [to] *know the head gardener!*

On a recent visit to the gardens, I recalled with pleasure that magic day [so] many years ago. As I thought back on my walk with Grandpa and Mr. Shin[er,] it occurred to me that God protects and nurtures us in much the same w[ay.] Like the gardener, God provides all that we need. He tends us when we suf[fer] infestations of ill-will, poor health, and other woes. He creates within us a n[ew] spirit; He expands our horizons with new goals.

Truly it is a privilege to know the Head Gardener!

Whether I'm withering or flourishing, let me remember it is You, Lord,
the Head Gardener, who always nourishes and protects.
—BRENDA WILBEE

JULY 2

"Before I formed you in the womb I knew you."
—JEREMIAH 1:5 (RSV)

When our granddaughter Kerlin phoned from Nashville, Tennessee, to say that she and her husband Jordan were expecting a baby, I was as excited as a great-grandmother-to-be could be.

"As soon as we learn the sex," Kerlin said, "we'll let you know."

This was a new dimension for me. When my children came along, you could only guess at an unborn baby's gender. They, in turn, expecting their own children, had opted not to know. Five months before the due date, Kerlin called with the news that she was carrying a boy. It was no longer "when it's born," but "when he's born."

Soon Kerlin and Jordan chose a name. Somehow, awaiting Adin Marshall Richter was different again from waiting for "the baby" or even for "him" to come. He had an identity, a name to sew on a blue blanket. I even wrote him a letter: "Dear Adin..."

The birth was still four months away when they set the date for his baptism. "We thought you'd like to make plane reservations ahead," Kerlin explained.

So much advance planning, so many details already decided—how strange it all seemed to me! Strange...and troubling. "Is it right, Father," I prayed, "to know so much so far ahead?"

I knew you, the answer came at once, *before you were born. Before you were conceived. Before the mountains and the seas were in place.*

Five months too long to plan ahead? For an awestruck moment I had a sense of the unimaginable vistas of time as matter was flung into space and galaxies formed, and the components of the earth were forged in exploding stars. How far ahead did God plan for the creation of life...of humankind...of you and me?

Take away my fears for the future, Father. It is already in Your care.
—ELIZABETH SHERRILL

He was praying in a certain place, and after he had finished, one of his disciples said to him, "Lord, teach us to pray, as John taught his disciples."
—LUKE 11:1 (NRSV)

I've always believed that you affect people more by what you do than what you say. I think that's particularly true of prayer.

When I met my husband Charlie ten years ago, I'd venture to say he wasn't praying a lot. But because I prayed, he started to pray with me. Eventually we were praying together daily, though I occasionally suspected that he was praying just to please me. Did he really believe in the power of prayer?

I learned the truth earlier this year when we were flying back to Connecticut from Key West, Florida. We made our Miami connection and were about fifteen minutes into the flight. I was dozing and Charlie was gazing out the window. Suddenly the pilot announced, "Folks, the flight crew has detected a burning odor in the back of the plane, so we are returning to Miami. Please don't panic and don't be surprised when you see fire and emergency vehicles on the runway."

Amid the fearful chatter of the other passengers, Charlie and I were quiet. He gripped my hand. We were silent for the next twenty minutes until we landed safely.

When we were on the ground, I turned to him and asked, "Why didn't you say anything all that time?"

"Well," he answered slowly, "I thought that under the circumstances, we better concentrate on praying."

I guess he has been getting it all these years, after all.

Listening Lord, thank You for showing me how to pray.
—MARCI ALBORGHETTI

JULY 4

Behold, the Lord thy God hath set the land before thee...
fear not, neither be discouraged.
—DEUTERONOMY 1:21 (KJV)

A couple of years ago I was visiting two of my children in California, Jeanne and Andrew, and their families. Jeanne's Adeline was three years old and Andrew's Ethan was two and a half. We drove to a little town to watch the fireworks on the Fourth of July and ended up sitting on a brick ledge in front of a grocery store for the best view.

When the booms and flashes began, Ethan started shaking and was soon in tears. I tried to comfort him, but even Grandma's lap couldn't provide shelter from the sensory overload. Then Jeanne put the two little ones together in the front seat of a huge grocery cart shaped like a big toy car. Adeline put her arm around Ethan, and before long they were giggling and staring at the fantastic light show with glee.

Sometimes I'm afraid of things too: noisy politicians, war, rising taxes, hurricanes, health problems. Then I remember: today is the Fourth of July, Independence Day, the day we officially became a nation under God, indivisible, with liberty and justice for all. We're in this together and our government, our democracy, *under God*, is designed to give us a chance to tackle the problems, big and little, that concern all of us.

Just like Adeline and Ethan, I find strength in numbers and comfort in the shared goals that we Americans enjoy. God bless America!

Father, keep me thankful for this nation that protects us
while keeping our freedoms intact.
—PATRICIA LORENZ

JULY 5

How great are his signs! and how mighty are his wonders!
—DANIEL 4:3 (KJV)

I learned something about myself this summer: I really like firework
When we visited San Diego in July, we saw fireworks almost eve
night, either at the ballpark, the symphony concerts by the bay, or a near
amusement park, all from our condo's living room window. I'd hear the *boo
boom* of a fireworks show and run to the window to watch. After a few nigh
my family lost interest, but I never missed a show. I was enthralled watching t
white bursts change to blue, then red, or seeing hundreds of gold shooting sta
fall together from high in the sky. "Mom, you have more kid in you than we de
my son Ross said.

Then late one night, as I was closing the front window, I glanced out at t
ocean. I had started to turn away when I realized that the bright silvery pa
shimmering on the water was moonlight. The waves sparkled as if strewn wi
diamonds. How had I not noticed this before? The following night I made su
to catch God's late-night light show, and I wasn't disappointed.

Fireworks are fun. But even better are the shows God puts on almost eve
day in the huge, puffy white clouds that hang over the mountains near my ho
in Arizona, and in nearly every sunset. Now I find myself running to the wind
a lot more often; the show is spectacular.

Every bit of Your creation reflects Your awesome power, Lord.
—GINA BRIDGEMAN

In God I trust; I will not be afraid.
—PSALM 56:11

Tommy, our orange outdoor cat, had been gone a few days. I saw him coming out of the woods, hopping on three legs. "What'd you do to yourself?" I said, sitting on a railroad tie on the edge of our drive, waiting for him to come to me.

"Meow," he cried painfully as he hopped over.

The wound, bloody and swollen, was coated with dirt and held the beginnings of infection. "This is going to hurt," I said. Tommy had come to us three years earlier as a wild kitten, and I'd won his trust. Now he was my porch buddy, climbing all over me, purring. But he'd never been to the vet. Today would have to be the day. I dreaded it, for good reason.

In a crate in the car, Tommy screeched and scratched like a wild thing. At the vet's, he peered out of his crate like a small bobcat, hissing, raising his back, his green eyes lit with fear. I left him to be neutered as well as to have his paw fixed. Hours later I brought him home, calmly sedated. Gently I laid him on a clean bed in the garage, where he slept nights. The next morning I found him cowering behind a pile of boxes. He stared accusingly.

"It's okay, Tommy," I said, approaching him. "I'm your friend." He limped away as fast as he could.

Two days went by. I was sitting on my porch, lonely without my buddy. Then I saw him coming up the sidewalk, his wound obviously better. He climbed the porch steps and slinked my way. Holding my breath, I kept reading. He leapt to the cushion beside me, I stroked his back. His quirky motor started up, and he stepped into my lap. We were friends once again.

"Tommy, Tommy," I said, a lump in my throat. "Welcome back."

Lord, when trouble surrounds me, may I trust in You,
rather than falling back on my fears.
—SHARI SMYTH

July 7

The lines are fallen unto me in pleasant places; yea, I have a goodly heritage.
—Psalm 16:6 (KJV)

Last summer I spent two nights in Red Wing, Minnesota, the slee[p] Midwestern town where my mother grew up in the 1920s and 1930[s]. My room in the historic St. James Hotel overlooked Levee Park, which hug[s] bend in the Mississippi River.

My mother had often talked about her grandmother's visits to Red Win[g]. Grandmother Helene would sit for hours near the river's edge in Levee Par[k], staring across the water. She had emigrated from Norway's breathtaking fjo[rd] country to the prairie of South Dakota, and I suppose she never lost her longi[ng] for the sparkle and dance of water.

On my last morning in Red Wing, I was able to sit down on a bench in Lev[ee] Park, Bible in hand, for some solitary reflection. A young man approached m[e] and asked if he could play his trumpet at a nearby picnic table. "Fine with me[," I told him, "if you'll play a tune for me." Perhaps he had noticed my open Bib[le] because as the rich round notes rolled from his horn and sailed out across t[he] water, I heard the old hymn "Blessed Assurance."

The young trumpeter knew nothing about my great-grandmother Helene [or] her faith in Christ. But his song evoked for me the image of a short, plump lad[y,] her hair caught in a neat white bun, with a faraway look in her eyes as she gaz[ed] at the river in this very place, and offered her prayers to the Lord.

I felt a deep peace. "Blessed assurance, Jesus is mine." My great-grandmoth[er] Helene knew it to be true and, some seventy years later, so did I.

*Loving God, may the praises of my Savior come
through me to my children's children's children.*

—Carol Knapp

JULY 8

Love bears all things.

—1 Corinthians 13:7 (RSV)

*M*y husband Lynn and I celebrated our thirty-third wedding anniversary over a long weekend in a little mountain town in the Colorado Rockies. On Saturday afternoon, we wandered into a gift store. In a jewelry case along one wall were some silver-and-gold rings. For years, I'd been wanting such a ring to wear on my right hand.

"Try one on," Lynn urged. An hour later, we walked out of the store, with a bright and shiny silver-and-gold ring on my finger. "It's perfect!" I gushed to Lynn. "Thank you!"

It wasn't until we were driving down the mountain toward home the next day that I spotted a tiny flaw in the ring, a pin-prick-sized hole in the gold on the front side. "Oh no," I moaned, showing Lynn the flaw.

"I can hardly see it," he assured me. But all the way down the mountain, I stared at that flaw, and it seemed to grow bigger and bigger before my eyes. "I wonder if it was there yesterday and I just didn't notice it in my excitement?" I said.

For the next several days, I struggled with the imperfection in my ring. When I looked at it, all I saw was that tiny hole.

"We'll just take it back," Lynn finally told me, exasperated with my monomania.

His words made me realize that I had a choice: I could fixate on the flaw or focus on the ring's overall beauty. And with its tiny flaw, the ring was the perfect gift to celebrate the longevity of our marriage and remind me of a choice I face every day.

Lord, in marriage, and in all relationships,
help me overlook the flaws and focus on the good.

—Carol Kuykendall

Your attitude should be the same as that of Christ Jesus:
who, being in very nature God...made himself nothing,
taking the very nature of a servant, being made in human likeness.
—PHILIPPIANS 2:5–7

In Charles Dickens's novel *Bleak House*, a hypocritical character who acts of charity benefit only faraway causes and never people at hand known for her "telescopic philanthropy."

I know something about this. Tsunami or hurricane devastation? I write check and think, *Oh, if only I could go there and help*, all the while knowing th I'm glad to be insulated from meeting a real need in any hands-on way.

This penchant came to the fore last week when I received an e-mail fro the Colonel, a World War II veteran I know from church. Since the accide that had totaled his car, he'd lost his license. His wife was debilitated. Now request: could I possibly drive them to Walter Reed Army Medical Center for a appointment on Monday?

Why, that's clear across town! Before bed that night, I explained my excus to God: There's construction on Nebraska Avenue. The parking's impossibl It will take most of a day. But when I glanced up, the moon shining from fa beyond the oaks in my yard sent me a silent message: *Go for an attitude generous servanthood. Not telescopic, but near and neighborly.*

Monday morning, I cheerfully picked up the Colonel and his missus. W three went clear across town and back, after ice cream at a favorite cafe.

Jesus, teach me more about Your servant heart.

—EVELYN BENCE

They must enjoy having guests in their homes and must love all that is good.
—Titus 1:8 (TLB)

*D*uring the 1950s when I visited Grandpa and Grandma Knapp in Blandinsville, Illinois (population six hundred), I was amazed at the number of drop-in visitors they had. In the winter, they'd visit in front of the coal stove that plunked and hissed in the middle of the living room. In the summer, neighbors walked over to sit a spell in the porch swing. Grandma would bring out the pitcher of lemonade and an extra chair or two from the dining room so everybody could sit down.

Every day they came: old farmer friends who'd retired like Grandpa and moved into town; shopkeepers on their way home from work; the preacher from the local church; the town librarian.

In 1998, when my youngest child went off to college and my home became an empty nest, I wondered what had happened to that custom of drop-in-anytime hospitality. Why is it that we think we need a week to prepare for guests, and that we must have every nook and cranny in our homes white-glove-inspection clean, and that we must feed our visitors elaborate meals every time they come to visit?

I decided right then to encourage everyone I knew to stop in anytime. Whenever I saw my friends or neighbors or acquaintances, I'd say, "I mean it. If my car's in the garage, I'm home. So stop in."

Well, people started doing it. Now, three or four times a week I get a surprise visit from someone. I'm not expected to have the house clean or food prepared. Usually I just boil water for tea, pour lemonade, and pass out graham crackers, if that's all I have on hand. And without all the stress and fuss, my guests and I can just visit our fool heads off, enjoying every glorious minute.

> *Thank You, Lord, for the gift of hospitality and, most of all,*
> *for the amazing variety of interesting people*
> *You've brought through my front door.*
> —Patricia Lorenz

Behold, you are beautiful, my beloved.
—SONG OF SOLOMON 1:16 (RSV)

"I have to tell you something that happened the other day," my friend Pat said while we waited for our kids in the school parking lot. "I was walking into the cafeteria to get coffee, and I saw your husband standing outside smelling the roses." She smiled. "What a sweet moment. I mean, how many times do you see a man do that?"

"He's like that," I said, unable to think of anything else to say because her story both surprised and touched me. *What a charming, even romantic picture,* I thought. Had I forgotten that Paul is like that? And exactly how do I see him? More likely smelling of cut grass and gasoline after he's spent Saturday morning mowing the backyard and trimming the bushes. Or paint-speckled with sawdust in his hair after working a fourteen-hour day on his latest theater set.

After seventeen years of marriage, it's easy to let the everyday details bury the treasured reasons why I married him: his love for God; the joy he shares singing and playing the guitar; that he knows the names of all the constellations and where to find them on a starry night.

Now I carry a new picture of Paul in my mind. When my day gets hectic and I might be annoyed by some little thing he forgets to do or say, I try to see him as others do, as God sees him. Not as the guy who forgets to close the kitchen cabinets, but as the one who remembers to stop and smell the roses.

Loving God, help me to see the good in all You have created,
and to love others as You love me.
—GINA BRIDGEMAN

July 12

If ye have faith as a grain of mustard seed...
nothing shall be impossible unto you.
—Matthew 17:20 (KJV)

During the summer, wild mustard grows freely along the roadsides in Wyoming. Even by late July, when many other species have shriveled and died, the mustard continues to thrive in broiling heat and sandy soil.

After sidestepping a particularly dense mustard plant that was crowding me off the sidewalk one summer evening, I remembered the necklace I had worn as a child: a spherical glass pendant that encased a tiny mustard seed. It had fascinated me, and I decided to share the miracle of the mustard seed with my fifth-grade religious education students. All I needed was a Bible and a box from my spice cabinet.

Once my class was settled, I gave each child a mustard seed and listened.

"What is it?"

"I think it's from a pickle jar."

"What does it do?"

After a few minutes I asked the children to look up Matthew 17:20, the memory verse for the week. We opened our Bibles and read aloud. Somewhere a brain-bulb flashed on.

"Hey! It's a mustard seed!"

"Sure is little."

I pointed out that the bushy mustard plants in the nearby pasture had grown from seeds like these. "Hold your mustard seed. Look at it again, boys and girls. This is all the faith you need to move mountains."

Someone whispered, "Wow!"

"That's all? Just that much?"

"Totally awesome."

Totally awesome, indeed.

Lord of Creation, thank You for giving me little things
to help me understand the big ones.
—Gail Thorell Schilling

But God hath revealed them unto us.

—1 CORINTHIANS 2:10 (KJV)

Parakeets were never at the top of my favorite pet list. But when someo͏ I know needed a new home for her two birds, Hercule Poirot and M͏ Jane Marple, I took them, wire cage and all. The birds nuzzled and chirped day long—until the time I left the cage open and Hercule and Miss Marple ma͏ a run (or should I say, fly?) for it.

I tried catching them with my hands; they flew across the room. I tr͏ throwing a light cloth over them; they seemed to be laughing as they flew by ͏ put cups of birdseed on the curtain rods. Then I got a broom, taped it to a b͏ plastic laundry basket, covered the basket with some pink netting torn fron͏ dress I hadn't worn in a decade, and thought, *They'll never get away from this!*

Well, they did.

My neighbor, to whom I'd never said much more than "hello," knocked my door. "I heard such a racket through the wall," she said, "that I wondere͏ everything was all right."

It's hard to say "Everything's fine" when you're answering the door, holdi͏ a blue laundry basket festooned with pink tulle and fastened with duct tape͏ a broom handle, two parakeets flying feverishly around your head and cups birdseed falling to the floor. But with my neighbor's help—she somehow ͏ Hercule to land on her finger and Jane followed shortly after—I got the bi͏ back safely to their cages.

What did I learn from my adventure? Well, I don't know very mu͏ about parakeets. And never say no to a helping hand—or finger—no mat͏ the embarrassment.

God, thank You for birds that fly as they were meant
to and for goodhearted neighbors.

—LINDA NEUKRUG

What is man that thou art mindful of him,
and the son of man that thou dost care for him?
—Psalm 8:4 (RSV)

Growing up, I often heard the story of my mother's lost Shirley Temple doll. Given to her during the Depression, it was much treasured. But her grandmother wouldn't let her play with it lest she break it. When I was in high school I decided to find my mother another Shirley Temple doll. But in every antique shop I searched over the years I invariably found nothing and left with my name on yet another list. Then one summer day, just a few years ago, I got a call.

"Don't sell it!" I shouted into the phone, yanking off my gardening gloves and kicking off my boots. "I'll be right up!"

The doll was in mint condition. I bought her on the spot. But during the long months between summer and Christmas, when I would surprise my mother, I did some research. To my dismay I discovered that there were more than fifty different kinds of Shirley Temple dolls! What was the chance I'd found the right one?

I don't know who was more surprised when Christmas finally rolled around, my mother or I. She stared down into the opened box. "My doll!" she whispered, and I nearly burst into tears. I'd found the right doll after all.

"But, oh...," my mother said all of a sudden, hands poised frozen over the doll, "I might break her." After sixty years, my mother was still hearing her grandmother's admonition.

A few moments went by. Then my mother very gently lifted Shirley Temple from the nested box, and carefully let us all "play" with her.

Thank You, Lord, for caring about the little things,
like finding the right lost childhood doll.
—Brenda Wilbee

JULY 15

Then said Jesus, Father, forgive them; for they know not what they do.
—LUKE 23:34 (KJV)

My doctor had ordered a new pain patch that had amazing resul The fun-loving Roberta was back, full of pep and planning, a when I decided to go on a weekend shopping extravaganza, I asked my sis and a new friend to come along.

We had a great time, but on the dark, rainy drive home, my new patch off. Not realizing it would lessen its effectiveness, I secured the old (and ve expensive) one to my arm with some adhesive tape. It wasn't long before I h a violent headache and was pulling off the side of the road. My sister took o the driving and I curled up in the backseat.

Soon I heard my friend remark to my sister, as if I wasn't there, "We never going to get home at this rate. Does she get any worse than this? I do know how you stand it." Her words hurt me in a place down deep that I did know existed. I'd planned our trip down to the tiniest detail, tiptoed to t hotel kitchenette each morning to brew a pot of coffee, and brought a cup wi a cinnamon roll to my friend's bedside, carried her packages when her ar got tired.

Then seemingly out of the blue, Jesus' words, spoken from the Cross, flash into my mind: "Father, forgive them; for they know not what they do." It was if I were hearing them for the first time. Of course! My friend couldn't kn what I was going through—she'd never been ill herself. And maybe she had meant to be unkind but was just frustrated, or even scared.

When I got back to work, I printed that Scripture on an index card and tap it inside my desk drawer. It never fails to take my eyes back to the Cross, to forgiveness beyond my understanding.

What freedom there is, Lord, in Your model of forgiveness in the midst of pain.
—ROBERTA MESSNER

JULY 16

*Therefore, my beloved brethren, be ye steadfast, unmovable,
always abounding in the work of the Lord, forasmuch as ye know
that your labour is not in vain in the Lord.*
—1 CORINTHIANS 15:58 (KJV)

The Centennial Celebration was to be the biggest gathering my childhood church had ever had, with four full days of activities. I planned to travel back from the West Coast to New York to attend, and for weeks I daydreamed about what the Evening of Remembrance might include. What big events and dynamic speakers would people bring to mind? Perhaps the "Flying Evangelist" who took us on plane rides? Or the many talented musical groups who had come from various Christian schools to share their faith with us? Maybe the dramatic candlelight New Year's Eve service we once had?

But I was in for a surprise. The cozy, hushed auditorium sheltered many precious faces from my past. Some now had white hair; others who were once toddlers now looked down at me. And as each one stood, they named individuals: Ida, the quiet, godly nursery teacher whom no one could recall *not* being there. They remembered the untiringly serving Pearl. And several people mentioned Betty's quiet faithfulness as a Sunday school teacher. "Betty's always here, always the same," one woman said with appreciative teariness. "That's meant a lot to me."

Nothing was said that evening about stupendous events or "big names." It dawned on me how very much we crave dependability and quiet steadfastness. These were the treasures to remember, the goals to try for.

I left that evening with a new perspective, and with a proud hand on Betty's freckled arm. You see, Betty's my mom.

*Dear Lord, have I been pursuing "Christian showiness," hoping
to win more favor and unforgettableness? Help me choose the better thing.*
—KATHIE KANIA

Day to day pours forth speech, and night to night reveals knowledge.
—PSALM 19:2 (NASB)

M y husband Bill has made me a night owl. I grew up a city girl ar
then became a wooded-lot suburbia woman, so only here in th
Shenandoah Valley have I discovered the joy of the ever-changing night sky.

On many nights from May to September, a cool breeze from West Virgin
dips softly into the valley, and when I'm ready for bed, I take the chair cushic
and a soft blanket and pile into the Adirondack chair. My clear star view is to th
northeast, over our rooftop. I settle in and wait.

As my eyes adjust to the darkness, I see an occasional aircraft bound fo
Washington or Baltimore, threading its way, blinking, through the dar
Sometimes a star-white satellite sails silently far above. Then the stars wink o
one...two...ten million. On the clearest nights I can stare in awe at the dense
parts of the Milky Way. Bill and I thought they were clouds the first time we sa
them, until we dug out the binoculars and discovered myriads upon myriads o
stars crammed together millions of light years away.

I know the Big Dipper; I find it and follow the bowl's line out to the star that
always stuck between my chimney and the roofline: Polaris, the pole star. Eve
if I doze off and the universe turns, when I awake Polaris is still there. I call it n
"Jesus star," the one true constant.

I sit in silent praise, thanking God for His immensity and for His closenes
Slowly my eyes shut, gently I sink down, and soon I am asleep—safe in th
Father's love under the dome of His universe.

Father, let me remember that above me always, day or night, city or country,
lie the uncountable stars that show forth Your lavish love and the Pole Star
that reminds me of Your steadfast presence.

—ROBERTA ROGERS

The fruit of the Spirit is love, joy, peace....
—GALATIANS 5:22 (KJV)

One summer day, my aunt Eunice and her husband George gave a family picnic. Eunice had worked for days making sure that everyone's favorite dish was waiting. She had even set a place underneath a leafy tree for our dog Bandit: a blanket folded into a bed and a big bowl of cool water welcomed him with love.

"Vintage Eunice," my husband David said after he told that story from the pulpit of the First United Methodist Church in Florence, Alabama. David's funeral sermon was filled with lovely stories of Eunice's life, but it was the story of the dog that brought tears of knowing to the congregation's eyes.

Ever since I first got to know Eunice, after my mother married Eunice's brother Herb Hester, I saw her as the kind of person I'd like to become. Now David's words helped me to see what that would be like.

How many times have I worked myself silly, cleaning everything in sight, so my guests would admire my housekeeping? To become like Eunice, I'd have to pay less attention to dust bunnies and cobwebs and concentrate on creating a place of warmth and welcome for my friends.

How many times have I monopolized conversations with stories of "me"? To become like Eunice, I'd have to take the time to listen, holding on to each word as if it were the finest ever spoken.

How many times have I gloated over my possessions? To become like Eunice, I have to take more pleasure in giving away my treasures than in keeping them.

The truth is, by living the way she lived, Eunice offered me a choice: I can either spend my days concentrating on what makes me look good, or I can work to create situations that make others feel good.

Father, when You show me the fruits of the Spirit in another's eyes,
help me not only to admire but to emulate.
—PAM KIDD

JULY 19

In those days a man will say to his brother, "You have some extra clothing, so you be our king and take care of this mess."
—ISAIAH 3:6 (TLB)

One thing about being single and an empty-nester is that you get to fill all the closets. No sharing; every inch is mine. And what happens over the years is you end up with far too many clothes. I have clothes for every season, every reason, every style, size, and event.

I should take my cue from my stepmother Bev, who, at age seventy-eight, always looks like she just stepped out of a fashion magazine. When it comes to clothes, she's a minimalist. For instance, for summer she has five or six really nice spotless T-shirts; I have about thirty. Some are in the same condition as my dad's shop rags. How can you ever get rid of the T-shirt your daughter painted in high school? Or the one you bought at the Eiffel Tower? Or the one your son bought you for Mother's Day fifteen years ago?

Well, I'm going to try. My goal for this year is to reduce my clothes-chaos from three closets full to perhaps one and a half. I'm going to try to find something that looks really good on me and stick with that style. I'm going to give the rest away to Goodwill or Human Concerns so that others who have little can have more. I'm going to share a few special things with friends, who, unlike me and my dreams, have already lost the extra twenty pounds.

Yes, I am going to conquer my closets! My new mantra: less is more. I feel lighter already.

Jesus, thank You for keeping me well clothed. Help me to be more like You and share my bounty with others who have less.
—PATRICIA LORENZ

"I'm putting my rainbow in the clouds."
—GENESIS 9:13 (MSG)

*J*ulie's daughter Katie was my first grandchild to marry. We all got caught up in Katie's plans, except for one thing: She had her heart set an outdoor wedding at sunset. Nothing could dissuade her.

"What about rain?" I asked her gently.

"It's not going to," Katie answered with a smile.

A week before the wedding, Julie told Katie that showers were in the forecast. dded my grim amen.

"It's not going to rain. I've prayed about it, y'all."

Four days before the wedding, I phoned to tell Katie that rain was actually recast for her wedding day.

"It's not going to rain, Nanny. Thanks, though," she said politely.

Then a day before the wedding, when I ran out to get the mail in between owers and glanced up to scan the sky, I lit up like a Christmas tree. There, nging in the darkish sky, was a double rainbow! Back inside, I telephoned lie. "I know," she said, not even bothering to say hello.

Saturday arrived, a bit dreary-looking. As we left the house, I grabbed an nbrella that blended in with my ice-pink dress. At seven o'clock, about two ndred of us sat in white chairs in front of a large gazebo. The wedding music, ayed by a small ensemble, filled the air. Jamie, the handsome groom, waited th folded hands alongside his brother, the other groomsmen, the bridesmaids, d the minister. I checked the sky one more time. The dark clouds behind us emed to have stopped moving as if on command. Then Katie and her father lked over the lush green grass toward the gazebo and her future.

Father, help me to expect Your rainbow in all life's storms.
—MARION BOND WEST

Commit thy works unto the Lord, and thy thoughts shall be established.
—Proverbs 16:3 (kjv)

I've always loved music. As a child, I struggled with piano lessons, b my hands were too small to stretch an octave on the keys, and I nev could seem to loosen their stiffness enough to make the music seem other tha labored. I gave it up when I got old enough to protest against the lessons.

One year I shared a monastery guest house with a young man name Douglas, who wanted to be a jazz trumpeter. He moved in with hundreds CDs and a shiny trumpet. I was eager to hear him play. Douglas practiced f four hours every day, two in the morning and two in the evening. But for t entire month I was there, he played only scales, every morning, every night. A those hours of practice went into nothing more than scales.

Just before I was due to leave, I asked him why he never played anythi else. He answered, "I want to be a very good trumpet player, and I don't have natural gift for it. So I have to work at the basics very hard for a very long time

I went away humbled by his dedication to making music, aware that, just I hadn't had the talent to play easily, I also hadn't had the gift of working ha enough to make up for my flaws. Douglas may not get the career he wants, b it won't be for any lack of trying. His God-given determination will carry hi through obstacles that turn away a lesser heart.

Show me the gift You've given me, Lord, and give me the perseverance to pursue
—Rhoda Blecker

JULY 22

A man approached Jesus and knelt before him.
"Lord, have mercy on my son," he said.
—MATTHEW 17:14–15

B *less them,* I silently prayed as I walked into church and saw two strangers among us, up near the front. The Hillearys had adopted brothers, ages five and four. Just arrived in Virginia from Cambodia, they understood hardly a word of English. During the songs, the curious boys surveyed the congregation, each perched on his specially reserved seat: the hipbone of a new parent. Throughout the Scripture readings and the sermon, the brothers didn't say a word or make a fuss.

When the sermon was over, I opened my Book of Common Prayer to the "Prayers of the People," which start with the invitation, "With all our heart and with all our mind, let us pray to the Lord, saying, 'Lord, have mercy.'"

From a front pew, a woman read a petition: "For the peace from above...let us pray to the Lord." She paused.

"Lord, have mercy," we responded.

She read another line: "For the peace of the world...let us pray to the Lord."

"Lord, have mercy."

The rhythm was quickly obvious, even if you'd missed the instructions. So I was surprised to hear the pattern broken after the sixth response. It was the older Hilleary brother. In the brief silence between the response and the next prayer, he went solo: "Lord, have mercy."

Then again and again, for the next six petitions. After the congregation asked for a common mercy, the child echoed his own private request. The boy, embarking on a new life—in a new land, with a new family—didn't know the meaning of his prayer. But that only made his final echo more striking—for him and for every child of God of every age.

"Defend us, deliver us, and in thy compassion protect us,
O Lord, by thy grace."
—EVELYN BENCE

JULY 23

*Not one of the good promises which the Lord had made
to the house of Israel failed.*

—JOSHUA 21:45 (NASB)

I didn't want to sell the old beige car. I had bought it shortly after I becam
a widow—the first one I ever bought by myself. Now my husband Ge
thought I should have a newer, safer car. But the old car and I were good friend
Why, I had even driven it when I went to meet Gene for the first time. Wh
my son Jeremy was in a terrible accident, my trusty car got me to him in reco
time. When my daughter Julie's newborn son died at birth, I found sanctuary
that faithful old car as Gene and I drove to the hospital and then to the cemete
the next day. When Julie delivered beautiful, healthy Thomas a few years late
I made the joyful drive to see them in my car. It was crammed full of memori
and its bumpers were covered with stickers that witnessed the faith that ha
gotten me through.

In a moment of weakness, I took Gene's advice and bought a new car. B
I absolutely refused to leave my old car on the lot, abandoned and unwante
I drove it home slowly and thoughtfully, while Gene drove the snazzy new c
with the sunroof. As I drove, I asked God to send people to buy my car wh
would love it, be excited over it—and leave my bumper stickers on it. I cou
hardly believe it when He seemed to say, *Okay*. I parked my car in the yar
and we put a FOR SALE sign on it, and I went inside to vacuum and try to wo
through my feelings.

I turned off the vacuum when Gene came running into the house with a fi
full of money and explained, "This is a down payment. A couple stopped just
I parked your car. They've been praying—asking God to show them a car. Th
don't have a lot of money, but they have a lot of faith. They're in love with yo
car and, get this, they love your bumper stickers!"

*Father God, help me to learn that when You say You'll do something,
it's as good as done, no matter how trivial my request. Amen.*

—MARION BOND WEST

July 24

Blessed be thou of the Lord, my daughter.
—Ruth 3:10 (KJV)

*W*hen I was in my early twenties and newly married, I longed to be a mother. But neurofibromatosis stole that dream. I busied myself with creative pursuits like home decorating and designing a dollhouse complete with working lights, colorful rugs improvised from placemats, and silhouettes crafted from black-and-white cameo earrings.

One weekend there was a home show at our local arena. My five-year-old niece Allison attended with her parents. To her great delight, she won a door prize donated by the local miniatures shop: a gift certificate for anything her heart desired.

A few days later when Allison came to spend the night, she brought along a medium-sized, black-and-white checked box. "This is for you," she explained. I lifted the lid to find a dollhouse-size mom and dad with a little girl and boy. "It's a family for you."

I had never admitted to anyone how I'd longed for a child, yet this dear one had sensed it and tried to heal the hurt in my heart. No, my sadness at being childless didn't vanish at once. But when I put the dolls on display in my dollhouse, for the first time I knew that someone had acknowledged my pain.

Today, that five-year-old girl will soon be the mother of her third child, a little girl. I'm going to find that dollhouse and my "little family." I think I know someone who would enjoy it—and a second thank-you.

Thank You, Lord, for the times when life comes full circle
and I get to remember my blessings again.
—Roberta Messner

JULY 25

*Can you bring forth the constellations in their seasons
or lead out the Bear with its cubs?*
—JOB 38:32

Yesterday we took a picnic lunch up to Elizabeth Furnace in Virginia's George Washington National Forest. I was packing up the remains when I glanced under the picnic table. There, and just outside around the table, were thick chunks of dense black fur.

There are bears in our mountains. Our son John saw one a couple of years ago on a bluff above where he was fly-fishing, and in the past year our family had several more encounters: my husband Bill and I saw one hopping over the guardrail on Route 211 over Thornton Gap; our son Tom saw a cub shimmying down a tree in the north Georgia hills; and my brother Nat saw one on a farm in Pennsylvania.

We are city folk, and bears both intrigue and frighten us. Most of the time we frighten them too. Our bear, John's bear, and Nat's bear scurried off when they saw us. But what Tom, alone with his mountain bike, heard scrabbling in the brush may well have been the mama bear, wanting to protect her young. Using his bike as a shield, he walked on down the path. Suddenly, his cell phone, which had been out of service range for hours, rang. It was his wife Susan calling to see how he was doing. Since making human noises is a good way to send bears scurrying, Tom told her of his encounter in a loud, trying-to-sound-calm voice. He heard no more scuffling in the undergrowth. And he had no cell service until he was back on the highway headed home.

None of this is enough to deter us from enjoying the mountains and woods. We're cautious, we've learned what to do, and we know how to pray. The rest is in God's hands.

*Lord, teach me to be wise and alert, but to continue
on my daily path trusting in Your love and protection.*
—ROBERTA ROGERS

*"Blessed by the Lord be his land...with the choicest fruits of the sun...
with the finest produce of the ancient mountains, and the abundance of the
everlasting hills, with the best gifts of the earth and its fulness."*
—DEUTERONOMY 33:13–16 (RSV)

A forty-minute hike?" my mother gasped. "I didn't know we'd have to hike there!" My family and I were in the Puerto Rican rain forest and had just learned we'd have to trek it to La Mina, the island's tallest waterfall.

"It'll be fine," we convinced her. "You have your asthma pump. We'll just take it slow." It had been more than twenty years since we'd been in Puerto Rico as a family, and we were having a wonderful time rediscovering the island of our roots.

We started the hike with a burst of energy. Even my mother was zipping through and actually leading the way. Our trek was anything but straight and level; the trail twisted and turned and led up and down steep hills. We helped one another cross narrow paths and climb over large slippery rocks as we laughed, talked, and encouraged each other to keep going. Streams of light found their way through the tropical palms. There were lush, shiny leaves the size of small umbrellas, and we passed babbling brooks and small waterfalls. But the best part of the hike was simply being with my family.

We finally reached the waterfall, and after a moment of admiration we immersed our tired bodies in the cool, refreshing water. "You see," I said to my mother, "wasn't this worth it?"

My mother didn't hear me. She was under the waterfall, letting it spill over her head like blessings from God.

I am awed by Your creation, God. Thank you.
—KAREN VALENTIN

July 27

And I will give them one heart, and I will put a new spirit within you.
—Ezekiel 11:19 (KJV)

I felt empty, self-centered, all wrapped up in me, me, me. God seemed remote. *I need You to do something, Lord. I don't even know what.* Silence.

One lonely Friday morning I finally curled up with a book a friend had sent for no apparent reason. *Some Wildflower in My Heart* by Jamie Langston Turner captivated me. I read all day—slowly, like a second-grader. Nearing the end of the book on Saturday afternoon, I savored each word as I would an expensive chocolate. When I finished, I couldn't bear to put it down, so I sat holding it close to me, fully aware that God had worked His way into my heart—even the stubborn part—through this remarkable book. I'd rediscovered the key to Christian joy—genuinely loving others, even the unlovely, from the reservoir of God's unconditional love.

That very afternoon I visited an unbelieving neighbor, a classic grouch. I took flowers to a sick friend I somehow hadn't been able to make time for before. Back at my desk, I wrote out a generous check for a missionary and sent letters of encouragement to each of my six grandchildren. Finally, I looked my astonished husband right in the eye and told him a few of the reasons I love him so completely.

I decided I had to call the author of this life-changing book to say thank-you. Then my common sense took over, and I attempted to talk myself out of the idea. How would I locate her? Exactly what would I say? Where would I begin?

Five phone calls later, Jamie Turner and I were talking excitedly like old friends. We spoke from the heart for nearly an hour that Saturday afternoon. I could hardly believe it when she insisted that my call had made her day. I know that her book—and her graciousness—had made mine.

Father God, fill my heart with Your love so that I may
pass it on to friends and strangers. Amen.
—Marion Bond West

JULY 28

One thing have I desired...to behold the beauty of the Lord.
—PSALM 27:4 (KJV)

*A*fter a long drive, I arrived at my sister's house and found her on her knees in a freshly turned flowerbed.

"What are you planting?" I asked.

"Roses," Libby said, wiping her forehead with the back of her gloved hand.

I looked at the sturdy stems and green leaves. "What color will they be?"

She laughed. "Any color they want!" Libby proceeded to tell me that she had 	ten the flowers at the dump.

"The dump?" I asked, incredulous. "But they look so healthy!"

She told me that the biggest grower in the area tossed out any plant that 	n't meet their strict standards. "But these will be lovely. Just wait and see." 	e patted the dirt affectionately.

That was several years ago, and now whenever I visit my sister in the summer, 	ge, beautiful roses grace her yard. Pink, yellow, even mottled red and white 	es. These flowers, picked from the trash, are thriving, offering their beauty to 	eryone who sees.

Master Gardener, open my eyes to the potential for beauty
in places where I might never look.
—MARY LOU CARNEY

And God saw every thing that he had made, and, behold, it was very good.
—GENESIS 1:31 (KJV)

One summer Sunday morning I took my Sunday school class of first- and second-graders to our church's spectacular flower garden. Tucked away behind the church, the garden has fragrant roses, marigolds, petunias, zinnias, nasturtiums, and lavender. We trudged across a carpet of grass to a picnic table under an old shade tree. I handed the two boys and six girls paper and pencils.

"I want you to go into the garden with a partner and choose a flower. Write something about it. What is its shape? Is it tall or short? What is its smell? What does it remind you of? Then come back and we'll compare what you've found." My aim was to spark a wonder in them at the variety and beauty of God's creation.

The girls spread out into the flowers like butterflies, giggling and comparing. The boys, Turner and Gregory, got no farther than the grass. I watched them plop down just out of earshot and talk as if they were in a two-man huddle. Knowing their penchant for sports, I was sure that baseball, not flowers, was their topic.

After the allotted time was up, I summoned them back to the picnic table. "I think we'll let Turner and Gregory go first," I said.

"We picked a clover flower," Gregory said. A clover! It never occurred to me to call such a lost-in-the-grass thing a flower.

"What did you write about it?" I asked.

"We thought it looked like a ballerina," Turner said.

"The wind is its music," added Gregory.

Creator God, help me to stop underestimating
Your children and the other works of Your hands.

—SHARI SMYTH

July 30

Weeping may endure for a night, but joy cometh in the morning.
—Psalm 30:5 (KJV)

Our newborn son Henry was inconsolable. We hummed, sang, rocked, swaddled, played white noise. Henry still cried.

The doctor assured us it was just colic, but I began to worry that something was terribly wrong. Why was Henry so unhappy? Why couldn't I soothe him?

"Don't take it personally," my mom said. But how could I not?

Our family got used to it. When I had to get the shopping done, I took Henry to the store, where he screamed as I held him in one arm and piled groceries into the cart with the other. I learned to live on two consecutive hours of sleep and relied on my nightly bath for twenty minutes of quiet—pure heaven.

The day before Henry's three-month checkup, he woke up, opened his eyes, and smiled. He sat contentedly and fell asleep easily in my arms.

"What's wrong with Henry?" Solomon asked.

"I don't know." I felt his forehead.

Henry had a happy day with only a few whimpers and then slept through the night with little fuss.

"Is he okay?" I asked the pediatrician the next day.

"He's fine. Why?"

"He's like a different baby."

"Sometimes they just outgrow colic," the pediatrician said. "Their nervous systems mature and they realize everything is fine."

Henry smiled with an innocence that only a baby who's kept a family up for three months straight can have. His beautiful dark brown eyes studied me with a look of wisdom and pride, as if to say, "See, Mommy, we both passed the test!"

Dear God, when my burden is heavy, remind me that every trial has an end.
And thank You for a happy baby and a good night's sleep!
—Sabra Ciancanelli

*Honor the Lord with your substance
and with the first fruits of all your produce.*
—PROVERBS 3:9 (RSV)

Charlie, Texas, has a population of about 120, mostly farmers and fruit growers. Once a year, if and when the crop comes in, the Charlie Peach Festival draws five hundred to six hundred people from the surrounding towns to eat homemade peach cobbler and peach ice cream, courtesy of the hardworking folks who run the orchards. People drive for miles to watch the ice cream crank-off and the pea-shelling contest, and to join in a little bit of country fun. The festival under the shade trees is like stepping back in time.

Charlie is about fifteen miles north of my home in Wichita Falls, and we city folk continue the trek to Charlie's fruit stands throughout the summer to buy fresh-picked produce. When it's really hot and the orchard owners are tired of sitting at their roadside stands, they leave little cigar boxes out alongside the baskets of sweet, juicy fruits and vegetables with signs that say, HONOR SYSTEM, PAY FOR YOUR PURCHASE HERE.

There's always money inside the cigar boxes. That's one of the best things about Charlie, I think: along with the old-time country fun, people there still think we're all neighbors who care about one another, and we can be trusted. It's a nice feeling, sweeter even than a Charlie peach.

*Father, help me always to bring out the best
in people by expecting the best from them.*
—MARJORIE PARKER

August

My soul yearns for you in the night; in the morning my spirit longs for you.
—ISAIAH 26:9

Will you pray with me?" an attractive young woman asked timidly during a break at a women's retreat where we'd been talking about turning our "I can'ts" into "I cans." We found a quiet corner, and her words tumbled out, describing a life filled with difficulties. She was a single mom with four children, working full-time at a job with some pressing problems, and the man in her life had just broken their engagement. "I can't figure out what to do," she admitted, wiping away tears. "I feel so lonely and overwhelmed."

My heart ached for her, and we spent the next several minutes praying together, asking God to show us some "I cans" in the midst of her "I can'ts." When we finished, I took out a piece of paper, wrote "I CAN" across the top and handed it to her. "Let's think together," I suggested, and soon she had these ideas written down on the paper:

Three things only I CAN do:

Take responsibility for my self-care.

Let my needs be known to those who can help.

Ask for help.

Three ways I CAN ask another person to help me:

Spend time with me.

Spend time with my children.

Pray for me.

Three ways I CAN have fun:

Go to the movies.

Go out to eat.

Attend special events.

As she tucked her "I CAN" list into her Bible, I prayed...

Lord, with You, we can turn our "I CAN'TS" into "I CANS!" Thank You.
—CAROL KUYKENDALL

August 2

He that dwelleth in the secret place of the most High
shall abide under the shadow of the Almighty.
—Psalm 91:1 (kjv)

My youngest son John has completed his graduate work and has taken a position with a company in the Washington, DC, area. The job is exactly right for him, and we were all delighted when he was offered the position. Then came September 11, 2001.

To be honest, I worry about John. He's living in what is probably the least safe place in the country, and there's nothing I can do to protect him.

I guess there comes a time when a mother has to let go and trust. But trust whom? The DC security forces? Can I really even trust God to keep my son safe? After all, I'm sure that many of those whose loved ones were killed on September 11 were praying people. Why should I believe that God would protect my son and not others?

The answer, as I see it, is there is no absolute certainty in this life. There is no physical place that is completely safe, and there never was. What I do know for sure is true safety is found only in God, and that His safety is of the soul and spirit, not necessarily of the body. Of course, I'll continue to pray for my son's physical safety, but I'm also trusting, in this unsafe world, that my children's souls will always be safe in the One who created them. In the long view, that's all that really matters.

Holy Comforter, I entrust the souls of all those I love
to Your unfailing care, now and always.
—Marilyn Morgan King

AUGUST 3

I have learned, in whatsoever state I am, therewith to be content.
—PHILIPPIANS 4:11 (KJV)

*M*y work as a writer for decorating magazines takes me into ma[n]y homes. Although each of them is lovely, I'm usually happy to g[et] back to my little log cabin that once served as a fishing lodge.

But when a packet of pictures taken at our latest prizewinning home arriv[ed] one day last year, the peaceful palette of pink, robin's-egg blue, and white was [so] captivating, I immediately transported myself there, enjoying an imaginary c[up] of coffee on the screened-in back porch that I was certain looked out on a lak[e].

The owner, Jan Giacalone from Flint, Michigan, proved as delightful as h[er] cottage. "Tell me about the view from that porch," I asked during our pho[ne] interview, fighting a twinge of envy because a new housing development w[as] going up beside my cabin.

"The view?" she answered with a chuckle. "The view is of a doctor's offic[e]. I'm smack dab in the middle of the city!"

Jan went on to tell me that she loved the water, too, and even moved [to] Florida a few years back to be able to enjoy her favorite vacation spot. "Bu[t I] found out that paradise isn't paradise unless you have people to share it with[,]" she said. The Giacalones lasted in Florida three months, and then Jan and h[er] husband moved back to a place two doors down from where she grew up. Sh[e's] close to her mother and sister, and her daughter lives on the same block.

And that spacious lakeside home of Jan's? It's all of nine hundred square fe[et.] But like the little log cabin that I'm enjoying anew, thanks to Jan, it's paradise[.]

Wherever I am is paradise, Lord, as long as You and those I love are with me.
—ROBERTA MESSNER

"But come on, all of you, try again!"
—JOB 17:10

I appreciated the phone call from my publisher, warning me before I opened the letter that was in the mail. Even so, the disappointing news devastated me: my most recent book was on its way out of print. A book of conversational prayers that I'd cried over, lost sleep over. My brightest and best work—or so I thought—no longer readily available in stores.

"An early retirement," my optimistic friend Anne said, as if the book had a life of its own.

"A premature death," I countered, trying to name the depths of my grief.

The loss took its toll. I removed the framed book jacket from the wall in my home office; it seemed easier to look at a bare nail than at the cover, a photo of two light-hearted women. Though I was forty pages into a new manuscript of family essays, I shut down. I'm just an editor now, not an author.

"I'm never writing again," I told Anne when she called later that week.

"Don't be so sure. Give yourself some time," she said, neither discounting my pain nor allowing me to dwell in never-never land.

A month later she asked what I was writing.

"Nothing. Not yet."

She dropped the subject, but I knew it would come up again. And sure enough, it did. "You writing yet?" she asked next time we met for doughnuts and coffee.

Her gentle persistence sparked a smile and a new answer.

"Tomorrow," I said. "Tomorrow I'll try."

I wrote a paragraph. Just one at first, but it was the start of another essay that bolstered a new book proposal. And now this devotional. And even a new prayer.

God, thank You for the nudge away from "never" and toward "try again."
—EVELYN BENCE

*Every three years once came the ships of Tarshish bringing gold,
and silver...and peacocks. And king Solomon passed
all the kings of the earth in riches and wisdom.*
—2 CHRONICLES 9:21–22 (KJV)

We have an abundance of Solomon's riches in our community the form of peacocks, and they can be an outright nuisance. Li the time the children called from the driveway, "Mom, come quick! He's beautiful." Feathers spread out like an iridescent fan, the peacock was strutti and prancing. Then, feathers flattened, he fiercely pecked at his reflecti shining from the passenger door of our car. He didn't like the competition another bird in his territory. I didn't like the damage to our car. I chased hi He chased me. He won!

On the other hand, the music of Beethoven, Mozart, and Tchaikovsky w never sound the same as when played under the stars one memorable nig in August. The maestro of the California Philharmonic Orchestra raised h baton, and the opening of the *Eroica* symphony had us spellbound. That's whe the peacocks joined in. From the trees where they had perched for the nigh they mewed and screeched in raucous disharmony. They continued on duri Mozart's *Violin Concerto No. 3*. We in the audience loved it when the maest raised his baton to the treetops as though to cue them. Too bad that whe darkness fell and we came to *Capriccio Italien*, the peacock *obbligato* diminishe to a few muted mews.

Oh, the whimsy of creation! A conundrum, that a most beautiful bird has screeching awful voice and the modest little meadowlark thrills us with lilti song. How wondrous is God's curious world.

*For soul-soaring music with peculiar twists, for picnics and people,
and all our fine pleasures, we praise You, O Lord.*
—FAY ANGUS

*Let him have all your worries and cares, for he is always thinking
about you and watching everything that concerns you.*
—1 PETER 5:7 (TLB)

The bridge to nowhere crosses a steep gorge of the East Fork of the San
Gabriel River in California, high in the mountains several miles from
ere we live. The concrete span extends 230 feet from a rock buttress to the
ge on the other side. Designed to connect a proposed highway between ski
orts, the bridge was completed in 1936 and has never carried a single car. In
arch 1938, torrential rains raised the river to a forty-foot churning disaster.
ads under construction were destroyed and the project abandoned. Only the
dge remained, useless, leading nowhere.

Over the years I've spent hours building such bridges, brooding on what
uld've—would've—been, if only I'd done this, that, or the other. Most
ently I felt smug satisfaction in booking a travel package at a reduced rate.
ur days later another special came up for two hundred dollars less! It was too
e to switch. I grumbled about the injustice to a friend. "Your fretting is getting
u nowhere," she said. "Go and enjoy your trip." She was right.

I'm resolved to abandon useless bridges that take me nowhere. Instead I'll
ild bridges of trust, faith, and confidence in the common sense the Lord has
en me with which to map my daily life.

*Holy Spirit, I trust Your guidance on the roadways of life. How I rejoice
that Jesus is the bridge that leads me to the heart of God!*
—FAY ANGUS

Surely goodness and mercy shall follow me all the days of my life:
and I will dwell in the house of the Lord for ever.
—PSALM 23:6 (KJV)

Sitting front and center at old Uncle Hubert's funeral was my aunt Rut
a tiny woman flanked by her two elderly sons. All three sported a clou
of fluffy white hair.

The minister began the service. "The Lord is my shepherd, I shall not want–

Aunt Ruth jumped in: "He maketh me to lie down in green pastures
Embarrassed, she lifted both hands to her mouth. Uncle Rodney, on her righ
tucked a comforting arm about her slight shoulders to let her know the outbu
didn't matter.

The preacher continued. "He leadeth me beside the still waters. He restore
my soul."

"He leadeth me in the paths of righteousness—" Aunt Ruth blushed th
time and bowed to hide her face. To her left, Uncle Bill reached for one of h
hands. Affectionately, he patted her gnarled old fingers.

"—for his name's sake," continued the preacher. "Yea, though I walk—"

Aunt Ruth couldn't help herself. Every time the preacher started in, sh
interrupted. The words of the Twenty-third Psalm were so alive in her soul sh
couldn't keep still, no matter her embarrassment and my amused smile.

Suddenly, the minister looked up from his Bible with his own smile for Au
Ruth, and he held out his hand in invitation. "Thou preparest a table before m
in the presence of mine enemies: thou anointest my head with oil...."

Aunt Ruth sat tall—though still very tiny—between her two sons. "My cu
runneth over," she joyfully joined in. "Surely goodness and mercy shall follo
me all the days of my life: and I will dwell in the house of the Lord for eve
And ever and ever and ever and ever and ever!" She clasped her hands and the
opened them like the wings of a butterfly. "Forever!"

Thank You, Lord, for this invitation to dwell with You forever,
and for Aunt Ruth's faith. May I, too, know this comfort when in need.
—BRENDA WILBEE

*Therefore all things whatsoever ye would that men
should do to you, do ye even so to them.*
—MATTHEW 7:12 (KJV)

When I was in college, I worked as a waitress in a large, busy restaurant. The owners trained the staff well, but they were not very tolerant of mistakes, and on every table there were cards for the customers to write down their comments about the food and service. Most customers didn't bother with them.

One evening, however, I brought a couple the wrong soup, and they became furious. They said they were going to complain to the manager about me, and reached for one of the cards. I fought hard to hold back my tears because I was afraid I would lose my job, but I did my best to be courteous.

Another couple at the next table must have heard the remarks, because when I took their order, they smiled and told me to take my time bringing their food because they weren't in a hurry. That gave me time to pull myself together.

Later, as we were closing, the restaurant manager said he had two comment cards for me. One accused me of being careless and stupid. The other described me as thoughtful and efficient, and said I had been attentive in spite of a difficult encounter at another table. "This second card saved your job," the manager told me.

Ever since then I have made an effort to thank people who do their jobs well, no matter what those jobs may be. I try to be specific about what they have done well. Sometimes I put my gratitude in letters. I don't know whether my efforts have saved anyone's job or made a difference in anyone's life, but they mean something to me. I know how it feels to be appreciated for something I've done, and I just like to pass on the feeling.

*Dear Lord Jesus, You are so quick to applaud me, for even my smallest
accomplishments. Help me to be like You with others. Amen.*
—PHYLLIS HOBE

AUGUST 9

I devoted myself to study.
—ECCLESIASTES 1:13

I had—at the tender age of fifty—enrolled in a Master of Religi[on] program. Now I was struggling to find time for all the reading a[nd] research and writing for my class on the Gospel of Luke and the Acts [of] the Apostles.

It was 5:00 a.m., and I sat on the floor of my family room, surrounded [by] reference books. Some were left over from my undergraduate days; some h[ad] been bought as I taught church classes over the years. But most of them h[ad] come to me when Mother died six years ago.

How she loved the Bible! She would spend hours "running references" on [a] certain word or Scripture. Many times when I visited her, I'd find her sitting [at] the dining room table surrounded by books and legal pads covered with purp[le] ink. *She would be so proud that I've gone back to school*, I thought, *especially to stu[dy] religion. Too bad she isn't here.*

The words in front of me blurred. I swallowed back my tears and reached f[or] the book closest at hand. It fell open to a page where a yellow bookmark reste[d.] I looked at the bookmark: "My Darling Daughter," the heading said. I look[ed] closer; it was a poem. A poem for me. *Why is it here in this book? Why had Mother given it to me?*

The last lines of the poem seemed to come from Mother's own lips: "You a[re] a shining example of what every mother wishes her daughter was/And I am [so] very proud of you." And then, in purple ink, she had signed it: "Mother."

I smiled and settled in to read, knowing that God would help me g[et] everything done. And Mother would be proud.

Even though our loved ones are with You, God,
thank You for those moments when they seem so very close at hand.
—MARY LOU CARNEY

Even to your old age and gray hairs I am he, I am he who will sustain you.
—ISAIAH 46:4

With a brush and a blow dryer as my weapons, I've been waging a yearlong war against middle age. So far, middle age is winning, as hormones have their way with my head, both inside and out. A cowlick has suddenly developed a mind of its own, a couple of spots are thinning, and what little body my hair once had has lain down and died. Every morning as I stand in front of the mirror, I get so frustrated that I don't know whether to throw something or cry.

"It's just hair, for crying out loud. It doesn't really matter," I tell myself. So what is the matter? One day it comes to me: This isn't about a head of willful hair; it's about a life that I can't control. It's feeling that things that seem to come so easily to others—friendships, nicer homes, professional success—don't seem to come to me at all. It's silly, because they do, of course, and they will, but try to tell that to someone in a midlife crisis.

Finally, even though this isn't really a hair issue, God sent me one little thought about my hair that helped me win the skirmish: just let it do what it wants to do. So I suddenly found the courage to do something I've wanted to for a long time—have my hair cut really, really short. Now I wash it, gel it, and... let it do what it wants to do. No more battles. No more frustration. In fact, my carefree hair reminds me every day to quit trying to control my life, and to let God do with it what He wants.

Father, help me to be satisfied with You and what You bring my way.
—LUCILE ALLEN

Is there no balm in Gilead; is there no physician there?
—JEREMIAH 8:22 (KJV)

In my first week of clinical training as a phlebotomist, a medical technician who draws blood, I had done little more than observe the more seasoned phlebotomists as they drew blood from nervous patients. When it was my turn to draw blood on my own, I was excited and full of confidence, eager to use the skills I had worked hard to learn.

Carrying my tray of equipment, I headed for the patient's room. As I stepped inside the door, I was confronted by a hostile, defiant young woman who declared that she was not having her blood drawn again. I tried to explain that her doctor had ordered more tests, but she abruptly cut me off and ordered me out of her room. I was stunned and shaken and humiliated at having to return to the lab in defeat.

The days that followed went more smoothly, and I became more skillful as I practiced different types of draws on different patients. Still, I was unable to forget the patient who had caused me to crash and burn on my first solo flight. *What had been her problem, anyway?* I wondered.

Then one afternoon a coworker and I were called to the emergency room to draw blood from an elderly woman with chest pain. When she saw us approach her cubicle with our tray of needles and syringes, her jaw clenched in anger. But as I prepared for another attack, something in me recognized the terror in her eyes. Bending over beside her bed, I slipped my arms around her shoulders. As I began talking to her in soothing, reassuring tones, she broke into sobs. Carefully, Christina drew her blood while I held her hand, letting her know that everything was all right.

It was too late to make a difference to the scared young woman upstairs, but I knew now that there was a lot more to being a phlebotomist than knowing how to use needles, syringes, and tubes.

Father, remind me often that love is the best medicine in every situation.
—LIBBIE ADAMS

AUGUST 12

Pray without ceasing.
—1 Thessalonians 5:17 (kjv)

I'm looking forward to going to the monastery with you," I told my friend Ellen, "but I don't know how much praying I'll be able to do!" We had planned this retreat for months, but now with my four-month-old Mark along, I doubted I could participate much.

We arrived before dinner and chatted with the nuns in the kitchen, the sisters cooing over Mark. Sister Helen explained the scheduled services but also encouraged us to pray in between services. "In fact," she said, "I'm learning that my whole life can be prayer." She gestured to the sisters dishing out bowls of steaming soup, setting the table, arranging bread in baskets. "Cooking, washing dishes, whatever our work—it can all be prayer." *Perhaps that's true in a monastery,* I thought, *but in the world out there?*

The next morning I had to leave the chapel several times to walk or feed Mark. Later, in my room, it seemed whenever I started to pray, he needed attention.

I began pondering Sister Helen's words. Could my tending to Mark's needs itself be prayer? Outdoors I saw a sister hanging laundry, her black robes billowing and the blue sheets flapping in the wind as she pinched them on the line. Could God's Spirit blow through my stream of tasks, filling them with prayer?

Later in front of the guest house, I saw a sister showing a young man how to prune the rosebushes. Inside I met friends of the monastery from Cleveland, Ohio, heading downstairs with carpentry tools. "Hope the noise doesn't bother you," they explained. "We're building an office for the nuns." But as I listened to clipping shears and the pounding hammer, I heard the sounds of prayer.

At home I began approaching my work differently. I tried to start each task by offering it to God. Soon I'd be absorbed in work—clicking away at computer keys, reading a recipe, answering the phone, helping children share a toy—yet my heart and hands would still be praying.

May my work be prayer today, Lord, each task a reaching out to You.
—Mary Brown

Fear ye not, stand still, and see the salvation of the Lord.
—EXODUS 14:13 (KJV)

*Y*esterday morning as I was driving to a meeting, I spilled a mug water onto my lap, so I pulled over, stopped, and opened the door brush the water off my coat. But I'd neglected to put the car in PARK; it began move and I fell out!

At first I held on, trying to get back in, but the car, still in gear, was movi downhill and gaining speed. In a moment of sudden clarity I saw myse pinned under the car and made the decision to let go. As my hand let go of t runaway car, my heart grabbed hold of something solid within me. Instantl felt a strong trust that no one would be hurt. My little car brushed against so bushes, careered across the street, and was stopped, finally, by a wire fence.

Thank God no one was hurt, I thought as I checked for damage to my car a the fence. It wasn't until I got in the car and started driving that the emotio came: fear of what could have happened; anger at myself for not putting the c in PARK; anxiety about what my husband might say.

Later I realized that the suffering I felt was not from the near-accident itse but from my thoughts about it. During the actual danger I'd been awake ar alive and alert. Now I was replaying the scene and adding my own negati thoughts to it. I was causing my own suffering, and I didn't know how to st it. Then I remembered that moment of letting go of the car and simultaneous grabbing hold of something solid inside of me. And that solid somethi helped me now to let go of my self-inflicted suffering.

My runaway car experience brought me a gift: the sure knowledge that I ca trust the solid presence within me, the Spirit who can help me to let go wher need to.

When I need to let go, help me, Holy Spirit, to find
that solid place where You reside within me.
—MARILYN MORGAN KING

Ye are the light of the world.
—MATTHEW 5:14 (KJV)

*M*y mother walked into my kitchen and set a cardboard box on the counter. "Here's that old lamp you said you wanted," she said.

For weeks I'd been living on shaky ground. David felt it was time to put our five-bedroom house on the market and look for something smaller. I was having a hard time letting go of our spacious home. Sure, we needed to start scaling down and planning for retirement, but I just didn't want to let go of the happy times our big house afforded.

I opened the box and unwrapped the old hammered-brass lamp. I could still remember the exact spot where that lamp sat in the house trailer we lived in when I was three. In those days apartments were not easy to find in the small towns where my father's job took us. A little silver trailer seemed the perfect home. I remembered my mother sitting beside me on the sofa for hours reading to me; the smell of biscuits as she pulled them on the small tin sheet from the undersized oven; the laughter of my parents' friends snuggled around the little kitchen table playing cards; feeling safe at night, tucked into the cozy bunk bed, right below my big brother Davey.

I found myself smiling with pleasure as I polished the lamp. I could remember where it sat next—near a picture window in the little three-bedroom ranch house my parents bought. Later it sat on a desk in a four-bedroom lake house; then it brightened a corner of the den of a five-bedroom home nearer town.

As I followed the lamp's passage through time, it dawned on me that the good life I've lived within its circle of light hadn't a thing to do with the size or snazziness of the structures we occupied. A hospitable heart turns the smallest, plainest room into a joyful home. Houses don't make happy times. People do.

Father, let my attitude light the way for happy times—
anywhere You choose to send me.
—PAM KIDD

Except ye...become as little children,
ye shall not enter into the kingdom of heaven.
—MATTHEW 18:3 (KJV)

*M*y eight-year-old granddaughter Saralisa spent some time with u last year. The first thing she wanted me to do was to go to the cree with her. It's just across the road from our house, so hand in hand, we dance and skipped our way there.

Oh, the sound of the flowing water! It's the most beautiful music I know. sat on the bank as Saralisa took off her shoes and socks and stepped into th cool stream. The morning sun was shining in golden patches, causing the mic at the bottom of the clear water to sparkle like pure gold. Saralisa had brougl along a small skillet with which she "panned for gold," just as her grandmoth had done more than sixty years ago.

Suddenly, I was a child again! With only a little hesitation, I took off n shoes and socks and joined in the fun. Of course, we both knew it wasn't re gold, but that didn't matter one bit. Our true gold was in the pine-scente mountain air, the sunshine, that inimitable sound, and the feel of the cool wat over our bare feet.

Thank You, God! I thought to myself. For this moment in all eternity, th seventy-two-year-old grandmother is a child again. Time, like an artist on th brink of creation, stands still. And ringing down the centuries, I hear tho precious words, "And God saw every thing that he had made, and, behold, was very good" (Genesis 1:31).

Dear God, may I make time to be a child today,
letting in all the wonders of Your great creation!
—MARILYN MORGAN KING

If we hold fast.
—Hebrews 3:6 (nasb)

Discouragement rode along with me on a steamy August day as I drove to have my hair done some thirty-five miles away. Lately, it seemed possible to hold on to God and His promises.

When I stopped for a red light, alarm suddenly replaced self-pity as something whizzed into my car through the partially open window. I screamed, and a white-haired man in overalls standing on the street corner called out, "It's only a katydid, lady."

The light turned green, and I took off, quickly opening the windows and the sunroof. The six-legged hitchhiker backed herself resolutely across the passenger's side of the dashboard and hunkered down unflinchingly against a corner of the windshield. I sped up, and wind blew through the car. The katydid only tightened her grip. I had no idea what katydids do. *Will she sting me? Hide in my hair? Crawl into my clothes?* The faster I drove, the more stubbornly Katie held on. I closed the windows and the sunroof and slowed down, keeping my eyes moving from the highway over to Katie. When I applied the brakes suddenly, she put one dainty foot forward to steady herself.

At the hairdresser's, I parked in the shade and decided to leave the windows down and the sunroof open. When I returned forty-five minutes later, there she sat. "You're very determined. I like that," I said softly.

About five miles into our return trip, Katie suddenly bounced up and down like a child who'd finally decided to take off from the diving board. "Wait, Katie!" I said. I pulled off the road, opened the window, swallowed hard, and ever so slowly slid a church bulletin in front of her. Amazingly, she put one leg on it, then another, until she'd walked securely onto the paper. Steadily, I inched it over toward the open window. Hesitating a moment, she flew upward. Watching her courageous venture into the unknown, my faith unexpectedly soared skyward too.

Only You, Father, could send encouragement on the wings of a katydid!
—Marion Bond West

He calls his own sheep by name and leads them.
—JOHN 10:3

Wayne and I chose a family name for the middle names of each of our children. Jody Rose, our oldest daughter, was named for my mother. Jenny Adele was named for Wayne's mother. Later, as Jody grew, it became apparent that she resembled Wayne's side of the family far more than mine. My blond, blue-eyed daughter was all Macomber. Jenny, on the other hand, with her dark hair and eyes, resembled the Adler side of the family. It seemed to me that we'd picked the wrong names for the girls.

The thought was even stronger when Jody entered her teens and often clashed with my mom. As Jody matured, however, her relationship with my mother mellowed and the two grew especially close.

Shortly after my father died, we moved Mom to an assisted-living complex in Port Orchard, Washington, where we live. It was Jody who stopped by the complex two or three times a week to visit Mom; it was Jody who took her to her doctor's appointments if I was out of town; and it was Jody who sat with Mom and me after Mom suffered a stroke and slipped into a coma. During Mom's final minutes on earth, it was Jody who sat by my side and prayed with me as God's angels ushered Mom into glory.

At the funeral, as my daughter offered the eulogy, I sat with tears in my eyes. Wayne and I had given our daughter the right name after all. God knew all along that she was meant to be Jody Rose.

*Father God, how grateful I am that You know us all
better than we know ourselves.*
—DEBBIE MACOMBER

AUGUST 18

Not unto us, O Lord, not unto us, but unto thy name give glory.
—PSALM 115:1 (KJV)

I have a secret admirer. Well, it's not quite like the time in eighth grade when I received an anonymous Valentine with only a typed question mark for a signature. This nameless person sends me Bible verses or thoughtful notes carefully typed on postcards. I'm guessing he or she is a *Daily Guideposts* reader, because that's just the kind of encouragement readers often send. But instead of a signed letter, these are short, simple spirit-boosters. "Life is 10 percent what you make it and 90 percent how you take it." Or the one I've taped the door of my laundry room where our dog Cookie sleeps: "One reason a dog such a lovable creature is that his tail wags instead of his tongue."

I've often thought how unusual it is that someone whose name I don't even know can so frequently make me smile. But even I didn't realize the power of these messages until the day I received a disappointing letter telling me I would not be included in a book project I was hoping to work on. I was crushed, barely thinking as I flipped through the rest of the mail. Then I stopped at the familiar-looking postcard with this message: "God never closes one door without opening another." That old line had never held such power for me, healing my heart with the balm of hope. Now the rejection didn't feel so bad.

I began to wonder why my anonymous friend wants no credit for these small kindnesses that have meant so much. Then it occurred to me—because the credit belongs to God. As God is the Source of all good things, everything we do, whether or not it has a name on it, is His. No act is truly anonymous. I may never know who sends me those day-brightening little cards. But I know where they come from: from the Spirit of God from whom all good things flow.

God, let Your Spirit inspire me to help others, in simple ways, along the path.
—GINA BRIDGEMAN

But though God has planted eternity in the hearts of men, even so, man cannot see the whole scope of God's work from beginning to end.
—ECCLESIASTES 3:11 (TLB)

I'd never ridden a four-wheeler before. I climbed up onto the back and held on tightly to my twelve-year-old son Thomas's stomach.

"Mom, just relax. You'll be fine."

"Are you sure you know what you're doing?"

"Yes, ma'am." He clicked the gear with his foot.

"Is your helmet fastened right?"

"Yes, Mom. Let's go. You'll like it." He drove me around our wooded property. *Ah, Thomas knows me pretty well. He's not going fast.* He reached ahead and carefully pushed back tree branches so they wouldn't slap us. As Thomas headed downhill, he drove slowly as though leading an old horse down a rocky cliff. He wound around and stopped at the little creek. We didn't talk—we didn't need to.

I relaxed and thought back over the past year. So many changes: My grandparents had both died; our middle daughter left for college. Thomas seemed to be taking charge, riding me around, leading the way. I began to trust his skills. I admired his confidence and kindness.

My thoughts raced ahead. Years ahead.

One day I'll be really old, Thomas will be grown and even have children of his own. I don't want anything else to change. *Talk to me, God.*

A truth came just as gently as the leaf floating down the creek. When the end comes, there will be a place prepared especially for me, a perfect place. I will love my new home even more than the majesty of these woods. No fear. Like Thomas, my Shepherd will be right beside me.

O Lord, You know the outcome. You won't leave me. It's going to be good, isn't it?
—JULIE GARMON

I hope to see you soon and then we will have much to talk about together.
—3 JOHN 1:14 (TLB)

Charlie and his wife Carol have been my next-door neighbors since I moved here several years ago. We got along well, and their two sons used to mow grass in the summer.

Then one day Charlie and I had a dispute over something I can't even remember. We stopped speaking. Carol and I waved when we drove past each other on the road, but Charlie looked the other way. It was an uncomfortable situation, but I didn't know what to do about it.

God did.

The couple who had bought the farm across the street from me, Bob and Rosemary, were expecting a baby, their first, and all the neighbors were excited because we hadn't had a new baby on our street for a long time. When Rosemary called me from the hospital to tell me she and Bob had a son, I was thrilled—until she asked me to call a few neighbors to tell them the good news.

"Don't forget Charlie and Carol," she said, not knowing we weren't on speaking terms. "They've been on pins and needles."

I called everyone on our street, except Charlie and Carol. Finally, I couldn't put it off any longer; I had given my word to Rosemary.

I dialed the number and held my breath. Charlie answered in the pleasant, friendly way I remembered. I hurried to tell him about the new baby before he could hang up on me. He didn't. "Gee, that's wonderful," he said. "It was nice of you to call."

"Actually, Rosemary asked me," I said, "but it's nice to talk to you."

"Same here," Charlie said, and we went on to talk about all kinds of things that had happened in our lives. Our years of silence were over. God had found a way to make us neighbors again.

Heavenly Father, when I put distance between myself and others,
please take our hands and bring us back together again. Amen.
—PHYLLIS HOBE

The wise heart will know the proper time and procedure.
—ECCLESIASTES 8:5

"I did it, Mom! I found an apartment, and got the phone, the water, an electricity all turned on in one day. They should have the air conditionin fixed by tomorrow, and we have a microwave, so I don't have to buy one!"

Dave's phone call left me as breathless as he was. Our last son was out on hi own, an army officer at his first base, near Dothan, Alabama.

"Dave," I said with a grin, "I bet you don't remember when you were abou four years old, and you and I had just ridden up the elevator to Dad's offic He showed you his computer and phone and how he worked there every da Suddenly, you looked up at me with your lip quivering, 'When I grow up can stay with you?' Tears swam in your brown eyes.

"I knelt down and wrapped you in a hug. 'Why, sweetheart, when you'r grown, you'll want to be out on your own. What has frightened you?'

"'Oh, Mommy,' you wailed, 'how will I know which buttons to push?'

"I assured you that as you grew, you would slowly learn how to be an adul how to understand and affect the world around you properly, which button to push on phones and computers, for microwaves, in elevators and car Obviously, you've learned!"

We laughed.

But recalling David's small-child concerns about how he might survive i the adult world made me think of my own worries for the future. How will handle growing older? Can I adapt to changes in my life? How will I know whic buttons to push?

Then I smiled to myself. Just as we reassured David that he would know th proper procedure to succeed in his daily circumstances, so my heavenly Fathe will grant me the same grace and learning.

Heavenly Father, remind me often that You give me Your grace
and wisdom step by step, each in its proper season, all my life long.
—ROBERTA ROGERS

Now the Lord God had formed out of the ground
all the beasts of the field and all the birds of the air.
—GENESIS 2:19

Now that we've moved back to my husband's family ranch, the kitchen window is one of my favorite lookouts. The southwest view is of rolling pastures and wheat fields, with a dirt road cutting a dusty path up the hill to the horizon. I see horses and cattle grazing, wildlife of all kinds flying and scampering. I've watched stormy weather blow in and unhampered winds rearrange leaves and piles of hay.

This August morning, I'm watching some unusual immigrants for this north Texas area: egrets, fluttering to their daily landing spot beside the grazing bulls. Many settle on the grass beside the huge animals' feet, waiting for them to kick up insects as they walk. Others line the fence, watching.

As I look across the pasture, I laugh out loud. Three egrets have perched on a bull's back as he lies in the grass, their white feathers and long necks in stark contrast to their host. The bull appears hospitable to his odd guests. He lies quietly, soberly chewing, his tail swishing. I wonder what he's thinking. Does he know the birds will keep the bugs from bothering him?

Watching the bull, I begin wondering: *Am I as hospitable to the stranger who comes into my space? Do I sit quietly and listen to the new ideas brought in by a new church member? Do I welcome the friendship of a new acquaintance not quite like me?*

I tend to be set in my ways, and I like to be in control of things. I'm also a little shy and reluctant to get out of my comfort zone. But I've decided to try to emulate the bull and the egrets. They've shown me I can work the bugs out of almost anything if I partner with others.

Father, forgive me for my reluctance to try new things and forge new relationships. Help me to welcome whatever You send my way.
—MARJORIE PARKER

AUGUST 23

God's laws are perfect. They protect us, make us wise,
and give us joy and light.... They are more desirable than gold.
—PSALM 19:7–8, 10 (TLB)

I am sorely tempted to buy a lottery ticket! The jackpot is millions of dollars, and I'm arguing with God. Just think of the blessing. Not only for my family, grandkids, and all, but for the things I could do with the money for those in need around the world. *Try me, Lord. Test me. I could handle a million or two!*

> *You've more than millions in blessings, dear child.*
> *Count all the stars on a clear, cold night,*
> *the diamonds of dew in the morning light.*
> *The smiles of friends, and strangers alike*
> *that gladden your days and make them bright.*
> *Gather the words of your answered prayers,*
> *more than millions through the years.*
> *The promises given in my Holy Book,*
> *thumb through the pages and take a good look.*
> *You're wealthy, dear child, way beyond measure,*
> *these are the blessings to share and to treasure!*

Guess I don't need that lottery ticket after all.

> *Thank You for the riches You have given me, Lord,*
> *that no mega-million-dollar jackpot could ever buy.*
> —FAY ANGUS

Then our mouth was filled with laughter.
—PSALM 126:2 (RSV)

While watering my husband Gene's three beloved tomato plants, I discovered that some of the tomatoes were missing. To my horror, I spotted Lovey, one of our dogs, chewing on a tomato! Just then, Red Dog came trotting up proudly holding a nice-sized tomato in her mouth. "No!" I screamed, but both dogs continued devouring their newfound treats.

When Gene came out later to admire his tomatoes, he stooped down for a closer look. "Marion! Who's been picking the tomatoes?"

Looking in the other direction, I mumbled, "The dogs."

"What?"

"Just the green ones." I tried to smile.

Not even a hint of a smile from my husband. I quickly explained, "Well, they do look exactly like the green tennis balls we throw for them to retrieve, and they probably figured...."

"What are you going to do about it?" he said.

Right then Lovey came up to offer Gene a tomato she'd dug up from its hiding place, and I sashayed back into the house and considered bolting all the doors. A few moments later in the kitchen, our eyes met for what seemed like forever. "Normal dogs don't eat tomatoes off the vines," he explained grimly.

Don't laugh, Marion. This is serious business. "I know, I know...."

I thought I glimpsed a hint of laughter in Gene's eyes. I ventured a half smile, and so did he. I snickered. Then my husband started laughing out loud, and I fell over onto the kitchen counter, laughing helplessly.

Father, one of Your most remarkable gifts is laughter—especially in marriage.
—MARION BOND WEST

AUGUST 25

The eyes of all wait upon thee; and thou givest them their meat in due season.
—PSALM 145:15 (KJV)

Every time I spent a day with Grandma Ellen, she offered me peppermint. She always had a plastic bag of them in her purse. Though I rarely ate them, it seemed as if every time we went to the store she bought another package. If I asked her if she really needed more, she'd just add a bag her cart and say, "Well, they're on sale."

After Grandma Ellen died, I helped sort through some of her papers. I w working at Grandma's desk when I heard Mom groan. Turning to look, I sa her pull a plastic bag from Grandma's purse. "What in the world am I goin to do with all these peppermints?" she asked. A few minutes later, I heard louder groan. Several more bags of mints waited in a drawer. Mom had four Grandma's stockpile! "How am I going to get rid of them?" she asked.

At church that Sunday Mom had an idea. A lady sitting in the pew in fro of us seemed to be having some trouble with a cough, so Mom tapped her gent on the shoulder and handed her a mint. The woman smiled and unwrappe the mint quietly. Soon her cough was soothed, but the wrapper's crinkling ha caught the attention of a small child down the row, so Mom passed a peppermi that way, too. The next week, Mom gave a mint to another coughing friend an two more children. After the service, several ladies enjoyed mints with the coffee in the social hall. Mom left a handful in the Sunday school candy dish.

A couple of months after Mom's "mint ministry" began, we went groce shopping, and as we approached the candy aisle, I asked Mom if she had give away most of Grandma's mints. She chuckled but didn't answer. Somehow wasn't surprised when I saw Mom reach for two bags of mints. She looked me, grinning, and said, "Well, they're on sale."

Father, thank You for Grandma's peppermints. Though I don't like to eat them they're wonderful to share!
—KJERSTIN EASTON

August 26

Although the fig tree shall not blossom.
—Habakkuk 3:17 (KJV)

*M*y son Jon, our beloved prodigal, happened by our house unexpectedly one summer day. Smiling and walking confidently as
his life were totally okay, he put down a brown paper bag in the kitchen. "It's
u, Mom, isn't it, who loves figs so much? Aren't they beautiful?" He held one
his huge, square hand.

"Yes, Jon." I touched it softly, our hands touching.

"Taste it," he urged.

"Okay," I said and then asked, "Do you remember the Scripture from
bakkuk about the fig tree without blossoms?"

"Sure, I know it." No matter where Jon's unwise choices take him in life, his
e for Scripture remains. He picked up a paring knife and carefully sliced the
into perfect halves, offering one to me.

I pointed to the pretty bits of pastel scrunched up inside. "Those are the
ssoms, Jon."

"No way, Mom! Sounds like something you made up."

"It's true. I discovered it accidentally at the library." We both stared at the
en fig in his hand. "Do you know what it means?" I asked.

He smiled and nodded. I knew that look; he understood fully. Even so, I said,
od's at work..."

Jon finished the thought: "...even when we can't see a thing happening."
Nothing else was said; nothing else was needed.

Lord, I don't understand what happened when Jon and I ate that fig,
but I believe it was a powerful promise from You.
—Marion Bond West

"I will pour out my Spirit on your offspring,
and my blessing on your descendants."
—ISAIAH 44:3

To the west of our country property, separating our backyard from a field of neatly groomed raspberry bushes, stand five enormous poplar trees. My husband and I planted the saplings when our five children were small—one for each child. Now as I look at the sturdy trees reaching for the sky I wonder where the time has gone. The youngest of our children left home to get married two years ago.

Our children's interests take them far away from home, to Africa, Europe, China. Often I don't hear from them for months at a time. I worry about their safety. I worry that my imperfect mothering has not prepared them adequately for life's pitfalls. Sometimes I'm perplexed at the decisions they've made or the direction in which their lives are going. I want to shield them from trouble. But I can't.

At times like these, I like to read the promises God has given me concerning my children. I've highlighted them in my Bible and typed them out separately for easy access—three pages, single-spaced. They include the following:

"All your sons will be taught by the Lord and great will be your children's peace" (Isaiah 54:13).

"My eyes will watch over them for their good, and I will bring them back to this land.... I will give them a heart to know me, that I am the Lord" (Jeremiah 24:6–7).

"Your descendants...will spring up like grass in a meadow, like poplar trees by flowing streams" (Isaiah 44:3–4).

As I gaze at the sturdy poplars in our backyard, I reflect how little I had to do with their growth. Beyond their initial nurturing, I simply committed them to the Master of trees.

Father, into Your gentle, capable hands I commit my children.
—HELEN GRACE LESCHEID

"My Father, if it is possible, may this cup be taken from me. Yet not as I will, but as you will."
—MATTHEW 26:39

After making a miraculous recovery from a major stroke and two brain surgeries a couple of years ago, my husband Lynn was recently diagnosed with a malignant brain tumor. Again the doctors performed surgery, removing most of the tumor. Over the next several weeks, a whole bunch of new words started to define our lives: grade three brain cancer, pathology reports, chemotherapy, radiation, MRI results, life expectancy statistics. We are still reeling from all these new realities.

"How are you?" people keep asking me. I'm not sure how to answer the question. I know I should sound deeply spiritual, totally trusting God's will for our circumstances, regardless of the outcome. But here's the reality: in spite of my faith and trust in God's promises—that the ultimate outcome will be good—I feel afraid of the pain that might be experienced between today and that outcome.

Then I remember that Jesus probably experienced similar fears. In the Garden of Gethsemane the night before He died, He honestly expressed both His fear and His faith to God in prayer. Fear in the moment, but faith in God's plan for the ultimate outcome. His fear must have been about the pain He knew He would experience between that moment in the garden and God's good outcome. Expressing that fear seemed to strengthen His faith.

So when others ask, "How are you?" I sometimes tell them about my fears. But more importantly, I regularly tell God.

Lord, You know my fears. Please strengthen my faith.
—CAROL KUYKENDALL

The word of our God shall stand forever.

—ISAIAH 40:8

*M*y Bible is falling apart. And no wonder; I received it at Sunday school on September 29, 1957. With colorful plates, maps, a concordance and student dictionary complete with illustrations from ark through Zion, was perfect for a child.

Of course, I'm no longer a kid. Over the years the inexpensive leatheret cover has broken off along the edges. The gold-leaf gilding on the title rubbed off years ago, and "Holy Bible" has become a dull gray shadow. In fact, the entire front cover sloughed off a couple of months ago, taking the first forty nine chapters of Genesis with it. I stuck it back with cellophane tape, but even that has loosened, so I keep my Bible together with a rubber band. My shabby Scriptures.

They should look a lot worse. For the first thirty years I owned this Bible thumbed through it only casually, mostly at Sunday school. Then a dear friend introduced me to daily devotional reading—just as I was going through divorce with four small children to care for. Bible reading became part of my early morning routine. Over the next fifteen years I underlined and highlighted my favorite passages, all the verses that really made a difference to me. Now I wouldn't trade that Bible for a more handsome or sturdier edition. It's my constant companion, my never-failing guide through life. No matter what struggles I'm going through, I can always turn to it for the help I need.

Yes, my Bible may be falling apart, but thanks to the wisdom in its pages I'm not!

Dear Lord, thank You for Your Word hidden in my heart.

—GAIL THORELL SCHILLING

Don't scold your children so much that they become discouraged and quit trying.
—COLOSSIANS 3:21 (TLB)

'd been having a difficult day, and in every mistake I heard a message of failure. Work returned for improvement: you'll never get it right. Losing my temper with the children: you're a lousy mother. Groceries partly put away and no dinner ready: you plan your time so poorly.

Rummaging in a box of old toys for something to entertain then-one-year-old Mark while I cooked, I found a little blue car. Suddenly, I remembered our daughter Elizabeth pushing it along a wooden bench in the tiny church we attended while living in New Zealand when she was three years old.

One Sunday she wandered from our pew to the open door and began singing loudly about the bees buzzing outside, causing all heads to turn. After the service, an elderly woman with regal posture, elegantly attired in a green silk dress, approached us. I feared she would reprimand Elizabeth for disturbing everyone.

Instead, smiling, she sat next to Elizabeth, and in her proper British accent asked her name. "And how old are you?" Elizabeth held up three fingers. "Just three! Goodness! It is difficult for someone just three to sit so quietly." Elizabeth nodded solemnly.

"But, my, you are learning, aren't you? And please keep singing. We so enjoy your lovely voice!" She rose and patted my arm. "She's delightful. She's trying. Each week it will get easier."

As I brought the blue car to Mark, I resolved to be easier on myself and the children. And I could hear dear Mrs. Holland cheering me on: "Keep trying. Each day you'll do better. You are learning."

My patient, loving Father, help me to pour out encouragement
on everyone around me, even myself.
—MARY BROWN

Therefore I will look unto the Lord...my God will hear me.
—MICAH 7:7 (KJV)

Last year our grandson Andrew attended Monash University in Melbourne, Australia, on the opposite side of the earth from our home in New York. So many miles between us, I thought, places and experiences I couldn't imagine!

So it was a kind of shock—newcomer that I am to the Internet—when an instant message popped up on my computer screen one morning soon after Andrew got there.

"Hi, Gran! I'm loving this place! I've put some photos on my blog."

Blog? Andrew explained that it's short for *web log*, a kind of journal kept on the Internet, and, sure enough, in a moment I was looking at pictures of him and some new friends...the landscape around the school...a car trip just the day before. I didn't have to imagine his new setting, I could see it, share it all with him.

Most wondrous of all to me was that as we instant-messaged back and forth, we were in contact right then. How different from my efforts to reach my father and mother from Africa in the early 1960s! I had to find a ham radio operator who would patch a call to someone in Egypt to be relayed to another set, and so on until hours later I'd hear the phone ringing in my parents' house in the United States—on the chance that they were home.

Instant messaging, I thought, as Andrew and I chatted electronically across the globe, is much more like the experience of staying in touch with God. Right now, wherever I am in my travels over the earth and over the years, I can communicate with Him and receive His reply. Unlike phoning between continents in the 1960s, I know that the Father I want to reach is always there. The only requirement: I must remember to go online.

Lord of the journey, what message do You have for me right now?
—ELIZABETH SHERRILL

September

SEPTEMBER 1

And forget not all his benefits.
—PSALM 103:2 (KJV)

As my husband and I were traveling through the southern part of Illinois on our way home from vacation, we stopped for breakfast in a truckers' cafe. While we were waiting our turn at the cashier's stand, my ears tuned in as an older man greeted a young woman with, "How are you *mostly?*"

When we got back into the car I told Ken what I had heard, and we discussed how we would have answered for ourselves. We were tired and dreaded getting back into harness after vacation. We had some aches and pains. We were concerned about my mother and some problems our children face.

But mostly, we decided, we were fine! God loved us. We loved each other. We had challenging work to do. We were members of a church that cared. We had shelter, food, clothing, and a car that ran. And even with the aches and pains, we could function.

How are you mostly? Remember, mostly is what counts!

Dear Lord, help me to take time to remember Your blessings.
—BARBARA CHAFIN

Our Father... Hallowed be thy name.
—MATTHEW 6:9 (KJV)

*M*y flight had been delayed yet again, and the boarding area at JFK was filled with disgruntled travelers. In a corner, two young men in long black coats and wide-brimmed hats bowed rhythmically toward a wall, rapt in worship. I didn't know the words the young Hasidic Jews were saying, but because they prayed I suddenly saw, not a noisy airport corridor, but a hallowed space.

When I first learned the Lord's Prayer years ago, I puzzled over the words "hallowed be thy name." "To hallow," says the dictionary, "is to make holy." How could the name of God be "made" holy! Wasn't it already holy—the holiest thing I could imagine?

Jesus must be telling us, I realized, not that our prayers create holiness, but that prayer opens our eyes to the Father's holiness inscribed on everything around us: people, trees, skies, airports.

In a crowded terminal, two young men invoked God's presence among fretful travelers and blaring loudspeakers. Silently I joined in with the Lord's Prayer. "Our Father..."

And at the word *hallowed*, I did indeed see differently. I saw the overhead monitor screens and the plastic chairs bolted together in rows in a new light—the light of His infinite love for everyone there: the tired-looking Arab family with the crying baby, the harried clerk at the check-in counter.

God's arms are over and around and beneath us every moment of our lives. To hallow His name is to open our eyes and look.

Our Father, show me Your holiness in unexpected places today.
—ELIZABETH SHERRILL

SEPTEMBER 3

Blessed are the peacemakers: for they shall be called children of God.
—MATTHEW 5:9 (KJV)

Blessed are the piecemakers." So reads a small framed needlepoint hanging on my mother-in-law's kitchen wall.

"Did you know this is spelled wrong?" I ask.

"I never really noticed, I guess," she says, laughing a little.

I laugh, too. Then I wonder if it really is a mistake. It's certainly true. I think of all the people who do their small part to make our world spin around, including myself. Sometimes my small part feels too small. I want to be bigger, more important, taking care of the whole pie. But I'm not. I'm taking care of my small piece, raising my child, singing in the church choir, teaching adult classes. Often the task seems so small and insignificant: to color with my son, to sing on Sunday morning. Neither will change the world.

Then I think of my brother-in-law Danny. He's mentally handicapped, employed at a sheltered workshop with hundreds of other people like him at all levels of ability. They're working on a huge order for one of the big carmakers. Dan's job is to separate foam pieces. Then a more skilled person stacks the pieces. The next person, more skillful yet, staples them to a plastic form. The next attaches those forms to other forms by machine. And on it goes, each worker doing what he or she is capable of: the seemingly smallest piece but at that moment the most important. Then all of it goes back to the manufacturer, and by the time they're done, they've built a car. Each worker is part of the whole, making a piece of the pie.

Blessed are the *piecemakers*, you wonder? Where would we be without them?

On this Labor Day, Lord, help me to be content to do my small part,
knowing I'm a "piecemaker" in the work of Your larger creation.

—GINA BRIDGEMAN

have nourished and brought up children, and they have rebelled against me.
—ISAIAH 1:2 (KJV)

*W*hen I was forty-two years old, I had my first experience with motherhood: I married a man with two children—a boy, eleven, and [g]irl, fourteen. I'd like to report that we quickly became a happy family, but it [di]dn't work out that way. It seemed that no matter what their father or I wanted, [th]ey invariably wanted the opposite. But I was optimistic. "What children need [is] lots of love and prayer," I told myself. But even that solution didn't work. [Un]fortunately, I felt more and more *responsible* for my stepchildren. I believed it [wa]s all up to me to make our household happy.

Then one day, something happened that turned things around for me. It [di]dn't change the children, mind you, or even the situation—it just put things in [pe]rspective and helped me stop blaming myself for being a failure as a parent.

What was it? The first three chapters of Genesis! They told me that God— [th]e model Father, the ideal Parent who can't make a mistake—brought two [ch]ildren into a perfect world (no TV, no drugs, no peer pressure). He did [ev]erything right, but it wasn't enough to turn Adam and Eve into the children [he]'d hoped they'd be. They rebelled, choosing their own way instead of His.

What a comfort this was. The story of Adam and Eve not only helped me [ac]cept my limitations as a parent, it also taught me how to respond: as God [di]d—with love, patience, and forgiveness.

Are you trying too hard? Carrying the weight of the world on your shoulders? [Ea]se up, and ease God into the picture. Then love, give, be the best human you [ca]n possibly be. Trust God to make up the difference.

Father, I've been carrying too much. Let me be the most loving
I can be, and give the impossible to You.
—SUSAN WILLIAMS

The light shines in the darkness, and the darkness has not overcome it.
—JOHN 1:5 (RSV)

*T*hey called him the "Singing Miner," a husky, broad-shouldered ma who swung a pick at a coal-face all day, his mellow tenor making th heavy work lighter. In the pit, at home, at church—wherever he was—Mauri Ruddick sang: gospel music, praise choruses, standard hymns, any music th glorified God.

"What's your favorite song?" I asked him.

"'Christ Whose Glory Fills the Skies,'" he said without a moment's hesitatio "You watch any miner just before the rake takes him down into that shaft. He be craning his neck for a last look at the sky."

Maurice Ruddick should know, I thought. He worked the deepest pit North America, Nova Scotia's Springhill Mine, at best spending most of th daylight hours deep in the earth. And at worst...

My husband and I were in Nova Scotia to write about the explosion Springhill's Number Two shaft. Seventy-four miners had died; Maurice and s others were trapped for ten days, two and a half miles underground. "Dee earth dark is deeper than black," Maurice told us, "a dark without promise."

What sustained him and the others through the blackness, the thirst, th fear that rescuers would give up? Charles Wesley's hymn. "True Light." "Da star." "Day-spring." "Radiancy divine." Over and over he sang the shinir words. "Beams of mercy." "Perfect day."

"When you can't see any light at all," Maurice said, "that's the time to affir that it's out there, just the same."

It's an insight I've turned to ever since. Though I can't sing like Mauric I can remember when I'm ill that God is health, when I'm needy that He's th supply, when discouraged that God is joy. And when the world looks dark, tha the light of Christ cannot be overcome.

Give me songs, Father, for the truths I need to hold on to.
—ELIZABETH SHERRILL

SEPTEMBER 6

I trust in the mercy of God for ever and ever.
—PSALM 52:8 (KJV)

*M*ore and more these days I find myself thumping my chest with the palm of my hand and saying, "Mercy!" This was my mother-in-law's regular expression of faith. Whether she'd spilled a cup of coffee or heard of a major disaster, she rallied her ability to cope with a series of chest-thumping "mercies." Conversely, upon finding her misplaced glasses or getting a phone call from a long-lost friend, her string of "mercies" was more hand-fluttering than thumping and had a jubilant cadence that put a smile on her gentle face, all of which, I'm sure, brought joy to the heart of God.

When I heard the good news that my grandchild who had spent the semester struggling at school had received the President's Award for good citizenship, I could barely contain my hand-fluttering string of "mercies." Likewise, on hearing of the automobile accident of a friend (fortunately not hurt), one huge chest-thumping "Mercy!" said it all.

The dictionary says mercy is "a blessing that is an act of divine favor or compassion." I find myself constantly putting my prayerful concerns under the mercy of my Lord, knowing that what I am unable to do, He is able to do for me.

"I will sing of the mercies of the Lord for ever: with my mouth
will I make known thy faithfulness to all generations" (Psalm 89:1 KJV).
—FAY ANGUS

September 7

But Samuel was ministering before the Lord—a boy wearing a linen ephod.
—1 Samuel 2:18

When my children's father was killed in a motorcycle accident, we we devastated. Part of our lives died with him. We cried, and then tried to go on living. I went back to work, and my children went back to scho Chase to kindergarten and Lanea to middle school. In that cloud of pain, it w difficult to pray. We retreated to our private places, silently trying to make sen of what was senseless, until Chase rescued us.

One evening after work, I sat in my darkening room. There was a knock the door and then Chase entered, wearing a hideous plaid jacket. He called it "comedian jacket."

"What did the penguin say when it fell down the stairs?" Chase said.

"I don't know. What did it say?" I asked, playing straight man.

Chase grinned. "Help! I've fallen and I can't get up!" he answered throug missing teeth, clad in that ridiculous coat.

It wasn't much of a joke, but I laughed. I laughed hysterically. I laughed un I cried, and we breathed deeply while we hugged.

It was the only joke Chase knew. He told it to our family over and over agai Night after night, he knocked on my door, wearing the same jacket and telli the same joke. Night after night, until we were completely rescued—until we regained hope and the courage to live.

Thank You, God, for children who minister to us and make our hearts merry.
—Sharon Foster

Let me dwell in Your tent forever.
—PSALM 61:4 (NASB)

When Keith and I first discussed moving out of Los Angeles after he retired, I had mixed feelings. I was not so wedded to the city, but I loved our home. We'd remodeled it so that it was exactly what we wanted, and was really the only house I'd ever lived in where I was altogether happy. The idea of selling it made me uneasy. "I think of our home as a place of safety, a place that surrounds me with its walls and holds me gently," I said. "I'm afraid to go away from it."

Keith smiled, the way he does when I get frantic over something and he has a point to the terra-cotta plaque on our wall that reads: "Be still, and know that I am God." Keith said, "It's not the house that shelters you."

And I knew that he was right. It was God who held me safely when I was at home—and also when I went away from it. And God would continue to shelter me, whether I lived in Los Angeles or anywhere else.

Thank You, God, for the loving shelter in which You are letting me live my life.
—RHODA BLECKER

Thou, O Lord, remainest...from generation to generation.
—LAMENTATIONS 5:19 (KJV)

*W*hen I went to college, I didn't have much money. Every semester I wondered where my next tuition dollars would come from. But I was rich in one thing: my mother's prayers. When she found out that I often studied past midnight and got up before dawn to study again, she had a practical solution. "I'll just pray that you get two hours of rest for every one hour of sleep." Knowing that made those short nights more bearable, somehow. And I always managed to get through my days—and my tests.

Now my daughter Amy Jo is in her first year of law school. Her days are filled with legal research, detailed lectures, hours spent writing briefs. And her nights are often very short. When she confided this to me on the phone the other day, I instantly knew what to say. "I'll pray that you get two hours of rest for every one hour of sleep."

So that's what I'm doing. And I know—firsthand—that God will answer this prayer.

Thank You, God, for a mother who prayed for me.
And for a daughter who needs my prayers.
—MARY LOU CARNEY

And we, who...reflect the Lord's glory,
are being transformed into his likeness.
—2 CORINTHIANS 3:18

*P*eople who come into my art studio often ask me, "What is your most helpful tool?" They wonder, *Is it the brush? The easel? The tube of white?* To their surprise, I point to the mirror that is always set up several feet in front of my easel.

When I am laboring deeply and happily on a painting, I can become so engrossed in what I'm doing that although the painting looks right as it sits in front of me, something may be very wrong. My staring and concentration actually rob me of objectivity. But if I look at my painting in the mirror, the flaw will pop out. It's like seeing it through another's fresh eyes! I can see what's wrong and make the correction.

I have another frank, honest mirror: my Bible. I couldn't do without its telling reflections. The tendency to become inwardly focused and think, *I'm not so bad; why, I'm just as good as so-and-so,* is jolted by 2 Corinthians 10:12 warning against comparative bragging: "We dare not make to classify or compare ourselves with some who commend themselves...."

By contrast, my "God doesn't care about little old me" is proven out of perspective when held to the loving mirror of I John 4:10: "He loved us and sent his Son as an atoning sacrifice for our sins."

The mirror's truth sometimes hurts; it means backing up and starting again. But I can't make the corrections if I don't know where the problem is. Artwork or life, I need my mirrors.

Dear Lord, let the mirror of Your Word do its work, that my life might reflect You.
—KATHIE KANIA

SEPTEMBER 11

From everlasting to everlasting you are God.
—PSALM 90:2

September 11, 2001: the day the World Trade Center and the Pentagon were targeted by terrorists. The day death and tragedy swept over our country like a dark plague. At work, we all bent toward the small radio that kept giving us the too-terrible-to-be-true news. But it was true. As the editor of two websites—one for kids and one for teens—I longed to meet—quickly—the challenge of helping young people cope with this horror.

Like everyone else in the office, I went home at noon. And if the radio reports were bad, the TV images were unthinkable. Finally, late in the day, I went for a walk along the shores of Lake Michigan. I had decided to write an open letter to our young web visitors, but what could I say? I could make no sense of it all, how could I help the kids?

The sun was just setting, a huge, perfect ball, red as a ripe tomato. Magnificent in every way, it sank slowly, purple clouds easing it into the horizon. My heart still heavy, I turned back toward my car. That's when I saw them: two teenaged girls sitting in the sand, playing guitars. Their heads were bent forward as their fingers strummed and their voices blended in harmony. As I got closer, I heard the song:

Our God is an awesome God,
He reigns from heaven above,
With wisdom, power and love,
Our God is an awesome God.

And suddenly I knew what to say in my open letter: God is still in control. God doesn't want you to be afraid. I turned back for a last look at the sunset-streaked sky. And He will be near you—in ways more awesome than you can imagine!

When the foundations of the earth shake, God,
You are our rock and our salvation!
—MARY LOU CARNEY

SEPTEMBER 12

Forbearing one another, and forgiving one another.
—COLOSSIANS 3:13 (KJV)

*B*y temperament my husband is much like Winston Churchill: a brilliant wit, stubbornly persistent, impatient—and grouchy in the morning. Churchill once confessed that he had to give up having breakfast with his wife because he was "just too out of sorts" early in the morning. Same here.

John takes the newspaper and his coffee to his special den upstairs, where he can rant and rave and harrumph at all the goings-on in the sports section without disturbing my own peace and morning tranquility.

Churchill was devoted to his beloved "Clemmie," and John has never given me cause to doubt his love. Nevertheless, the Churchills had their quarrels, and we Anguses have ours. Not that it's ever my fault, you understand. John says, "She's too proud to say she's sorry, and I never have reason to!" Ha.

Once at a dinner party, Churchill kept walking his fingers, knuckles bent, across the tablecloth toward Lady Churchill. Distracted and curious, her dinner partner asked what on earth Sir Winston was doing. She replied that they had had a quarrel before leaving the house, and he was acknowledging that it was all his fault. He was on "bended knees" to ask her forgiveness.

A friend of mine has another solution to the apology problem. "When my husband told me, 'The trouble with you is that you're never willing to say "I'm sorry,"' I fixed it. I wrote 'I'm sorry' umpteen times on a piece of paper, then cut it into strips. I put them in a tumbler on the dining room table and told him, 'There, when you need one, take one!'"

I use "sorry slips" in a tumbler, and John uses Churchill's "bended knee." When he pulls out one of my slips, or when he creeps his knuckles at me, it works. Now if only we'd learn to do this early on, we'd avoid most quarrels in the first place!

Enlarge my understanding and compassion, Lord.
Help me to forbear and, most important, to forgive.
—FAY ANGUS

September 13

All the ways of a man are clean in his own sight, but the Lord weighs the motives.
—Proverbs 16:2 (nasb)

O ur family possesses an odd trait: the backs of some of our heads are as flat as a wall—no pretty round curve whatsoever. My mother passed the flat-headedness right down to my brothers and me and to one of my children. But I didn't realize I had it for quite some time.

I was newly married and choosing a new hairstyle. The hairdresser said that she'd have to be careful to cut the layers to flatter the back of my head.

"What are you talking about? What's wrong with the back of my head?"

"Well, it's sort of flat-like." From behind me, she looked at my eyes in the mirror with a smirk.

"I didn't know I have a flat head," I said as I felt my head. "My mother never told me. She has one."

She studied my problem area and fluffed my hair. "There's nothing you can do to fix a flat head! That's for sure."

When I got home, I studied the back of my head in a mirror. Sure enough– flat as a frying pan. My husband confirmed the news. "Yeah, I thought you knew it."

"How would I know? I've never seen the back of my head!"

Twenty-five years of marriage have passed since that revelation in the salon. My head's still flat, but I've finally grown to see some unappealing hidden traits in my attitudes, too. I can be stubborn in areas in which I should surrender. I like to be right. I try to fix people. Sometimes I'm sweetly controlling. For a long time I didn't see these traits. But, unlike my head shape, I can do something about them.

> *Father, You help me look in the mirror of my heart.*
> *Thank You for caring enough to point out the truth.*
> —Julie Garmon

Lo, he passes by me, and I see him not; he moves on, but I do not perceive him.
—JOB 9:11 (RSV)

We were putting on a French farce in one of the many theater classes I took when I was a playwriting major in college. I had been part of the crew that built and changed the sets, so I was in the wings when I heard whispers from another part of the backstage area as the second act began.

The entire act hinged on an incriminating letter, which three actors moved from place to place with split-second timing to keep a fourth actor from finding it. We were close to the point where the first actor had to move the letter for the first time, and the props people had just discovered that they had forgotten the letter. The set was closed on three sides, so there was no way to sneak it into place. "What will happen when Denny reaches for it and it isn't there?" the prop person moaned. We crowded downstage, just behind the curtain, to see what was going on.

Denny walked to the fireplace, where the letter was supposed to be waiting beneath a candlestick, hesitated for a moment, then grasped the air firmly, turned, and passed the nonexistent letter to the actress who was to hide it in the bookcase, without missing a line. She caught on instantly, took the nothing, and hid it just as she was supposed to. Throughout the rest of the act, the "letter" changed hands five more times, with everyone cooperating in the illusion that it was really there.

Between the second and third acts, the stage manager went out front to mingle with the audience. When he returned, he was shaking his head. "No one even noticed that the letter wasn't there," he said wonderingly.

Denny had changed into his third-act costume and overheard the remark. "Not so odd," he said. "We all just believed that it was there, so it was."

It was the first time in my life I ever found a practical demonstration of the presence of things invisible, and I never forgot it.

Dear God, keep my spirit alive to the reality of the things my eyes cannot see.
—RHODA BLECKER

Pray without ceasing.
—1 THESSALONIANS 5:17 (KJV)

I looked up at the clock on my classroom wall one more time, squinting to see the time through the glare of afternoon sun. It was one o'clock and still no word from my son Christopher, who was taking his firefighter certification test—a challenging and competitive test that required mental and physical stamina. As a rookie firefighter, Christopher had to pass in order to continue his training. I looked up at the clock again. Only a minute had passed. My students were taking a history test; the room was quiet except for the sound of pencils scribbling furiously and the loud *tick-tick-tick* of the clock.

I prayed silently, as I had all morning: *Lord, bless my students and my son with a clear mind and a steady hand as they take their tests today.*

When the final bell rang to signal the end of the school day, I had still not received word from Christopher. I decided to call.

"Oh, hi, Mom," Christopher said. "Sorry I forgot to call you. I got busy here at the fire station after I found out that I'd passed my test."

I was overjoyed, but also annoyed. I had spent the day in constant prayer while waiting for a phone call that never came. Right before I was about to embark on a "Do you have any idea what my day was like waiting for your call?" lecture, I remembered the advice of a wise friend. "If a problem brings you to prayer, then it has served its purpose," she had calmly stated when offering counsel years ago.

Indeed, I had spent the day in almost continuous dialogue with God simply because I had a problem that led me to prayer. What a blessing!

Gracious and loving God, thank You for turning my problems into opportunities to become one with You in prayer.
—MELODY BONNETTE

Jesus saith unto him, Have I been so long time with you, and yet hast thou not known me, Philip? he that hath seen me hath seen the Father.

—JOHN 14:9 (KJV)

Elizabeth and I were on the subway, talking. As she launched into an animated explanation of some math concept she'd recently read about, part of my brain held itself in reserve and observed my seven-year-old daughter. *She's so incredibly different from me!* I thought. Her mind works differently, her emotional constitution is different, her social needs are different. She doesn't even look like me!

I love my daughter passionately, yet she and I are so unlike each other that I sometimes wonder if I leave any imprint on her at all. We're not like oil and water; we're more like oil and a giraffe, a living non sequitur.

As we neared our subway stop, I asked Elizabeth to get ready to get off the train. She jumped up off her seat and swung, grinning, around the pole designed to give standing passengers something to hold on to. I gathered our belongings, and we stood by the doorway. Just as the train pulled into our stop, a man who had been sitting across from us spoke. "I have to tell you how much I enjoyed watching you and your daughter. It's amazing how much her body language and her mannerisms are like yours! And then, when she jumped up, it's as if she underwent a transformation, and it's obvious that she is also completely herself."

I smiled my confused thanks, and we stepped out onto the platform. *Elizabeth acting just like me? Really?* I had seen and sensed none of it, and yet a total stranger was able to see my reflection in her. Wonders never cease.

Lord Jesus, I am only fully myself in You. May all people see Your reflection in me.

—JULIA ATTAWAY

Clothe yourselves with compassion, kindness, humility, gentleness and patience
—COLOSSIANS 3:12

My dear friend Helen Morrison died last year. I met her at my first job when I came to California twenty years ago. Helen never had a bad word to say about anyone. When I felt like having a good gossip about a coworker with a snappish attitude, Helen would say, "Oh, maybe he was having a bad day," in her lilting British accent. When I started to tell her about the carpool driver who leapt out of the van to chat with a friend and made me late for work, she said, "Isn't it nice to unexpectedly meet a friend?"

I once tried to get Helen to admit that a former boss we'd all found controlling and manipulative was...well, controlling and manipulative. "Come on," I coaxed, "you're not going to say you liked him!"

"Well," she said, "at times he could be a tiny bit difficult."

"A tiny bit difficult?" I exploded. "He tried to get his best friend fired! Helen, isn't there anyone you don't like?"

Helen seemed surprised by my question and considered it for several long moments. Finally she said, "When I moved to America by myself all those years ago, I knew no one. So I couldn't afford to be picky and choosy about my friends. That habit has stayed with me all these years, and it's served me well."

I must have looked skeptical because she lowered her voice and whispered in a conspiratorial tone, "Besides, Linda, everyone brings joy—some when they come and some when they go."

God, today let me say a prayer of thanks for those friends whom I loved when they came and cried over when they went.
—LINDA NEUKRUG

"Then you will present your petitions over my signature!"
—JOHN 16:26 (TLB)

When our daughter Gae began her second semester in Bible college, some five hundred miles from home, she needed to pay for her courses in advance. But she wouldn't know the courses she'd be taking until she arrived on campus, so she couldn't tell us the exact amount of her tuition. Too young to have her own credit card, she asked her father how she should go about paying.

As only a loving father would do, Leo sat down at the kitchen table and wrote his signature on the bottom of a blank check. "Here, Gae. Once you've enrolled, fill in the exact amount of your tuition."

"But what if you don't have enough money to cover it?" Gae asked.

"There's more than enough. Just trust me," replied Leo.

"Oh, boy!" Gae teased. "Maybe I'll spend it on a new car or something!"

"Just remember," said Leo, shaking his finger at her in mock warning, "I can put a stop payment on it."

"Oh, so you've got me all figured out!" Gae said with a laugh. After giving her dad a big hug, she started off to her bedroom to finish packing. "And don't worry, Dad. I'll find a good safe place for that check. Thanks again!"

That little scene replayed itself in my mind this morning during prayer time. Do I ask for too much? And yet the Bible says, "My God shall supply all your needs according to His riches in glory in Christ Jesus" (Philippians 4:19 NASB).

Is what I want within His will? And yet Psalm 84:11 (NASB) says, "No good thing does He withhold from those who walk uprightly."

If God has given me a blank check, why am I so unwilling to fill it out?

Heavenly Father, help me to believe that You are both willing and able to grant those petitions that will bring me closer to You.

—ALMA BARKMAN

And he called his ten servants, and delivered them ten pounds,
and said unto them, Occupy till I come.
—LUKE 19:13 (KJV)

There are days when I come home from work and just want to lie down. No, make that pass out. After a long day on the job, the bed, the blanket, and the pillows look awfully tempting.

Then I think about Bishop Howard Oby. I remember the first time I saw him, more than twelve years ago, preaching in a country church in North Carolina. His skin the color of coffee without cream, he stood about six feet tall, with short-cropped salt-and-pepper hair. Bishop Oby's hands often dangled loose at his sides, as if they were unconnected to his body. Except, that is, when he was using a hammer or playing the piano to accompany the choir, a soloist, or the congregation. In his church, he was preacher, repairman, and musician. On the quiet back roads, people whispered that Bishop Oby could lay those hands on sick people and make them well. They said he could stare at you and know you'd done wrong before you could tell him.

In addition to preaching and playing, Bishop Oby often chauffeured his flock, in his van, to and from church on Sunday and from their rural homes to town, to market, to the Laundromat throughout the week. Each Sunday he bathed, clothed, fed, and preached to one homebound member of his flock. And with all this, he listened patiently each time one of us called. He never said a word about money and received no salary.

Bishop Oby still doesn't say a word about money. Now, having spent forty-six of his seventy years in ministry, he just keeps moving, keeps serving, keeps praying—keeps doing what he can with what he has, he says, until the Lord comes.

Lord, help me to be a good investor of my time and to be faithful in Your service.
—SHARON FOSTER

September 20

Remember, O Lord, what is come upon us: consider, and behold our reproach.
—Lamentations 5:1 (KJV)

A while back, my college class reunion was scheduled on Memorial Day weekend. My husband had never been in my hometown since we've been married, so I was eager to show him around.

We first drove to our former eighty-acre property, now a park. At the entrance I told the attendant my family's name, adding, "These grounds used to be ours." I expected instant respect or at least some recognition. "That so?" he said. "You still need a pass."

Our next stop, the newspaper office. I asked for the editor and was introduced to a nice young woman. "Your plant printed the college annual when I was its editor," I said. "That so?" she answered. "That was quite a bit before my time."

On Sunday we visited the church where our family had been pillars in the congregation. Before entering the building, I bragged to Lawrence, "Dad and Mom and I helped in its construction, even nailing and painting. We all volunteered to save the expense."

Inside a greeter said, "Welcome!" He pinned "Visitor" tags on our lapels "to make sure our people will show you around," as he put it. *I know more about this place than you ever will*, I thought. Then I thought again. *These are the people who took up where we left off. If it hadn't been for them the church would be in ruins, our old place an overgrown jungle, and my old office an empty shell.*

"Thanks," I said to the greeter, really meaning it. Later I told Lawrence, "They've done well with the old town."

Father, I must remember that I'm always somebody in Your sight.
—Isabel Wolseley

SEPTEMBER 21

To him that is afflicted pity should be shown from his friend.
—JOB 6:14 (KJV)

Bad days happen, and this was one. My plane ticket turned out to have the wrong return date, I lost my gloves on the way to the airport, the ATM rejected my card, and it was raining hard. Worst of all, I didn't want to go on this trip to a large meeting in an unknown city. I hate flying at the best of times. My confidence was low and ebbing as the minutes passed. I felt uncertain, miserable, and also quite ashamed of myself.

At the airport, I went to check in, wondering if my electronic ticket would turn out not to exist. As I waited glumly in the line feeling as alone as one can feel in a crowded airport, arms came around me from behind and an exuberant voice said, "Oh, how great, Brigitte, you're on my flight!"

The sun came out. Eric was one of the people in my profession I had loved and admired since I met him fifteen years before. I knew he would never laugh at my fears, and I knew he'd help me get to where I was going. He did not fail me.

"We can share a cab at the other end," he said.

"That would be great. Maybe," I added, "we could sit together?"

"I'll see what I can do with my big smile," he said with a laugh.

The bad day was beginning to look like a good one.

Lord, thank You for the generous and affectionate people in my life.
—BRIGITTE WEEKS

The Lord is my helper, and I will not fear what man shall do unto me.
—HEBREWS 13:6 (KJV)

Last year my dog Suzy found a homeless kitten in the fields near our home, and the little fellow grew up to be a strong, healthy member of our household. So, a few weeks ago, when Suzy suddenly wanted to leave the road and plunge into the fields, I thought perhaps another animal needed help. "Okay," I said, "find it."

I held on to the leash but had to run to keep up with her. She was very excited and began to circle an area. Then she stopped and lowered her head toward something in the deep grass. It moved, and I realized, too late, that it was a young skunk. Poor Suzy got sprayed, not badly, but enough to make her and the rest of us uncomfortable for several days.

Suzy's experience is something I can appreciate. I welcome the opportunity to help people, but every now and then I rush to the side of someone who doesn't need me at all, and doesn't hesitate to tell me so. The anger and resentment hurts. But in time the hurt wears off, just as Suzy's special aroma did.

If I want to help others, I have to risk rejection. On the other hand, I just might rescue a kitten who needs a good home.

Lord, give me a spirit of gratitude for all those who have helped me,
and strengthen my willingness to help. Amen.
—PHYLLIS HOBE

"Write in a book all the words that I have spoken to you."
—JEREMIAH 30:2 (RSV)

*M*y husband John thought we'd seen the whales off the coast o
California; I was sure we'd seen them from Maui. He said we'
gone to Canada before the year we spent in Bolivia; I thought it was after we g
back. And that shoebox full of photos! Was this slate-roofed house in Austria o
Switzerland? And what were the names of this couple who'd been so kind to v
when our car broke down?

After years of such unsolvable mysteries, I'd finally begun to keep a trav
diary, a separate notebook for each trip, small pages so it wouldn't becom
a chore. It was still an effort some nights, after a day on the move, to get th
notebook out and record the highlights.

But the rewards! I have forty years of trip logs now, and opening any or
of them at random brings back people, places, small crises, discoveries, an
surprise encounters—most of which I'd forgotten.

Shortly after I began taking notes on trips, I started a spiritual diary. I jotte
down quotes, poems, insights, questions, prayers, confessions, words I believe
I was hearing from God—always with date, place, and shorthand summary o
the situation.

And like the external events in the travel diaries that would otherwise b
forgotten, these inner episodes come as revelations when I read them now.
had no idea how many prayers had been answered until I read entry after entr
and marveled at outcomes I could never have foreseen. I had no idea how trul
a journey this Christian walk is until I could trace mine over time. Not, ala
ever upward and onward. Like any journey, this one is beset with detours an
setbacks and disappointments. But full, too, of sudden glorious vistas, an
always with fresh glimpses of Him who is both the goal and the way.

Lord of the journey, what notes will I make today
on the trip whose destination only You can see?
—ELIZABETH SHERRILL

And he showed me a pure river of water of life....
—REVELATION 22:1 (NKJV)

*W*hen I walked into the break room at 8:00 a.m. and saw that the coffee machine was broken, I gasped. "What am I going to do without my coffee?" My coworkers laughed, pointing to the huge, hand-printed sign tacked to our barren coffeepot:

> *Yes, the coffeemaker is broken. No, we don't know what's wrong with it. Yes, we've ordered another one. No, we don't know when it will arrive. And, no, we don't know what you are going to do without your coffee!*

I laughed too. Obviously, I wasn't the first to utter those remarks.

My coworkers and I were still huddled in the break room when the next caffeine-deprived soul entered. And when Anna wailed, "What will I do without my coffee? I need coffee in the morning!" a coworker began singing "Ohhh, I neeeed coffee in the morning" to the tune of "I Love Paris in the Springtime." The rest of us joined in enthusiastically, if not melodiously.

When our manager walked in and said, "Oh no, the coffee machine's broken!" the whole room roared. And then almost as one, we stood up, ready to begin our workday fueled by laughter...almost as good an energy-giver as caffeine!

God, I'm thirsty for laughter. Please show me how to pour some refreshing humor on the minor irritations life may bring my way today.
—LINDA NEUKRUG

"Lord, let our eyes be opened."
—MATTHEW 20:33 (RSV)

*J*ust last week I gave a talk on creativity, urging the audience to open their eyes and to hone their insights. "Creative people can recognize repeating patterns and see similarities among things," I said knowingly.

So much for being the expert. This morning, for the first time ever, recognized a home-décor pattern that was utterly unintentional. Inside my front door hangs a round, rust-colored plate featuring a golden angel trumpeter. On the kitchen doorframe is a white-china angel holding a harp. Above the light switch in my office, I've put a mauve-and-teal angel plucking a lute. And on a nail just inside my bedroom, there's an angelic horn player, maybe Michael, molded from plaster. I'd put up these angels ages ago, without making the connection that all serve as doorway guards, minding my room-to-room comings and goings. And all four are musicians, poised to fill my home with heavenly chords.

The day is young. What other creative insights—angelic or otherwise—does the Lord have in store for this "expert"?

Lord, open my eyes to new creative insights that enrich my spiritual life.
—EVELYN BENCE

He said to them, "This is what the Lord commanded:
'Tomorrow is to be a day of rest, a holy Sabbath to the Lord.'"
—EXODUS 16:23

I was having Sunday lunch with friends, celebrating the baptism that morning of their daughter, when the waitress came in. "Emergency phone call for Mary Lou Carney," she said. My chicken salad stuck in my throat as I ran to the nearest phone.

"Honey," my husband said, the fear in his voice as clear as the phone connection. "It's Brett. He's been hurt."

Our son Brett has always been oblivious to danger, whether riding his three-wheeler or rock climbing, walking rafters in the houses he builds or driving his pickup truck on icy roads. "What happened?" I asked.

"Power nailer. He has a nail buried in his leg. He's in the emergency room now."

I headed for the hospital, praying all the way. *Please, God, let him be okay. Prevent infection. Help him bear the pain. Send a good surgeon.* But on another level, I was fussing at Brett. Why did he have to work today? If he'd been in church, this wouldn't have happened.

I rushed into the emergency room and was shown to a small, curtained area where Brett lay, a morphine drip hanging from his bed. A dent just above his knee made it clear where the nail—complete with brass barbs—was buried. All thoughts of lecturing him about keeping the Sabbath vanished as I took his hand.

Brett looked up and managed a smile. "Grandpa always told me not to work on Sunday."

I squeezed his hand...and bowed my head in gratitude to One who never takes a day off from watching over His children.

You are faithful, O Father, even when we are not. Forgive us for stealing
from Your ordained day of rest. Slow us down enough to bless us.
—MARY LOU CARNEY

SEPTEMBER 27

Grace be with thee.
—1 TIMOTHY 6:21 (KJV)

*S*ome of life's best gifts have come to me in small, undramatic moment like the words that came shortly after I began my first job from a woma whom I never saw.

"I hear you are working with the old folks at the county home," said a voi on the telephone. "I want to help. Write down my phone number and when or of those dear people has a need, you are to call and let me know.

And she did check back. At least once or twice a week my morning wou begin with one of her calls. If I knew someone who needed a new coat, or special book, or the comfort of a soft stuffed animal, all I had to do was ask. Sh was a self-appointed link among local churches, civic groups, caring individual and people in need. Requests made to this woman were always fulfilled withi a few days.

We had many telephone conversations before I learned that she was a invalid, confined to her bed. I was astounded. "How can you think of other when you have so many problems yourself?" I asked her one day when I wa feeling a bit down myself.

"My dear," she answered, "in the first year of my confinement I spent a my time feeling sorry for myself, until a very wise friend said to me, 'What happened has happened. You can face it with bitterness, or you can face it wit grace.' I knew he was right, so I gathered my courage and chose the latter.

"Moving the center of attention from myself to others, I found I could u the telephone to perform at least one useful act each day. One act of kindne blossomed into two, then three," she continued, "and now my days are full. S each morning when I wake up, I say these words, 'This is a new day. Face it wit grace,' just to remind myself what I'm about."

Today her words continue to bless me. To face the day means no regrets from th past, no resentments in the present, no fears of the future. It is to say each mornin,

What can I do for You today, God?
—PAM KIDD

SEPTEMBER 28

I will not leave you comfortless: I will come to you.
—JOHN 14:18 (KJV)

Forty years ago, when I was baptized, I welcomed Christ into my life. Since then I've claimed a line of an old gospel song by Herbert Buffum: "The Comforter abides with me."

Ten months ago I welcomed a cat into my life. Since Kitty arrived—from the home of my sister Alice—she's never ventured outside my house. I walk in the front door; Kitty greets me with an ankle nudge. I awake in the morning; she races me down the stairs. I take a phone call; she jumps on my lap. In short, she abides with me as a quiet, comforting companion; she is so present that I'm nearly always aware of her whereabouts, upstairs or down.

But Saturday afternoon Kitty wasn't perched on an upstairs windowsill or asleep on my bed. Downstairs, she wasn't in sight, and there aren't many places to hide. The front door was latched. I know she's here somewhere. I looked behind the couch, under the bed, in two closets. I called her. I hunted the house a second and third time, increasingly agitated. I called Alice. "I can't find her!"

"You know she's there. Keep looking," Alice advised ever so reasonably.

One more search, room by room. Sure enough, I discovered Kitty—nose poking out from between boxes in a closet.

Today I sing that old song with new appreciation for both of my abiding comforters: one small creature who is, admittedly, mortal; one immortal Spirit who is, unquestionably, faithful.

Jesus, You sent Your Spirit, the Comforter, to abide with me.
Help me lay claim to this truth with my mind and my heart.
—EVELYN BENCE

There are varieties of working, but it is the same God who inspires them all.
—1 CORINTHIANS 12:6 (RSV)

Last summer, I visited the Smithsonian's Museum of Natural History in Washington, DC, with my husband and our two sons. While looking at the mineral exhibits, I found a display of aragonite, a form of calcium carbonate that was particularly intriguing. There were several forms of aragonite shown, each strikingly different yet with the same atomic structure. One form consisted of milky spear-like crystals, while another was composed of opaque white strands that looked something like chow mein noodles. The same mineral, the same atomic structure, yet depending upon the environment in which they grew, very different appearances. Obviously, there is no one ideal form in which aragonite must appear.

That started me thinking about ideals I have set for myself. I used to struggle to be neat and tidy, thinking that "neat" was ideal and "cluttered" was somehow wrong. I'd spend precious hours cleaning closets, organizing desk drawers, and clearing off tabletops, only to feel guilty when they became cluttered again right away. Then a friend pointed out to me that my natural way of doing things—cluttered and untidy—wasn't wrong, just different.

My friend was right. It's not that I'm a slob or sloppy, because order and cleanliness *are* important. But I don't have to be a perfectionist or live by someone else's standard of organization. I can accept that my clutter makes sense for my needs and actually allows me to relax.

The New Testament says that God has created each of us different, like those varieties of aragonite. We each have our own traits, our own "splendor" like the sun, moon, and stars (1 Corinthians 15:41).

These days, instead of worrying about clutter, I can read, or have an extended quiet time with God, or play soccer in the front yard with my boys. And I think that's just what my loving Creator intended.

Creator God, let me take time to rejoice in my uniqueness today,
knowing that You created me exactly as I was meant to be. Amen.

—LISA ISENHOWER

He is green before the sun, and his branch shooteth forth in his garden.
—JOB 8:16 (KJV)

I t's nice to wait for the No. 5 bus that stops right along Riverside Park in Manhattan. The bus usually comes every ten minutes or so, and on this particular day I went out early so I'd be sure to get to my lunch date on time. But today fifteen minutes passed, then twenty. Now I was fidgety and anxious. "Calm down," I said to myself. "The bus will come. You have time. Take a deep breath. Look around."

I heard a racing and rustling. A squirrel trotted out of the park with a bright green globe in its mouth. "Is that a green Ping-Pong ball?" I wondered aloud just as an elderly man strolled by.

"No, it's a nut," he said. He kept walking, but in a minute came back with another green sphere, which he pressed open. "See, there's a nut inside. The squirrel's getting ready for winter."

A raucous squawking broke out overhead. I squinted up to see a feathery flash of vivid greens—spring green, yellow green, a glimpse of red. A parrot! Then another! I'd always heard about wild parrots in the park but had never seen any. A teenager and some children appeared. *"Pawwots,"* a little boy lisped to me. He wore a moss-green sweater.

By the time the bus pulled up, I'd not only been entertained during my wait, I'd been educated and delighted, and had fraternized with my neighbors. Plus, now I was alerted to green everywhere: a bit of moss on a bus rider's backpack; the glow of the stoplight saying GO; the lacy leaves of the trees bordering the park.

Instead of fretting, I'd enjoyed the gifts of the day. What a difference!

Dear God, thank You for the wonderful gifts of Your great green world.
—MARY ANN O'ROARK

October

OCTOBER 1

O Lord, be not far from me.
—PSALM 35:22 (KJV)

*M*y husband David and I have just worked out at our neighborhood YMCA, and I am waiting for him near the men's dressing room. I have not less than a jillion things to do before the day is over, and the thought of the long day ahead fills my insides with a familiar panic. I pace up and down the hall, and when I look up, I find myself staring at a sign posted on the wall. You ARE HERE, it says. A red arrow points to a certain location marked with an X on the building's blueprint.

I am still standing there looking at the sign when David comes. "This is crazy," I say to him, "but I feel so reassured knowing exactly where I am in this busy day." David laughs, puts his arm around my shoulder, and off we go.

Later, I am working at my computer when the buzzer on the dryer sounds. On my way to remove David's shirts, I smell the chicken dish cooking in the kitchen and change my direction to check on it. Passing the dining room, I notice that I haven't yet set the table for tonight's guests. A moment of cold fear falls over me. Can I really handle all of this? Then I remember the sign. "You are here," I remind myself as I open the oven door. The casserole is fine.

After I have the shirts on hangers, I return to my desk and jot down all the things I need to accomplish before the day ends, numbering them by priority. "You are here," I say out loud as I draw a red arrow to number one on the blueprint of my day.

Realizing that today actually can be managed, one task at a time, I stop and smile. "I am here," I say to God, "and You are here. Let's turn this into a good, productive day together." And we do!

Dear Father, my days are so full and I find myself overwhelmed.
Give me the peace that comes from knowing that where I am, You are,
and together we can handle whatever comes.
—PAM KIDD

OCTOBER 2

"He is able to humble those who walk in pride."
—DANIEL 4:37 (NASB)

*O*ur two daughters were perfect little girls, born just over two years apart. Friends and family called them angels. I dressed them alike and made sure to coordinate hair bows and socks with their outfits. Almost everywhere we three went, strangers praised my parental skills. I thought I deserved it. They're never rude in public or talk back, thanks to me.

I prided myself on my mothering ability. I didn't work outside the home, never shouted at my children, and drew smiley faces on their lunch bags every day. We went to church three times a week. When I'd see other parents struggling with their children, I'd think, *If you try hard enough like me, it works. Simply follow my example and there'll be no problem children.*

Then, at eighteen, each of my daughters started rebelling. It wasn't the quiet kind of rebellion, the kind to sweep under a rug. And the same friends and relatives who'd praised my mothering skills now called to tell me about the girls' bad behavior.

God, I prayed, *how could this happen?* Other parents may have messed up raising their children, but my children should be different. I tried as hard as I knew how. I don't deserve this.

My daughters' rebellion showed me the truth: puffed up by my own supposed success, I'd passed judgment on other parents. Now my embarrassment had exposed my sin of pride. It was a hard lesson, but I trust God has used it to make me a better person—and a better parent.

Father, Your Word puts it best: "When pride comes, then comes disgrace, but with humility comes wisdom" (Proverbs 11:2 NIV).
—JULIE GARMON

OCTOBER 3

...A time to laugh...
—ECCLESIASTES 3:4 (KJV)

I was baby-sitting three of my grandchildren, and it was time to bathe two-year-old Thomas. I got him and all his toys into the tub, and began to wash him, sitting at an angle on the edge so I could continue talking with Jamie and Katie, his sisters. Then, before I could catch myself, I lost my balance, slipped backward, and fell into the tub—fully clothed.

My granddaughters laughed hysterically. Thomas, observing them for a few seconds, threw his head back and joined in the laughter. As I sat in the warm water with my arms and legs extended, I felt this tremendous laugh making its way out. I leaned against the pink tiles and let it come. The four of us were joined together by our laughter, which lasted for perhaps three minutes and was exhausting and satisfying and unforgettable.

Of course, I wouldn't have laughed in my young motherhood days. I would have resented anything that made me look less than perfect, and would have been in a nasty mood for the rest of the evening, probably not speaking. And we would never have mentioned the incident again.

I'm glad I have finally learned—through experience, age, and God's grace—that there's a time to laugh, even at myself and my humanness.

Father, help me to see the lighter side of things.
—MARION BOND WEST

OCTOBER 4

It is not for you to know the times or the seasons,
which the Father hath put in his own power.
—ACTS 1:7 (KJV)

Celtic Christians, while believing that all things are sacred, honor certain places as especially holy. These are called "thin spots," where the line between eternity (heaven) and time (earth) is very thin. Standing in such a place allows one to experience, more fully, the presence of God. Wells are particularly honored as places of healing. While we were in Wales, we visited a number of holy wells. The one that felt most like a thin spot to me was St. Seriol's Well.

In April, I'd had surgery on both my feet. It was now September, and my feet were still very weak, to the point that fellow pilgrims often had to help me climb or pull me up after I'd fallen. Sitting at the edge of St. Seriol's Well, I surprised myself by suddenly removing my shoes and putting my feet into the water. I'd like to be able to say that I was instantly healed, but it didn't happen that way, and I admit I was disappointed.

Then a retired university professor who spoke to us that day called our attention to an interesting fact. The well water looked absolutely still and yet it was perfectly clear. How could it be so still without being stagnant? It was, in fact, coming from an underground spring. The water was actually moving, even though on the surface nothing seemed to be happening.

In the bus on our way back to the hotel, I realized that this was also true of healing. Even though on the surface, it may seem that nothing is happening, still the deep healing waters are truly moving according to the Creator's timetable, not mine! I wanted to remember this next time I prayed for healing.

It's October now, and even though my feet are still weak, they aren't hurting anymore. I choose to believe that my healing began at St. Seriol's.

Thank You, Beloved Healer, for all of the health-restoring miracles
that are on their way right now, though yet unseen.
—MARILYN MORGAN KING

OCTOBER 5

The wife must see to it that she respects her husband.
—EPHESIANS 5:33 (NASB)

*M*y husband Rick and I have been married for thirty years. I've spent entirely too much of that time thinking about his irritating behavior. I kept a mental list of what bothered me:

- We don't have inside doorknobs in the log cabin he built us.
- He stopped going to the barber and began cutting his hair in the bathroom sink.
- He jumps to new projects without finishing the ones he's already started.

My list grew. Seems there was no end to Rick's annoying habits—or to my nagging. Then I had lunch with a friend who raved about her husband. He brings her flowers and loves antique shopping.

"Yeah, but doesn't he ever aggravate you?" I asked.

"Sure, but the good outweighs the bad."

All afternoon her words moved in my heart. I began to remember the excellent things about Rick:

- He's generous; he gave a used car to a single mom.
- He attends our children's baseball and softball games.
- He teaches the Bible to high school boys.
- Every day the man makes me laugh.

I went through the alphabet and thought up positive descriptions:

A—He's available.

B—He's bold.

C—He cares about the down-and-out.

D—He's determined.

Now when I wipe his hair out of the sink or push open the knobless bedroom doors, I say: "Wow! You built this home just for us." "You have the gift of giving." "Your hair sure is thick."

May I honor You, Lord, by honoring my husband
with both my thoughts and words.
—JULIE GARMON

OCTOBER 6

Do not snatch the word of truth from my mouth.
—PSALM 119:43

The lemon pie I'd brought to a friend's house for dinner was very well received. And no wonder! The crust was made by Pillsbury and the filling with help from Betty Crocker. In fact, I guess you could say I'd "assembled" the pie rather than baked it. At dessert time the guests buzzed, "Linda, this pie is absolutely delicious! Did you make it from scratch?" But instead of flat-out saying, "No," I told myself I couldn't answer right away because I had a forkful of lemon pie in my mouth. Finally, I said with a smile, "Well, I didn't grow the *lemons...."* Then I soaked up the praise I got for my talents as a cook.

To me it was just a little fib. So I was surprised at my husband Paul's reaction. As soon as we were out the door he asked, "Why didn't you tell them the truth? That you hadn't made the pie from scratch?" I could tell from the puzzled look on his face that he wasn't criticizing me; he was honestly curious. So I carefully considered the question, Why hadn't I?

The answer, I discovered, was simple. I felt ashamed that I wasn't a better cook. I wanted to do everything perfectly, and I was afraid that my friends would think less of me if I admitted my shortcomings. But once I'd brought my reason into the light, I saw how foolish it was! After all, I didn't choose my friends for their cooking skills, but for other reasons, like their compassion, loyalty, sense of fun—and yes, their honesty. Even about the little things in life—like lemon pies!

Which is why, the very next day, I showed up on my friend's porch. "Would you like my recipe for last night's lemon pie?" I asked with a sheepish grin. She looked surprised and nodded, and I thrust a paper sack into her hands. In it? A box of Pillsbury pie crust and some instant lemon pudding.

*Thank You, God, for reminding me that I don't have
to be perfect to be loved by others—or by You.*
—LINDA NEUKRUG

OCTOBER 7

*Rejoice in all the good things the Lord your God
has given to you and your household.*
—DEUTERONOMY 26:11

*M*y father was asleep in the city, unaware that his children were secretly reuniting in my sister's home in the suburbs to plan his surprise party. Diane and I picked up our brother José from the airport that night, then anxiously waited for our sister Tilza and her family to pull up in Diane's driveway. They arrived after midnight, yet once they walked through the door the house exploded with excited squeals, long hugs, and a storm of kisses.

The next day we marched down the supermarket aisles like a mini-parade, filling our shopping cart with avocados, bags of chips, and bottles of soda. We spent the day preparing party details and enjoying one another's company. Mundane tasks like unloading the groceries or making guacamole became moments to remember. Long into the night, my brother's fingers danced over the guitar strings as we practiced the Puerto Rican folksongs we would sing for my father.

The day of the party passed in a flurry of activity. Decorations, Scotch tape, and tablecloths swirled around us in sweet chaos. Finally, that evening, the food was cooked, the guests arrived, and the candles were lit. There was nothing left to do but wait for my father's entrance. After we yelled, "Surprise!" the party moved as quickly as the festive music.

Soon this wonderful celebration filled with old photos, singing, and delicious food came to an end. The decorations we'd placed so carefully came down in minutes. Yet as we all pitched in to clean the room, I knew it wasn't just the party I'd remember in the years to come, but all the joy and laughter I shared with my family as we pieced it together.

*Heavenly Father, remind me to treasure not just the joy
at the end of each journey, but Your daily blessings along the way.*
—KAREN VALENTIN

October 8

And be ye kind one to another.

—Ephesians 4:32 (KJV)

When my neighbors Phyllis and Martin decided to get a dog, they knew exactly what they wanted: a small dog, female, young but not a puppy. They also wanted a dog who needed a good home. So they went to our local animal shelter and spelled out their needs.

A few days later they received a call from the shelter. A small, female, one-year-old dog had been brought in by a young couple who couldn't keep her because their working hours didn't allow them much time at home. Although it broke their hearts to give up the dog, they felt it was the only fair thing to do. When Phyllis and Martin saw her, they knew she was just the dog for them and took her home.

The next month they received a second call from the shelter. Another small, year-old dog—this one a male—had been brought in by someone who found it hungry and wandering along a road. "He's really nice and well-trained," the woman said.

Phyllis looked at Martin, and without a word they knew what each was thinking. "Let's just take a look," Martin suggested. They did and, of course, they adopted the dog.

Now and then, when I'm walking my dog, I meet Phyllis and Martin walking theirs, and they all look so happy—two little dogs who wanted a home, and two people who wanted their love. Sometimes, when we open our hearts, God has a way of filling them more abundantly than we could ever imagine.

Dear Lord Jesus, make me aware of all I have to share. Amen.

—Phyllis Hobe

OCTOBER 9

The Lord will watch over your coming and going both now and forevermore.
—PSALM 121:8

Just when I thought I had a good grip on the wisdom of the saying "Let go and let God," our twenty-six-year-old daughter Sanna moved to Tennessee to live with Whitney and me. She had a job, she paid her bills, she was mature and delightful to have around. But the guy she was dating...well, there's where I lost my grip.

All my efforts to steer Sanna away from him and into a church with a singles group backfired, forcing me to "let go and let God." In time, the relationship ended without my help.

"I really want to find the man God has in mind for me," Sanna said.

"I want that for you, too, honey," I said, swallowing the urge to steer. She was about to move into a large apartment complex. Lord knows what influences awaited. *Let go and let God, Shari.*

As moving day approached, Sanna decided to switch from an upstairs to a downstairs apartment. "But, Sanna, the upstairs has more light," I said.

"But the ground floor feels like where I'm supposed to be," she replied.

Time passed. Sanna began seeing someone new, a gem of a man. She joined his church. "I know he's the one for her," I said to Whitney.

"Let go and let God, Shari," he said.

Finally, on an evening I'll never forget, Glen and Sanna gave us the news: We're engaged!"

At their wedding reception, Glen toasted Sanna as the girl he'd been praying and hoping for. "And then she moved in next door!" he said.

Lord, even when I lose my grip, You never lose Yours.
—SHARI SMYTH

Refuse the evil, and choose the good.
—ISAIAH 7:15 (KJV)

"C an you believe this family?" I asked our friend Rich as I put down th
newspaper I'd been reading. We were chaperoning a church outing
waiting for the kids to get into the van.

"Who do you mean?" Rich replied.

I pointed to the headlines of the paper that announced yet another lawsu
pitting parents against son in a malicious battle over an inheritance.

"Oh," Rich said, "to be honest, I just don't have the time to read stories lik
that. There are more than enough positive things to keep me occupied."

I can't tell you how many times I've recalled Rich's response to that loca
scandal. Sure, there are many larger and more moving stories of how peopl
choose good over evil, but in Rich's small effort, I see possibilities for improvin
my own choices.

When others are saying mean things about someone, when a friend is bein
critical in public, when a family member is being pessimistic, I can refuse t
participate. I can say something constructive. I can turn the mood positive.

I can make choosing good such an ingrained habit that it becomes a par
of everything I do. I can tell the waitress how much I appreciate her servic
and let the man in the produce department know I enjoy the way he's arrange
the vegetables. I can ask a child questions, then listen to the answers; practic
smiling; say "thank you" a lot and mean it.

It sure does feel *good* to choose good. Why would I want to live any other way

Father, let me be one who chooses good.
—PAM KIDD

OCTOBER 11

We do not know how to pray as we should.
—ROMANS 8:26 (NASB)

For the past several years a few of us from our small congregation have made a point of gathering on Wednesday evenings for a time of prayer. Two couples are retirees, there are one or two singles, the pastor, a couple of church deacons, and a young family with six children. We meet in the church lounge, where we read some Scripture, sing a couple of hymns, and share prayer requests.

Being young and restless but well taught, the children usually say their short prayers first and then quietly slip downstairs where they amuse themselves without disturbing us oldsters.

But one evening little Sarah, about two years old, decided she would stay with the grown-ups. I confess I peeked at her once or twice. Her blond curly head was reverently bowed, her eyes tightly shut, her chubby hands clasped across the front of her pinafore. When there came a slight pause between supplications, Sarah herself began to pray. Although we couldn't understand her childish babble, she seemed so sincere that when she finished, the grandfatherly deacon responded with a hearty "Amen!"

Content that she had contributed her little bit, Sarah skipped off to join her siblings.

What was the gist of Sarah's prayer? Only God knows, and that's all that matters.

Thank You, Lord, that "He who searches the hearts knows
what the mind of the Spirit is" (Romans 8:27 NASB).
—ALMA BARKMAN

If thou hadst known, even thou, at least in this thy day, the things which belong unto thy peace! but now they are hid from thine eyes.
—LUKE 19:42 (KJV)

W hat can we learn from Christopher Columbus five centuries later In many ways it's hard to get in touch with the world he lived in— the pervasive cruelty, the fundamental disregard for individual human life, th religious zeal that executed nonbelievers. But in another way it's easy to pu ourselves in his place; all of us can identify with a man who failed to see wha was in front of him because he was looking for something else.

After years of struggle and disappointment, Columbus had led a sailin expedition westward and, as he expected, found land. Expectations, his an ours...so often misleading. Columbus believed he had reached the Eastern land described by Marco Polo, whose journals he carried everywhere. In fact, befor his very eyes were human and material riches beyond anything Polo had seen i Asia. But Columbus did not see what was before his eyes. Clinging to his flawe world map, Columbus spent his strength and broke his heart trying to mak incomparable reality conform to an image in his mind.

Fifteen centuries earlier, people in Jesus' day had made a similar mistak Like Columbus, faithful Jews had known struggle and disappointment in th long years of waiting for their Messiah. At last He came. But they were expectin something different—a Messiah king, a Messiah warrior—many never sa Him. The image in their minds blinded them to the truth before their eyes. "] thou hadst known," Jesus wept over Jerusalem "in this thy day!"

What, I wonder on this Columbus Day, *is God trying to show us in this our day What mental image of mine, what expectations—for my neighborhood, my family, m work—stand in His way?*

Let me learn from Columbus, Father, not to mistake my expectations for Your reality. Show me Your truth, which is always greater, higher, lovelier than my imagining.
—ELIZABETH SHERRILL

OCTOBER 13

Call unto me, and I will answer thee.
—JEREMIAH 33:3 (KJV)

W hen our daughter Amy Jo's marriage ended, she moved back in with us. She enrolled in a full-time master's program at a nearby university, but was feeling restless and unsure about the future. "You know," she said one night as she was setting the table, "I used to talk about going to law school. Remember?"

I did remember. She had only been about ten when she first brought it up. And although she'd mentioned it a few times during the years, it somehow had fallen by the wayside as she got a degree in communications, took a job, and got married. Now it was surfacing again. "I remember," I said, "but I'm not sure if that's what you should do now or not." Silently, I wondered where she would get the money. "Just pray about it, honey," I said, turning back to the stove. The words sounded frail. *Wasn't there something else she should be doing?*

A few minutes later, Amy Jo came back into the kitchen, beaming. She spread out the *Chicago Tribune* on the table and pointed to a classified ad: "Wondering if law school is right for you? Work for us and decide!" It was a large law firm in Chicago, an easy train ride from where we lived. So Amy Jo took the job, working for a year as a court runner. She loved it! Then she took the admissions test and enrolled in Valparaiso University, where she's currently studying law.

I've always believed in answered prayer. But these days I'm looking for those answers in lots of places. My Bible, of course. But also in the "thought for the day" that appears on my e-mail. Or in the overheard wisdom of an older woman in line at the grocery talking—on a cell phone—to her daughter. And, yes, even in the newspaper. As for the financial problem of law school—Amy Jo is on full scholarship, which is something we both prayed about!

> *Open my eyes, Father, to the unique avenues*
> *You use to let Your answers reach me.*
> —MARY LOU CARNEY

OCTOBER 14

And she tied the scarlet cord in the window.
—JOSHUA 2:21

The day our son Chris left for a tour of duty in Afghanistan with the army, my husband Gordon insisted that I buy fifteen yards of ribbon to make a gigantic yellow bow. As I tied the bow around the huge pine tree by the front driveway, I felt a stab of loneliness.

The next morning, as I was picking up the newspaper in the driveway, a neighbor stopped her car and asked about the ribbon. When I told her about Chris, she said, "I'll be praying for him." Soon everyone on the street had noticed the yellow ribbon, and another neighbor called to tell me, "We want to have a cookout to let you know we support your family."

At the cookout a seven-year-old girl named Amanda offered me a gift bag to comfort me. Inside was a dried Play-Doh pot, a thread with several beads on it, and a piece of foam with a slit in it. "A ring holder," she told me. A mother brought her two elementary-school boys over to me and each whispered a bit shyly that they were praying for Chris.

The day Chris returned from Afghanistan safe and sound, I got out a ladder and took down the yellow ribbon. By then it was stained from the rain and had pine straw stuck in it. I shook out the bow and took it down to the basement for storage as a reminder of those who comforted us and prayed for us during his absence.

Dear Father, thank You that when I share my personal struggles
with others, they support me with Your love.
—KAREN BARBER

*But the Spirit itself maketh intercession
for us with groanings which cannot be uttered.*
—ROMANS 8:26 (KJV)

Several years ago, I found myself drawn to an exquisite quilt in an antiques shop. It was hand-pieced from cheery feed sack fabrics in the Grandmother's Flower Garden pattern. Problem was, someone had machine-quilted it in a contemporary zigzag stitch.

I purchased it anyway and brought it to show a coworker who had just completed a quilting class. Sherry loved it immediately and volunteered to redo "Whoever originally pieced this quilt was a true artist," she told me. "Let me pick out that machine quilting and quilt it by hand for you." But it seemed too big a job to ask of anyone, so I brought the quilt home and stashed it in an armoire.

Soon after, Sherry went through some devastating experiences and had to give up her nursing career. One evening as I was dusting the armoire, the quilt nearly jumped off the shelf. A thought came to me: *give Sherry that quilt.*

I gave the quilt to Sherry without even beginning to understand God's purpose. Years later, her daughter told me about the role in which that quilt had served. During sleepless nights when Sherry's problems loomed so large and she couldn't imagine a new beginning, she would pick out those contrary zigzag stitches and replace them with her perfect hand quilting. And she prayed (or the first time in her life) that she would be restored, just as the quilt would be. "If it hadn't been for that quilt and your friendship, my mother would have surely committed suicide," her daughter said.

Today, Sherry believes in God, is active in church, and is building a new life—stitch by simple stitch.

*O Lord, sometimes Your nudges seem so small that I overlook them.
Help me always to follow Your direction.*
—ROBERTA MESSNER

OCTOBER 16

How delightful is a timely word!
—PROVERBS 15:23 (NASB)

It was turning out to be one of those dreaded "Can't I do anything right?" days. An important letter was returned to me, unstamped. In the grocery store I discovered my shoes didn't match, even though both were brown. Outside, I tried valiantly to unlock the door of a car that looked amazingly like mine.

Later, at the red light, I drummed my fingers impatiently on the steering wheel, but when at last the light turned green I couldn't remember where I was headed. I roared off anyway, so no one would guess my dilemma. After several blocks, I remembered where I wanted to go. Feeling almost smug, I pulled up at the dry cleaner. My victory was short-lived, however: I'd forgotten the clothes.

Back at home, I gathered up all my courage and phoned our insurance company to straighten out an unpaid claim. I concentrated intently as I punched the endless numbers that I hoped would connect me to a live person.

The lady who finally spoke to me was smiling; I could feel it all the way down in Georgia. Sweetly, she suggested, "Let me get you more experienced help. I'm new here."

"Oh no, please don't go," I said near tears. "You are so—nice—and patient and kind. Please help me." I didn't tell her that sometimes fast-talking people, especially short-tempered ones, scare me.

She laughed like a next-door neighbor. "Okay, then." She took care of my problem, and when we finished she said, "Have a blessed day. We're always home for you."

Lord, just a few kind words, even from a stranger, have changed
my entire outlook. Help me do the same for someone.
—MARION BOND WEST

It is more blessed to give than to receive.

—ACTS 20:35 (KJV)

Our trusted slogan "travel light" was unexpectedly challenged when we set out on a trip with our friend Brother Andrew. This was in the 1960s, when it was "impossible" for Christians from the West to meet with Christians behind the Iron Curtain. For years, however, Andrew had been doing just that.

This was to be a short trip, just into East Germany for a few days to watch him in action, so my husband John and I brought only a single small bag for both of us. Andrew was packing when we arrived at his house. Into a large suitcase on his bed he was putting shirts, sweaters, jackets—most with the store tags still attached.

"Why so many clothes for four days?" John asked.

"Oh, I won't be bringing any of this back," Andrew said.

The people we'd be visiting, he explained, like all believers behind the Iron Curtain, paid a tremendous price for their faith, forgoing good education, good jobs, good housing. "They have so little that even a pair of socks can make a difference." All he brought back from trips, he said, was a satchel with his soiled clothes, "so the customs inspector doesn't get curious."

I looked at the faded sweater Andrew was wearing. "You look like you could use a few new clothes yourself," I said.

Sure, he agreed; he'd buy a new sweater one of these days. "But you know what? I won't enjoy it half as much as I do buying a sweater for someone else. It won't be mine the same way. The only things you have forever are the ones you give away."

It's wisdom as we travel through life, too, I thought. Our talents, our experience, our time, our things—they don't mean much until they're shared.

Lord of the journey, what am I clinging to that You want me to give away?

—ELIZABETH SHERRILL

OCTOBER 18

For the Lord thy God blesseth thee, as he promised thee.
—DEUTERONOMY 15:6 (KJV)

When my husband Bob was first diagnosed with Parkinson's disease and I began to learn of the many ill effects it might have on him, I became very frightened. How would I be able to cope with the drastic life change awaiting both of us? I outlined my fears to God in prayer. And almost immediately I began to see those prayers answered.

One of my fears was that as Bob's condition worsened, we would be stranded at home. I had given up driving the car years ago, following serious eye surgery, and there is no public transportation in our area. Now a dear friend comes every Friday night after she leaves her job and takes me to buy groceries. Another call midweek when she is going shopping to see if she can buy anything for me. Trips to the doctor's office or short sprints to the mall are readily taken care of by other friends and neighbors.

And the blessings do not stop there! Church members remember us with cards, phone calls, visits, and hot food each time a supper is held in the fellowship hall.

A major problem with Bob's illness is that it causes the muscles to deteriorate, which results in his falling unexpectedly. A man across the street from our house responds immediately to my telephone calls—day or night—and helps me to lift Bob from the floor into his chair or bed.

And, of course, our daughter and granddaughter come almost every weekend and perform countless tasks about our house and yard.

Bob and I were gadabouts when we were healthy—traveling, dancing, participating in senior-citizen doings and church activities. Now all of that has ceased. But I am not restless or resentful. Instead, God has given me a sense of quiet peace and satisfaction, which, at this time in my life, I feel might be the greatest blessing of all.

Thank You, Father, for the blessings You send me daily. Please shower Your love on those who reach out to help us. Amen.
—DRUE DUKE

OCTOBER 19

And he led them forth by the right way.
—PSALM 107:7 (KJV)

I arrived at La Guardia Airport after a long and tedious meeting, wishing I could wave a magic wand and be home, or at least take a direct flight. Only there aren't any direct flights to our farm south of Copeland, Kansas. I had to go from New York to Denver, catch the 9:30 p.m. shuttle plane to Garden City, then drive fifty miles. With luck, I'd be asleep in my own bed by midnight.

The ticket agent checked the computer monitor, then shook his head. "Your plane is still on the ground in Denver. We're looking at a five-hour delay."

"I'll miss the last shuttle!" I wailed. "Can't you route me some other way?"

The agent worked for fifteen minutes. "Ma'am, it is impossible to get you to Garden City tonight. Is there any other destination that would work?"

Another destination? A light turned on in the dark room of my mind. My real destination wasn't Garden City, it was home! Twenty minutes later I boarded a plane to Chicago, where I caught a connecting flight to Wichita. My husband Don met me—and didn't gripe about the long roundabout trip! I tumbled into my own bed only an hour later than originally scheduled.

My life is often like that trip. Plans go awry, there are detours on the road, and the timetable changes without notice. But God graciously leads me every step of the way. I know I'll reach my heavenly home, my final destination, in His good time.

"All the way my Savior leads me; what have I to ask beside?" (Fanny Crosby)
—PENNEY SCHWAB

Though it linger, wait for it; it will certainly come and will not delay.
—HABAKKUK 2:3

When I was in junior high, I was a reporter for the school newspaper. I sat behind the bench during basketball games, close enough to hear the coach, close enough to see the sweat on the brows of the fourteen-year-old boys in the starting lineup. I was also near enough to see the hope, the anguish, the defeat that warred on the faces of those who had yet to get into the game—the benchwarmers.

They wore the team uniform and jacket because the coach had selected them and said they were good enough to be on the team. I'd seen them running drills, just like the starting five. They practiced shooting free throws, they ran laps, but still they sat on the bench, waiting. During the game, they'd jump to their feet yelling, cheering, and sometimes crying—but they didn't get on the floor. They sold candy and washed cars to raise funds for the team, but week after week, it was never their turn. "It's just not the right time. Just wait, I'm going to need you," the coach would tell them.

There's a change in my life that I've been preparing for and praying for, waiting for, and all indications are that it's coming; I just don't know when. I'm anxious, waiting to get into the game, and sometimes there are moments when I feel like going to the locker room and putting on my street clothes. That would be easier than waiting.

I think about all the preachers waiting to preach, all the practiced dancers waiting to dance, all the mothers waiting to give birth, and all the brides waiting to marry. All of us waiting to get into the game.

I look up toward the heavens. "I trust You, God," I whisper. "Coach, let me in the game!"

Lord, help me to be patient until my preparation,
my passion, and my destiny intersect with Your divine plan.
—SHARON FOSTER

OCTOBER 21

When I consider thy heavens, the work of thy fingers, the moon and the stars,
which thou hast ordained; what is man, that thou art mindful of him?
—PSALM 8:3–4 (KJV)

I had gone to bed early, exhausted from the sheer frustration of my workday. I was almost asleep when the phone rang. I heard my husband's voice downstairs, talking briefly, and then his footsteps in the hallway. "Honey, you asleep?" he asked as he opened the door.

"How could I be?" I asked, just wanting the day to end.

"Want to come outside and look at the moon? We're having a total lunar eclipse."

I was wide awake now. "Really?"

A few minutes later, Gary and I stood on the front lawn, the sky an amazing arc of black velvet studded with stars. And center stage was the pale, marvelous moon. I broke the silence and asked, "How did you know about this?"

Gary put his arm around me. "That phone call. It was some lady, all excited, telling me to go out and look at the moon. She was pretty embarrassed when I told her she had a wrong number."

I stood there looking at the sky, my frustration and exhaustion giving way to wonder and awe. God really was in control—of the universe and my own life too. "You know," I said, snuggling closer to Gary, "I don't think she got the wrong number at all."

How marvelous are Your works, God!
—MARY LOU CARNEY

Let us draw near with a true heart in full assurance of faith.
—HEBREWS 10:22 (KJV)

*S*ome days anxiety looms up out of the blue and snatches me. Sometimes I can't even describe my fear. It could be anything: My mother is having tests for an ulcer; I haven't allowed enough time for groceries so I'm stuck in line, late for my next appointment; the car keeps stalling; a friend hasn't called in a while, so I'm convinced he's angry with me.

During these frightening episodes, only one thing is sure to help: prayer. Not reciting familiar words or reading the Psalms or talking; my "anxiety prayer" has no words at all. I curl up in the corner of my sofa, facing the pretty stone gazebo on the small square of green separating me from Connecticut's Stonington Harbor. I close my eyes and imagine myself opening the sliding glass door. God stands in front of the gazebo, His arms open to me. I start walking, then running, to Him. He lifts me like the terrified child I am and swings me around through the air like the loving Father He is. Then He sits in the gazebo facing the water, holding me in His comforting arms until my breathing slows and my anxiety lessens. I feel His love, forgiveness, and grace just as surely as I hear the gentle waves and tinkling wind chimes.

I stay there with Him as long as I need to. I don't beg Him for help or tell Him my troubles. He knows. And when I open my eyes to my familiar living room, I'm always calm.

Father, never let me forget that You are just that:
loving, forgiving, and comforting.
—MARCI ALBORGHETTI

In my Father's house are many mansions: if it were not so, I would have told you. I go to prepare a place for you. And if I go and prepare a place for you, I will come again, and receive you unto myself; that where I am, there ye may be also.
—JOHN 14:2–3 (KJV)

My father was a carpenter, and he built six of our homes. He died two years ago, and my unyielding sorrow has taken on a more practical grief. I have to sell my home and "buy down." In short, I need my dad.

I need him to make repairs on the home I'm selling. I need him to inspect the homes I'm thinking about buying. I need him to brainstorm ideas for transforming cookie-cutter production into character and quality. But I'm on my own. Last week was particularly trying and, in tears, I asked God for perspective.

I was eleven when we lived in the Laurentian Mountains of French Canada. In the isolation of geography and language, my father homeschooled my sisters and me for five months. Part of our education was Bible memory. One of the first passages Dad assigned was John 14: "In my Father's house are many mansions."

How could I forget that Jesus was a carpenter like Dad? My grief and anxiety ebbed, for I knew that whatever I bought, it was not my final home. Also because I know my dad, I like to think he's lending a hand, and that he and Jesus are making things ready for my final move.

Dear Jesus, truly this world is not our home. The Cross was our down payment for something better, and You're now preparing that final home where we'll forever live with You and our loved ones.
—BRENDA WILBEE

The end of a matter is better than its beginning,
and patience is better than pride.
—ECCLESIASTES 7:8

*T*he barking woke me. I rolled over and tried to go back to sleep, but the open window made it impossible. Pulling the curtain, I looked down. Our neighbor Patty struggled on the sidewalk with two dogs, leashes taut in her hands.

"I might as well get up," I said to myself, shaking my head at our luck. Our neighbor seemed to have adopted two large, loud mutts. Maybe she's just babysitting, I hoped. Maybe it's just for the weekend.

When I went outside later to get the mail, I noticed Patty filling her bird feeders.

"Those sure are some dogs," I said, crossing the street.

Patty rolled her eyes. "It's going to take a few months before they're settled."

"Months?" I tried to hide my displeasure. "So they're yours?"

"The brown one spent eighteen months at the shelter. He got a home, but then the people took him back, so he spent another twelve months there. The other one was brought to the shelter with all kinds of problems. I asked for the worst cases, the ones no one would take."

"No one but you," I said.

She nodded and sighed.

For the rest of the summer, when the barking woke me, I reminded myself that patience was the least I could give to the cause. Eventually I learned to ignore it.

Just as the leaves were beginning to turn shades of maroon, I happened to look out the window and saw Patty and her dogs. It was the first time I'd seen them without hearing them first, and I couldn't get over the transformation. No longer tense and scared, the dogs pranced quietly, proudly, their heads high and straight as if they were escorting a queen.

Lord, help me to put up with little annoyances for the sake of a greater good.
—SABRA CIANCANELLI

OCTOBER 25

Every good gift and every perfect gift is from above.
—JAMES 1:17 (KJV)

*H*ats are difficult to make; it's hard to get the size just right. But I decided to knit one for Daisy. Maybe if it fit me, it would fit her. After all, she's one of my dearest friends, and our lives have fit together honestly and affectionately over the years. Perhaps the hat would do the same.

The yarn was soft and pretty, but hard to knit with. On my first try the hat got so big that I had to start over. Would I have enough yarn? This is a "thought hat," I reminded myself. It can be less than perfect and still get the job done.

Thought hats are important to me. I make very few of them. I don't work on them while watching television or chatting with my husband. I work on them alone and in quiet. Every stitch in Daisy's hat is a thought about the times we've shared: the amazing voyage in the Fiji Islands, the walk along the sandy beach in South Carolina, learning to kayak in Narragansett Bay. The changes we've looked at together: passing sixty (she got there first); being grandmothers (I'm here, and she's waiting and wondering); hard times (the deaths of her parents, my struggles with depression).

I've found that thought hats often work in two directions. Maybe Daisy's warm ears will bring back some memories for her too. We don't get to see each other very often these days. That's another reason why she's getting a thought hat for her birthday this year. It's white with colored flecks. I think it will suit her.

Lord, thank You for friendship, Your good gift, a blessing beyond words.
—BRIGITTE WEEKS

OCTOBER 26

And he took the children in his arms, put his hands on them and blessed them.
—MARK 10:16

T he theater was packed with squirming, fidgety, and chattering children. My husband and I should have realized that seeing an animated film on Saturday afternoon might mean that we'd be surrounded by little ones. "Do you want to leave?" I asked. "We still have time to go to another movie."

"No, let's stay. Maybe they'll quiet down," Roy replied.

I wasn't so sure. I'd had an exhausting week at work. School had just started, Open House was near, and I was still trying to learn all my students' names. *I came here to relax, not to be around noisy kids,* I thought.

I watched a little boy run up and down the aisle, wriggling to get out of his father's grasp. I shook my head. I was definitely not used to children this young anymore. My youngest was seventeen; I taught history to eighteen-year-olds. We had no grandchildren yet. I felt like we were in a foreign country.

The film started and, amazingly, the children stopped squirming and fidgeting and settled down to watch. Every now and then I'd hear a child whisper loudly, "Daddy, what was that?" or "Mommy, did you see that?" The preshow chaos turned into ninety minutes of giggles, spontaneous applause, and peals of laughter. I caught myself laughing loudly right along with the children.

I left the theater feeling rejuvenated. The film had been funny and entertaining, but it was the presence of the children that really lifted my spirit. My grandmother used to say that being in the presence of a child is like sitting with the angels. So until the time is right for grandchildren, I guess I'll be going back to the matinee.

Thank You, Lord, for the laughter of children.
—MELODY BONNETTE

OCTOBER 27

"Be strong, all you people...," declares the Lord,
"and work. For I am with you."
—HAGGAI 2:4

It was already after noon, and I hadn't been able to sit still and focus for more than fifteen minutes. How would I ever get in a good day's work with all there was to fret about? First I worried about the world situation: was anyone safe anymore? Then I turned to finances; I needed that tax refund this year more than ever. That reminded me of a health insurance claim I needed to fill out. I sorted through some papers, talked on the phone awhile, and finally took a walk around the block.

The exercise helped a little. Back inside, I opened my Bible and turned to the short book of Haggai. Hadn't I marked a verse once for a day just like today? Something to help settle my thoughts so I could work:

"Work. For I am with you."

That did the trick.

Lord, Your very presence settles me.
—EVELYN BENCE

OCTOBER 28

I have a message from God unto thee.
—JUDGES 3:20 (KJV)

T was turning into our garage, weary from shopping, when a scrap of paper stuck in the back door caught my eye. Immediately, joy, energy, and anticipation settled into my heart, and I wasn't nearly as tired. Smiling, I turned off the ignition and momentarily forgot about the groceries in the trunk and the packages on the backseat.

I stepped out of the car and reached for the note. It was scribbled on the back of an envelope in my husband Gene's familiar scrunched-up handwriting. Neither of us went anywhere without leaving a note for the other. This one said, "Hey. I've gone to the drugstore, the grocery, and to feed the cows. Julie wants you to call her. Your watch is ready to be picked up. Home before six. Want to eat out?" Then came the best part: a hastily drawn heart with an arrow through it and his initials at the top and mine at the bottom. I read it twice because—well, because I adore Gene and I like being reminded that he loves me.

Once, after Gene and I'd had a pretty hefty fight, he left a note on the door that said, "Busy day. Don't know when I'll be back. Gene." I turned the paper over, searching in vain for something like, "P.S. I love you." When Gene returned, stern-faced and moving around like the Tin Man, I ran into his arms, shouting, "Your note was terrible. The mailman leaves better notes than that!" He held me while I cried. Since then, Gene's notes have always contained that lopsided heart-and-arrow and our initials, a little message just for me.

Today, Father, help me to read the message You have just for me in Your Word.
—MARION BOND WEST

God hath chosen the foolish things of the world to confound the wise.
—1 CORINTHIANS 1:27 (KJV)

One afternoon I wandered into the arts and crafts room at a conference I was attending. I scooped up a handful of clay, put it on the pottery wheel, and began to spin a pot. When I finished, I had produced the most pathetically lopsided pot you can imagine. As I looked at it in disgust, the resident potter appeared. "I think I should just toss this thing in the trash," I said.

"I know how you feel. The first pot I ever made looked just like that and I hated it," she said. "But I decided to save it. In fact, it sits in a prominent place in my house."

She explained. "You see, I used to be a real perfectionist. I rejected whatever I did that didn't meet my own rigid standards. My lopsided pot reminded me that it's okay not to be perfect, that it's even desirable."

"Huh?"

"Well, think about it," she said with a wink. "If you're perfect, you won't have anyone like yourself to relate to. It would be awfully lonely being perfect, don't you think?"

As she walked away, I thought about my own imperfections, and how I berated myself for them. My house wasn't spotless (goodness, it wasn't even neat most of the time). And seven times out of ten I burned whatever I put in the toaster. Sometimes it took me three months to answer a letter. I'd gained a few extra pounds and broken promises to myself to take them off. I fussed at my family when they didn't deserve it...lopsided pots, all of them!

Of course it is important to try for excellence and improve, but it is also important to accept myself in spite of my imperfections, to relax my Herculean standards and join the human race. So you know what I did? I took that silly pot home and put it in my study. And funny thing—whenever people come to visit, they gravitate to that pot right away. Something in them understands.

You know what an imperfect pot I can be, God. Thanks for loving me anyway.
—SUE MONK KIDD

As for God, his way is perfect.
—2 SAMUEL 22:31 (KJV)

T was making Infection Control Rounds at the hospital where I work when I entered a private room. A nurse was bathing a patient who ha metastatic cancer and had slipped into a coma. I checked his IV to make sure hadn't been in place longer than the recommended hours, part of a patient-car audit I was conducting.

As I left the room, I paused, taking notice of how the nurse had wrapped th washcloth tautly around her hand so as not to irritate her patient's crepe-pape skin. She gently washed his arm and lifted it ever so tenderly to dry it. Then sh squeezed his fingertips twice, saying, "Your wife called earlier and asked me t give you the signal."

Some nurses might think such a patient was past the point of understandin words and touch and signals. But not this nurse. She had found the perfect way For her, administering a bath was a work of art.

Later that afternoon, I went back to the nursing unit to locate her. I found he in the storage closet, gathering up supplies to insert a feeding tube into anothe patient. "I've thought of you all day long," I told her. "I was so touched by th loving way you cared for your patient this morning, and I just had to tell you."

She lowered her head. "Oh, thank you," she replied. "I didn't think anyon ever noticed things like that."

That's going to be one of the great joys of heaven, God seemed to say. *You'll spen the first thousand years or so finding out how by following My celestial signals, yo made a difference in the lives of others.*

Lord, keep me listening to Your Voice.
—ROBERTA MESSNER

Be on the alert. Your adversary...prowls about...seeking someone to devour.
— 1 PETER 5:8 (NASB)

The Halloween tradition of trick or treating is just a little spookier and a whole lot scarier for children in Churchill, Manitoba, a town several hundred miles north of us. The rules are a little different too.

Rule one: no polar bear costumes.

Rule two: no white costumes such as ghosts, nurses, or brides. And definitely no seal costumes.

The reason? Polar bears. Churchill lies in close proximity to the world's largest denning area for polar bears. After spending the summer on land, in late fall the bears head back to the waters of Hudson Bay to hunt seals. By the end of October most of the twenty holding pens in the town's "bear jail" are already filled with occupants awaiting release.

To protect children going door to door on Halloween night, conservation officers and game wardens are out on patrol armed with dart guns to tranquilize any bears wandering into town. A helicopter does surveillance over the area. Local volunteers with two-way radios patrol in cars. Police constables carry shotguns to frighten away any furry white marauders. And while noise may help, authorities agree that the most effective deterrent against prowling bears is light. Each year more than a dozen fire trucks, ambulances, and police cruisers are positioned around the perimeter of Churchill, their bright lights flashing into the night.

I don't know about you, but sometimes when I read the morning newspaper, I feel very small and vulnerable. Should anxiety threaten my peace of mind, however, I find the best protection is to "walk in the Light" (1 John 1:7). It's advice that's equally effective whether dealing with polar bears or the powers of darkness.

Thank You, Lord, that You are the Light of the world.
—ALMA BARKMAN

November

Don't you think that God will surely give justice to his chosen people who plead with him day and night? Yes! He will answer them quickly!
—LUKE 18:7–8 (TLB)

*Y*ou can tell a lot about a person by looking at the front of his or her refrigerator. My seventy-seven-year-old stepmother Bev has magnets on hers from some of the countries she and my dad have visited over the years. My busy son Michael and his wife Amy have large magnetic alphabet letters at the bottom of their refrigerator for their little ones, Hannah and Zachary, to practice their spelling words. My friend Sharon has hundreds of tiny magnetic words on her refrigerator, so her whole family can create sweet, goofy, or sentimental poems.

My refrigerator is what reminds me to pray a dozen times a day, because the top two-thirds of it is a solid mass of four-by-six-inch photos. Everyone from 101-year-old Great-Aunt Peggy and ninety-five-year-old Aunt Helen to my two-year-old granddaughter Riley. My four children, their spouses, my other four grandchildren, my folks, brother, sister, their families, other aunts, uncles, cousins, and assorted friends all hold a place of honor on my refrigerator.

One is a picture of Jane Knapp, a friend I've never met in person. She interviewed me by telephone on her small radio station years ago, and we struck up an immediate friendship. In 2000, Jane's e-mails were gut-wrenching updates about her cancer. One day, after months of chemo, I received this note from Jane:

"The doctor called a few minutes ago and told me that the PET scan results showed new cancers in my liver, kidney, and lung. He said usually new cancers do not pop up at the same time, so I'm very discouraged, but have to keep believing in the power of prayer."

Jane's photo and all the others on that frequently opened door help keep my loved ones in my mind, heart, and prayers many times a day, every day.

Lord, bless, protect, and comfort every person whose face is on my refrigerator. And thank You, especially, for putting them into my life.
—PATRICIA LORENZ

NOVEMBER 2

Whatever your hand finds to do, do it with all your might.
—ECCLESIASTES 9:10

*W*orking as a registered nurse with seniors in assisted-care homes, I found two types of residents. The angry ones didn't want to be there and, in a way, I didn't blame them. They'd lost so much: hard-earned homes and possessions, independence, privacy, good health. And then there were people like Mr. and Mrs. Epp, who radiated quiet acceptance. What secret had they found to keep discouragement at bay?

One morning before breakfast I entered their room with their medication. At first I didn't see the couple. They were sitting together at a small table sipping coffee from Royal Albert china cups. "Mugs from the home won't do," said Mrs. Epp, smoothing the lace tablecloth, "nor will the coffee from the dining hall."

Mr. Epp nodded. "This is how we've always done it," he said proudly.

There's comfort in our simple routines, in the ordinary tasks of life. When I feel frazzled, I consider the Epps and enjoy a hot cup of tea, take a stroll in the park, or write a letter to someone I love. Sometimes the smallest things can make the whole day better.

Dear Lord, thank You for the familiar things that brighten my day.
—HELEN GRACE LESCHEID

His divine power has given us everything we need for life and godliness through our knowledge of him who called us by his own glory and goodness.
—2 PETER 1:3

'm on another diet. This one claims, "Never feel hungry." If that's the case, then why was it so hard for me to clean up the kitchen today? Why did I have to squeeze my eyes shut to put away the peanut butter and mash the macaroni leftovers into the dog food so I wouldn't gobble them up?

My grandmother would have sized up the situation using her own quaint terminology: "The trouble with you is that you're mouth-hungry, not stomach-hungry." And she'd be right. My stomach was not grumbling, nor did it have pangs. All I really wanted was to indulge in a great feast of flavors, textures, and aromas.

I have been mouth-hungry in other ways, too. When my typewriter broke, my husband suggested we buy a slightly better one that would do more things and still be within our budget. I wanted a word processor with features even a publishing house wouldn't need. Mouth-hungry. And when we bought a used pickup truck, the man said, "You can keep the fancy 'mag' wheels for two hundred dollars more."

"Sure," I said.

"No," my husband said.

Mouth-hungry. Going way beyond the need. Maybe I should take a better look at being content with what is obviously enough. I may lose a little weight along the way, too!

Lord, Grandma was putting it kindly calling me mouth-hungry—it's really greed. Help me to put Your kingdom first, and to be thankful for the many things I do have.
—KATHIE KANIA

NOVEMBER 4

Surely the Lord is in this place; and I knew it not.
—GENESIS 28:16 (KJV)

Though my youngest child always genuinely enjoyed attending and participating in worship services, my older children reached a point where they would dream up every excuse imaginable to avoid accompanying me to church. As a single parent, it took me a little while to catch on.

I quickly learned to tell who was sound asleep and who was pretending. Diagnosing diseases proved harder. Sometimes my children suffered from mysterious ailments that miraculously disappeared by the time I arrived back home to find them cheerfully curled up with the Sunday comics. Other times, thoroughly planned disorganization took its toll: "I can't find my shoes." "There's no time to shower." "No time to curl my hair." "My alarm didn't go off."

Even if the children were ready, they moaned as I edged them into the car: "It's boring." "It's too long." "I don't know what the pastor's talking about."

But one particular morning was the worst. My teenage sons reluctantly shuffled into church and pleaded to sit by themselves in the back. A little hurt, I agreed, rationalizing, *At least they're in church.* I sat with the girls in my customary seat up front. When I didn't see the boys in the Communion procession, I became suspicious. Much later I learned that they had slipped out of church shortly after the entrance hymn, hiked a mile to a fast-food joint for cocoa, and then hot-footed it back to church in time to stroll out with the congregation after the recessional.

It was nearly the same story five years later, when my older daughter Tess, by then a mother herself, paid her younger brother's airfare so he could join her at Christmas. She wanted family time on Christmas Eve; he wanted time with old friends. Tess stood her ground: "First, you have to go with me to the vigil service. Afterward, we'll have a turkey dinner with all the fixings. Then you can go see your friends."

"You sound just like Mom!" he thundered.

Tess admits she was delighted by the accusation.

*Father of all, give me the stamina to teach my children the way they should go—
even when they don't like it very much.*
—GAIL THORELL SCHILLING

Fear not: for I have redeemed thee, I have called thee by thy name; thou art mine.
—ISAIAH 43:1 (KJV)

Our little Mary recently celebrated her second birthday. She now has a new litany she repeats a dozen times a day in her sweet, high voice.

"I'm Ma-ry Fran-ces At-ta-way. I'm a toddler. I'm two years old."

Cute as it is, there is something extremely important to her in this self-definition. The day before yesterday she looked stunning in her green velvet Sunday dress, with her strawberry-blond curls tumbling down, and I said, "You look like a princess!"

She shook her head and solemnly replied, "I'm a toddler."

She is not a princess. She does not want to be a princess. She wants to be who and what she is: Mary Frances Attaway, a toddler who is two years old.

It strikes me that Mary is on to something that I as an adult sometimes forget. I fall, not infrequently, into the trap of thinking in terms of who I'd like to be, of the image I'd like to project, the person I'm trying to become or wish I had been. Mary is true to being the person God created her to be—she is who she is. As I hear her proclaim to her brother and sister, "I'm Mary Frances Attaway!" I marvel at her confidence in simply being Mary. Being Mary is what God asks of her, and that, in and of itself, is enough.

Surely God sees through my pretenses (even the ones to which I'm blind) to the Julia He created. Which causes me to wonder: *Why, then, do I ask God to meet me where I want to be, rather than where He has placed me?*

> *Lord Jesus, help me to die to self, that I may find my name*
> *written in Your Book of Life.*
> —JULIA ATTAWAY

NOVEMBER 6

The king's heart is in the hand of the Lord.
—PROVERBS 21:1 (KJV)

*Y*ears ago I became enthusiastic about a presidential candidate. friend and I did some grassroots campaigning locally. We organize prayer groups, gave out bumper stickers, and made phone calls. On Electio Day I woke up so excited I couldn't stop smiling all the way to the polls. Th evening I settled down cross-legged in front of the television to watch th returns, confident of victory.

Hours later my candidate conceded defeat, and I shouted back to th television the way my husband often did when his team lost a football gam Maybe the tide would turn, I reasoned. Maybe the morning paper woul announce a miraculous win after all. But there was no such miracle the next da Unless, of course, you count the one that arrived by telephone.

It was my campaigning friend. "Hi, Marion," she piped with all the eagerne: of Mother Goose to her goslings. I sighed heavily and shifted the phone to th other ear. "Listen," she insisted, "God is still God. He's not even surprised, an the Bible admonishes us to pray for everyone in leadership. Have you prayed fc our president-elect yet?"

Sitting there on the tall kitchen stool, my hand still on the phone I'd ju: hung up, I bowed my head and prayed for the man I hadn't wanted to win.

Lord, may Your holy presence abide in the hearts
of everyone elected to office today. Amen.
—MARION BOND WEST

NOVEMBER 7

*Making melody in your heart to the Lord; giving thanks always
for all things unto God.*
—EPHESIANS 5:19–20 (KJV)

My husband and I are pushovers when it comes to cats, especially when it comes to our Siamese cat Shushi. She has spent a good part of her thirteen-year lifetime curled up at the foot of our bed. The trouble is that now, in her old age, she needs to be let out around four in the morning, and in our old age, it is becoming increasingly hard for us to get back to sleep once we've gotten up to let her out.

Every time we decide to get Shushi off our bed, she looks at us with wide blue eyes, opens her mouth, and gives us a heart-tugging silent meow; a meow that is far more eloquent than the usual string of audible meows by which she lets us know it's time for chow or time to sit on a lap. My cat-talk friends tell me the silent meow should be interpreted as a polite protest or a plea for indulgence. Maybe with their cats, but not with Shushi. I know Shushi as well as anyone can ever pretend to know a cat. I take her silent meow as an expression of contentment and affection for those who care for her. It comes from so deep within her being that it has no audible expression.

Sometimes, wearing my husband's socks and his extra-large sweater, I cuddle up in a comforter these nippy early mornings and sit on the patio, my hands wrapped around a steaming cup of coffee. If I could purr, I would. In the quiet of the breaking dawn, before the hum of traffic, there comes from deep within me an overwhelming contentment, a spillover of affection for all God does as caregiver of my soul. The words I want simply are not there; all I have is my own silent meow. Looking up to a cloud-dappled sky, I offer it to God. Somehow, I think He's smiling.

When words fail me, loving Lord, please listen to the silent melody of my heart.
—FAY ANGUS

NOVEMBER 8

We...do not cease to pray for you.
—COLOSSIANS 1:9 (KJV)

The persimmon tree at the edge of our cabin causeway is heavy with fruit. Like a small miracle, it has survived the terrible deforestation of the year just passed. Over the spring and summer, I have watched in awe as the woods have staged a comeback of sorts. First came species of wildflowers I hadn't seen before. By summer most of the birds were back, and this fall there was enough foliage to offer a bit of color.

As I gather persimmons for a Thanksgiving centerpiece, small wonders of new beginnings push aside memories of the woodsman's saw. Good thoughts to take the place of bad. My thoughts fly to all the prayer habits that move me from life's disappointments toward the goodness that's always out there waiting to be claimed.

At the top of the list is "Praying for others." Each week I leave my prayer class with a sheet of paper that contains a prayer request from each member. It's virtually impossible to dwell on my own problems or feel sorry for myself when I'm praying for others.

"Pray for your enemies" is another good habit, not because I like to pray for my foes, but because I don't seem to have as many since I've been praying for them.

"Pray for the world." Mother Earth needs our prayers, as do the AIDS orphans in Africa, and all the people at home and abroad who are oppressed, hungry, and homeless. Prayer has changed me and now I am using prayer to change the world.

As for that personal prayer list, I hope you will consider making one of your own. Tape your list to the dashboard of your car, to the bathroom mirror, the refrigerator, your bedside lamp. Make God's "very good" world even better, one prayer at a time.

Father, as I grow closer to You, I want to be one who helps others to find new life in You. Point me ever in the right direction.
—PAM KIDD

NOVEMBER 9

As it is written: "No eye has seen, no ear has heard, no mind has conceived what God has prepared for those who love him."
—1 CORINTHIANS 2:9

My husband Roy and I visit New York City often now that our daughter and her husband are living there. And when we do, we always stop by St. Patrick's Cathedral. Inside its doors, the cool and quiet is a sharp contrast to the hustle and bustle of Fifth Avenue.

On our most recent visit, we stepped inside and walked down the aisle toward the front of the church and sat down to pray. I looked back over my shoulder at the long aisle we'd just walked down and said, "Can you imagine what it must be like to get married here? What a walk down the aisle that would be!" Our own wedding, as beautiful as it had been, held one disappointment for us: our pianist had missed her cue and we had walked down the aisle without any music.

Just then we heard a few chords of the pipe organ. I looked up at the choir loft in the back of the church. *It must be a rehearsal,* I thought. Standing up to leave, we faced the huge double doors at the back of the church with the long aisle before us. At that moment, as if on cue, the pipe organ began to play. Roy looked at me, "Ready?"

I looped my arm in his. "Yes."

My husband and I, arm in arm, walked down the aisle of St. Patrick's Cathedral to the most beautiful music we had ever heard. We smiled at the people in the pews, while those coming in stepped aside as we walked down the center of the aisle. When we reached the back of the cathedral, the music stopped as if on cue. We looked at each other in amazement. God had just given us our walk down the aisle—to the magnificent strains of the pipe organ at historic St. Patrick's Cathedral!

Life is a glorious journey as we walk in faith with You, Lord.
—MELODY BONNETTE

For therein is the righteousness of God revealed from faith to faith.
—ROMANS 1:17 (KJV)

*R*ecently, I heard a story about William Randolph Hearst, the famous newspaperman and collector who filled his mansion with art masterpieces. One day he learned of a painting that was supposed to be especially valuable and commanded his scouts to search for it. At last, one of them came back and reported that he had located the painting.

"Buy it!" commanded Mr. Hearst.

"You already own it," replied the scout. "It's in a crate in one of your warehouses."

My initial reaction to the story was amazement. How could Mr. Hearst lose track of such a treasure and not put it to use? Then I remembered the restless night I'd spent in a hotel the week before, worrying about the keynote speech I was to make the next morning at a conference. Had I prayed about the speech? No. Had I asked for God's support and placed my faith in Him, so I could relax and get a much-needed good night's sleep? No. So where was my faith, my greatest treasure of all? Locked up, I decided, in some dusty warehouse.

I resolved right then to get my faith out of storage, polish it up, and put to use.

Heavenly Father, today and every day I put my faith in You.
—MADGE HARRAH

NOVEMBER 11

I will call upon the Lord, who is worthy to be praised:
so shall I be saved from mine enemies.
—PSALM 18:3 (KJV)

*F*our-year-old Caleb and I were playing soldier when my daughter Rebecca called us for supper. We picked up the toy soldiers, flags, trucks, and planes, then sat down at the table. "I have an idea!" Caleb said as we joined hands for the blessing. "Let's pray like soldiers!"

"How do soldiers pray?" I asked.

"I'll show you," he replied. In a slow, deep monotone, he boomed out, "God... is...great...God...is...good...." We joined in, using our own deep, false "soldier" voices: "And...we...thank...You...for...this...food." We sounded silly, of course, and broke into peals of laughter right after "Amen."

Later, though, I thought about soldiers who pray. My brother Mike, now a retired marine, found time during the Gulf War to pray for my family. Our father, a B-17 pilot who spent nine months in a German prison camp, wrote to our mother on April 30, 1945, that prayers had been answered: "Our camp was liberated at noon yesterday by our dear soldiers. Thank God!"

Christians disagree about whether war is ever justified and about letting children play soldier, but we should never disagree about the need to pray for servicemen and servicewomen and for veterans. And at times we'll find it good to pray like some of them, too.

O Trinity of love and power,
Our brethren shield in danger's hour;
From rock and tempest, fire and foe,
Protect them wheresoe'er they go (William Whiting, 1825–1878).
—PENNEY SCHWAB

NOVEMBER 12

Restore us to thyself, O Lord, that we may be restored! Renew our days as of old!
—LAMENTATIONS 5:21 (RSV)

Our youngest son Glen restores antique pianos. While visiting him one year, I fell in love with a beautiful burled walnut piano he had on display in his showroom. The grain of the wood, the detail of the carvings, the contour of the cabinet all impressed me.

"Oh, but, Mom! You should have seen it when it came into the shop from that old farmhouse. The finish was peeling off from water damage. I had to strip it down and start from square one with the innards, but considering it was built in 1890, the outcome made all my work worthwhile."

That piano came to mind today when I was brought face-to-face with a similar piece of work. The legs were a little unsteady, the finish patched up, the joints wobbly, screws coming loose with age. Remembering how it looked several decades ago, I sighed. This wasn't just any old piece of furniture I was looking at, this was me.

I remembered what a friend said about the ravages of time. "Yes, my body is aging," he conceded, "but my spirit stays as young as ever, because God 'restoreth my soul.'"

No, my mirror doesn't lie. But realizing that God offers the opportunity each day to "start from square one with the innards," there might be some real improvements to my soul.

Considering I date back to 1939, Lord,
may the final outcome make all Your hard work worthwhile.

—ALMA BARKMAN

NOVEMBER 13

Hold thou me up, and I shall be safe.
—PSALM 119:117 (KJV)

It was a scary night! The Santa Ana winds whistled through our California canyon, snapping branches off the oaks and bouncing them across our bedroom roof. "One huge mess to clean up in the morning," my husband John grumbled as he tried to snatch a bit of sleep in between the thumps and bumps.

The next morning I stood shivering in my dressing gown on the patio, braced against the still howling wind, and looked at the tangled, twisted rubble that filled our pool and covered our lawn. The phone rang. It was Jan, the young musician who rents the little cottage that was once my mother's, just a few blocks from where we live in the hills of Sierra Madre.

"Come quick! The big pine tree across the fence is leaning over and maybe one or two more gusts of wind will crash it down on top of my roof."

"We'll be right over," I said. "Get out of the house—now—and wait for us in your car! That tree could fall and crush the cottage."

Protect him, Lord, I prayed. *And please protect our cottage.*

It took us exactly four minutes to get to the cottage. Jan, John, and I huddled together, feeling helpless as we watched the huge tree tipping over, perilously close to falling. "My drums are still in there," said Jan.

"Leave them. It's just too dangerous," my husband warned.

After an hour or so of waiting, Jan decided to go back in. A short time later, the huge tree fell. Jan rushed out of the cottage, and we all stopped and looked in awe. The spreading arms of the massive avocado tree that shelters the little cottage from the hot summer sun caught the falling pine and held it up, steady and firm. One side of our cottage roof was slightly cracked and dented, but Jan, his drums, and the cottage were safe, held in the arms of answered prayer.

Most blessed Lord, in the stormy seasons of my life and the lives of those I love, put the strength of Your arms under and around us and keep us safe.
—FAY ANGUS

"Why then did you not obey the voice of the Lord?"
—1 SAMUEL 15:19 (NKJV)

When I visited my parents, I noticed that my stepfather was doing something unusual. While my mother and I had coffee, I asked, "Joe, is that plain hot water you're drinking?"

He grinned. "Caught me." He explained that he was putting steaming hot water into a dark brown ceramic mug to fool himself into thinking he was drinking his usual coffee. It turns out that when Joe went to the doctor, he was told that he needed to watch his cholesterol. The doctor told him to follow certain rules—more vegetables, less fat, and no coffee—and sent him home, explaining that if that didn't work, he'd have to go on medication.

But what happened about a month later was a surprise. The doctor checked and rechecked him, then excused himself from the room. Joe was quite nervous by this point. "What's going on, Doc?" he asked.

After a few long moments the doctor returned. "Your numbers were so much better this time that I thought the nurse or I might have made a mistake with them. What on earth have you been doing to lower those numbers?"

Perplexed, Joe shrugged. "You know, more vegetables, less fat..." His voice trailed off. "Doc, I only did exactly what you told me to do."

And, eyes wide, the doctor replied, "But I tell that to everyone. You're the first person who actually listened!"

After they had a good laugh, the doctor clapped him on the back, and Joe and my mother went out for a cup of hot water to celebrate.

God, let me be a faithful follower of Your instructions today...
and the instructions of Your earthly helpers.

—LINDA NEUKRUG

I will not leave you nor forsake you.
—JOSHUA 1:5 (NKJV)

ring the bell to Susanna's apartment, carrying alphabet games and a simple reading textbook. For several months now, I've been tutoring my new friend, a refugee from Liberia, in reading and writing. Susanna is a relaxed and joyful student. When she mispronounces a word, she says, "I know it in my head and in my heart, but my tongue gets too happy!"

But Susanna is not happy today. In fact, her eyes shine with tears. In her rapid, fragmented English, she explains that four of her nieces and nephews have perished in a fire a thousand miles away. She has just returned from a brief visit there and shows me the funeral program, shaking her head in disbelief.

The stories tumble out and old grief resurfaces. In Liberia, her husband and six of her fifteen children were killed by war. Then she was torn from her family by the people in charge. "'You go here! You go there!' they tell us. My daughter and her children, we run away to this country." She had hoped to be safe here. Now this.

A lesson is out of the question. "Shall I go, Susanna, or shall I stay?"

"Stay a little while."

So I simply sit with my friend, whose losses I can't even imagine. For thirty minutes we do not talk, but think our own thoughts, pray our own prayers. Then she raises her head.

"It will be all right," she whispers. "God is here. God is here."

Father, I cling to Your promise never to leave us orphaned. Thank You for people of unbreakable faith like Susanna who draw me closer to You.
—GAIL THORELL SCHILLING

NOVEMBER 16

O Lord…. Thank you for making me so wonderfully complex!
It is amazing to think about. Your workmanship is marvelous.

—PSALM 139:1, 14 (TLB)

One of the most cherished moments of our day comes when, as a family, we join hands around the dinner table and give thanks for all the blessings God has given us. As the children were growing up, this became a choice opportunity for them to learn how to pray out loud, develop the gift of a grateful heart, and speak conversationally with God.

One evening when shepherd's pie, the children's favorite, was on the table, six-year-old Ian enthusiastically volunteered to say the blessing. After he had duly thanked God for the food and the highlights of the day, he paused—and then added, "And thank You, God, for the nice little boy You gave this family!"

"Nice little boy!" I gasped. "Where?"

"Right here." He grinned, pointing to himself. "I was thanking God for me!"

Doing the dishes later that night, I thought, *The boy has a point. We all come tagged with the designer label: "Individually Crafted with the Compliments of Your Creator."*

Suddenly, I was overwhelmed. Why, in all my years of thanksgiving, I have never ever thanked God for me! Hands dripping wet with suds, eyes spilling tears of wonder, there and then I quietly said, "Thank You, God, for all the workmanship You put into making me!"

Take time today to thank Him for the designer original—you.

It is too wonderful for us, Lord, when we think that You have numbered
each hair and designed each cell of all that we are. Thank You that You
are constantly shaping each of us into individual creations. Amen.

—FAY ANGUS

NOVEMBER 17

*This woman was abounding with deeds of kindness
and charity which she continually did.*
—ACTS 9:36 (NASB)

"S omeone left this on my desk," my husband David said as he walked
through the kitchen and tossed a gold box on the counter. My name was
written on the tag, but I couldn't identify the handwriting. I untied the ribbon;
inside was a colorful array of candy-coated almonds.

Smiling to myself, I popped one into my mouth and thought, *Someone is
having a "Deanna Day."*

Candy-coated almonds have been my favorite treat since childhood. I don't
remember how our friend Deanna discovered my preference, but candy-coated
almonds began appearing on my birthday, Christmas, Easter. Always packaged
in some clever way, the candy told me I was special, cared about, loved.

After Deanna died in a terrible car wreck, our church family began sharing
stories of her thoughtfulness. Deanna had regularly put envelopes of clipped
cartoons and jokes on David's desk to help with his sermons. For Gloria, it was
licorice. There were well-timed phone calls to shut-ins and holiday open houses
for the lonely. Deanna's kindness was endless, and her passing left a gaping hole
that I thought would never be filled.

Then I received the letter: "Dear Pam, I want you to know that God speaks
to us through your photographs.... Today is my Deanna Day. Remembering how
Deanna used to write thoughtful notes to people and how she always had a way of
making others feel good about themselves made some of us decide to take one day
a month to do something Deanna would have done. The fifth day of every month
is my Deanna Day and that's why I'm writing this note to you. Love, Mary Ev."

My almonds had come midmonth, so they weren't from Mary Ev. There was
really no way to know whom they were from, because the ripples of Deanna's
kindness were spreading through our entire church congregation and beyond.

*Father, the world is waiting for me to act on Your teachings.
Let me make today my Deanna Day.*
—PAM KIDD

NOVEMBER 18

Their faces are never covered with shame.
—PSALM 34:5

I never have been known for my athletic ability. (In fact, I was once asked to leave a bowling team because I lowered their average so much!) So when I saw the sign for a golf-putting contest to benefit a charity, I hurried right by.

But unbeknownst to me, my husband Paul paid the two dollars, one for him and one for me. We each got a chance to hit the ball down a long green strip of AstroTurf. (The contest organizers were trying to beat the distance in the *Guinness Book of World Records.*)

The first swing I took missed the ball completely. The emcee kindly gave me a second chance, and I clipped the corner of the ball and watched it dribble inches down the green.

My face flamed as the emcee announced to the huge crowd, "Say, she's got a real shot at winning the booby prize!" I yanked Paul's arm, and we scurried away. But not before I heard the emcee boom out my name: "Linda was our most valuable player! You know, if Arnold Palmer was up here, nobody would have the courage to go next. But after someone like Linda, people say, 'Boy, if she was willing to get up there and putt,' and we get more dollars for charity!"

For the first time in my life, I was able to laugh at my own ineptitude! Maybe sometimes it's just as helpful to be the worst as to be the best.

God, help me always to remember: I don't have to be the best in order to be valuable—to other people or to You.
—LINDA NEUKRUG

Through love serve one another.
—GALATIANS 5:13 (NASB)

*M*y husband Leo answered the phone. "Hello? Oh yes, Frances, I'm feeling much better, thanks. My beauty queen took real good care of me!"

Beauty queen? Huh?

His words jolted me right out of the fever-induced stupor brought on by a bad case of the flu. The previous week, Leo had been the one burrowed under the covers, shivering and sweating from alternate bouts of chills and fever. The same vicious bug had then bitten me.

Blowing and coughing and wheezing, I had managed to crawl out of bed just long enough to shuffle back and forth to the bathroom. Even in my weakened condition passing the mirror had been a shock to my system—red nose, sunken eyes, hollow cheeks, tattered sweater over baggy flannel pajamas, the bottoms tucked into big woolen socks. My hair was sticking out in all directions and my whole being was enveloped in the strong fumes of a decongestant.

Some "beauty queen"!

As more of Leo's conversation with Frances filtered into my brain, it became clear that he wasn't referring to my physical appearance. (After fifty years of marriage, we both know I'm no beauty queen!) His perception of beauty was being conveyed in phrases like "hot soup...tucking me in...calling the doctor... doling out pills...stroking my brow," the many little things one does to nurse a loved one back to health—the many little things Leo was now doing for me.

Help me, Lord, to look beyond the physical and see as You do
the beauty that is soul-deep in others.

—ALMA BARKMAN

*There came unto him a woman having an alabaster box
of very precious ointment, and poured it on his head.*
—MATTHEW 26:7 (KJV)

W hen our aunt Henrietta died at seventy-nine, my sister Amanda and I cleared out her apartment. To our surprise and dismay, we found a closet filled with boxes that contained almost every gift she'd received for at least five years.

"We gave these blue-striped towels last Christmas," Amanda said, peeking into an oblong box. "The ones she was using were thin and worn."

I spotted a familiar-looking gift bag. Sure enough, it contained the lavender-scented lotion I'd found at a specialty shop—unopened and unused, although Aunt Henrietta had written a gracious thank-you note. So it was with box after box. Rose-bordered tea towels, exquisite writing paper, carved picture frames—lovingly selected gifts were saved, apparently for a special time that never came.

How sad! I thought. Poor Aunt Henrietta never benefited from gifts that would have made her life more comfortable. Even worse, she missed out on the joy of remembering the giver every time she used the gift.

Then I thought of someone on the way to becoming as "poor" as my aunt: me. Didn't I insist that my family use the old towels and save the new ones for company? Hadn't I often set the table with chipped dishes while two "company sets" languished in the cabinet?

My basic nature is still a lot like Aunt Henrietta's. But I learned something important from her overflowing closet: The best way to honor the giver is to make full and joyful use of the gift. And it's the same whether the gift is a matchstick cross lovingly glued together by nine-year-old Mark or the wondrous gift of salvation given by Jesus.

*Lord, You received the gift of precious ointment with love,
and You gave Your life with love. Help me to honor all Your gifts. Amen.*
—PENNEY SCHWAB

So the last shall be first, and the first last.
—MATTHEW 20:16 (KJV)

*P*owder-puff football was a popular fall event at my high school. Every year the junior and senior girls put on uniforms, pads, and helmets and played each other on the school field.

I had a difficult time making it through gym class—unless it was folk dancing season—yet my heart was set on making the powder-puff team. My father offered me as many pointers as he could before he dropped me off at tryouts, but when he came back to pick me up, I threw myself into the car and burst out into tears. "It's not fair! It's not fair! I didn't make the team!" I wailed.

The next morning I had to force myself to go to school. No sooner had I walked in the front door than I was being called to the office. "Pam, one of the faculty sponsors said, 'Since you didn't make the team, we want you to be the manager.' All you have to do is round up the guys on the football team and get them dressed up to be cheerleaders at the game." Standing in the middle of the entire male football team, enjoying twice as much attention as the mud-caked girls out on the field, I was mighty glad that life wasn't fair.

Powder-puff football may seem a little silly, but I always think of that game when I read Jesus' parable about the vineyard owner who pays all his workers the same, whether they came to work early or at the end of the day. God's gifts don't depend on our output but on His heart. Sometimes we get a double dose of what we don't deserve.

Father, Your grace is for everyone: the first, the last, even me.
Now that's something to cheer about!
—PAM KIDD

NOVEMBER 22

We give thanks to you, O God.
—PSALM 75:1

Okay, I admit it: I don't like Thanksgiving. It's not that I have anything against gratitude; what I don't like is all the eating and the patting of bellies and then more eating. But my family loves Thanksgiving. Last year, my daughter Amy Jo suggested a progressive dinner, where we go from house to house for different courses of the meal. "And you might want to give Grandma a break this year and cook the main part of the meal." Forget the fact that I haven't really cooked in...well, a long time.

My husband Gary and I went out to dinner the night before my cooking adventure was set to begin. As we were driving home, we saw a young man, barely visible in the darkness, waving frantically. Gary guided our car across three lanes of traffic and stopped. Instantly, the young man was at our window. "Wow, thanks, man," he said. "Broken-down car. Been driving for twenty-four hours. Trying to get home."

We invited the young man and his buddy into our backseat and let them use our cell phone. After calling a tow truck, the boy's buddy tried to reach his dad. Finally, after talking to another relative, he handed us the phone. "My grandma...she had a heart attack. Everyone is at the hospital."

We were silent for a moment. Then, thinking of the long day ahead of me in the kitchen, I asked, "What's her name?"

"Emily," he said.

"Would it be all right if I prayed for her?"

Even in the darkness, I could see his shoulders sag a little less. "Yeah, that would be great." So all day long, as I prepared for the big meal, I prayed for Emily, for her health, her family, their holiday. Thanksgiving dinner turned out great. My family had fun going from house to house all day. And I didn't mind the overeating quite so much. I kept thinking about Emily and how God had given me the blessing of praying for her. Which gave me just one more reason to give thanks.

Thank You, God, for giving us the things we truly need.
—MARY LOU CARNEY

NOVEMBER 23

Delight yourself in the Lord and he will give you the desires of your heart.
—PSALM 37:4

*I*f ever a group of students needed a time to lighten up from the intensity of their studies, they are those at the California Institute of Technology in our neighboring city of Pasadena, where conversation revolves around such things as quasars, quarks, and the dynamics of particles in rigid bodies.

On their annual Ditch Day, seniors secure their rooms with complex codes that have to be solved in order to break in, then disappear from the campus. The challenge to the freshmen, sophomores, and juniors is to get into the dorms and claim or reject a bribe (generally a feast of some sort) left there to persuade them not to "prank" the room. (One year a senior came back to find all his furniture bolted to the ceiling.)

Professors also get into the fun. The late Richard Feynman, a Nobel Prize winner, offered one thousand dollars to any student who could build an electric motor one-sixty-fourth of an inch on each side. The challenge was successfully met, and the world's tiniest motor, the size of a grain of sand, is still on display at Caltech's Eastbridge Building. To the naked eye it is a black dot, much like the period at the end of this sentence. Through the mirrored magnifier it looks like a small piece of confetti with a line across the top. A notice reads: This Motor Is Worn Out and No Longer Runs.

From mind-boggling intensity, to fun and incredible frivolity, such is the capacity our Creator God has programmed into the human brain. It's all there for us to discover.

Almighty God, enlarge my capacity to see You in all things, great and small.
—FAY ANGUS

Ye should shew forth the praises of him who hath called you
out of darkness into his marvellous light.
—1 PETER 2:9 (KJV)

Living in the country is a new adventure for me. One evening, I noticed a small, black fur ball moving through our yard. I approached cautiously. It was a tiny baby skunk! Then I spotted another and still another. In all, six baby skunks that had somehow been orphaned greeted me.

I brought out a can of fish-flavored cat food and the visitors quickly gathered around. I discovered that they lived under our house in a deep dark hole. A vet instructed me how to move their food out farther from the house each time I fed them until they discovered the woods—and freedom.

I always marveled at their trust as they waddled and tumbled out of their dark hole, one by one. Spooning out cat food, I remembered a deep, dark hole of self-pity I'd found myself in after I'd become a widow. Although four years had gone by, I mostly kept to myself. One night, feeling so alone, I poked my head out of my hole and called some friends. Almost trembling, I asked if I could join them. I was so surprised when they all exclaimed, "Yes, yes! We'll come and get you. We love you!" Tears of gratitude had prevented me from saying anything except "'bye."

Maybe you've been "hiding" for your own reasons and are ready to come out. Take a deep breath, and with a prayer and God's courage, take that first step. Call a friend who's been waiting patiently; send in the application for that new job; volunteer to lead a church group. Start by trusting God.

When I am afraid, Lord, help me to reach out to others and move
toward Your marvelous Light in absolute trust.
—MARION BOND WEST

"I [wisdom] was his constant delight, laughing and playing in his presence."
—Proverbs 8:30 (TLB)

*R*usty is a purebred papillon, with large ears and long fur at his jowls that gives his face the look of a brown-and-white butterfly. He's the neighbors' dog, and they're away at work most of the day. Rather than whine and whimper at being left alone, Rusty has found someone to visit—us. Each time he crawls through the hole he dug under our fence, he brings fun and frolic into our lives. And that is often.

So much so that we're all agreed he's a time-share dog. If our neighbors aren't home when darkness falls, Rusty "sleeps over" with us. Whether he's running to catch a toy we've tossed or flirting with his own reflection in the swimming pool, he's our much-looked-forward-to entertainment. If I'm stressed or just plain down in the dumps, I follow Rusty's lead and take time to play, or I grab the leash and we go for a walk—tonics that lighten me up. And when I'm feeling lonely, like him, I visit a friend.

How lovely it is when unexpected blessings come into my life to cheer me up and put a smile into my heart. Help me to pass them on, dear Lord.
—Fay Angus

Truth lasts.

—PROVERBS 12:19 (MSG)

*T*sat on the edge of a circle of friends at a baby shower recently, watching Sara, a young mother-to-be, open her gifts. My friends and I exchanged wistful sighs as we passed around the gifts. So much had changed since we became mothers a generation ago.

Sara already knew she'd be having a girl, so there were many frilly, gender-appropriate gifts. She also received a baby monitor that lets you hear and see what the baby is doing in another part of the house, a bouncy seat that gently vibrates the baby, a wet-wipe-warmer to toast up the diaper changes, and a pillow designed to help prop up the baby while nursing.

The hostess asked us to go around and offer advice to this first-time mom. From moms of all ages came these tidbits:

- Trust your instincts.
- Write down the cute things the baby says and does. You think you'll never forget, but guess what? You do.
- Disappear for several hours at least once a week and leave the baby with Daddy. Try to do this during the baby's cranky time, so Dad "gets it."
- When people offer to help, let them.
- It's never too early to start reading to the baby.
- Ask for help.
- Cultivate patience.
- Go easy on yourself. Mothering is the hardest job you'll ever have.
- And finally, enjoy these years, they pass so quickly! (Aha! Some things never change.)

Father, Your timeless truth endures forever.

—CAROL KUYKENDALL

Restore to me the joy of your salvation.
—Psalm 51:12

I invited Kenny, a man without any family nearby, to spend Thanksgiving with my sister and me. That evening, as I drove him home, I told Kenny I was especially thankful that God had brought him into my life. Kenny had been helping me around the cabin with landscaping and odd jobs, and we had come to be good friends.

But an inner Voice wouldn't stop insisting: *tell Kenny about Me, Roberta.* So I began sputtering about God and salvation, hoping that I was explaining them in a way that would be clear and not offensive. I didn't want Kenny to think I'd invited him to dinner and then pressured him into something. So I closed my little speech with: "If you'd ever like to ask Jesus to live in your heart, just let me know."

Almost immediately Kenny's deep voice answered, "Well, how about right now, Roberta?"

In praying with Kenny, I felt the joy of my own salvation return. Suddenly, I was ten years old again and had just asked Jesus to live in my heart. "Jesus is the best Friend you'll ever know, Kenny," I promised.

"Even better than you?" he challenged.

"Oh yes," I said, "even better."

Precious Savior, remind me that the best way to keep thanking You for the good news is to pass it along to others.
—Roberta Messner

NOVEMBER 28

In the beginning was the Word, and the Word was with God,
and the Word was God.
—JOHN 1:1

*M*y sister Rebekkah and I had attended three funerals in less than a week. Each was a wonderful celebration of a life, but it bothered us that all the accolades were given *after* the person had died. "Let's tell each other what we admire about each other *now*," Rebekkah suggested.

She started. "You're the most generous person I know." A tear streamed down her cheek. "You're a great bargain hunter and, oh, what a dog lover!"

It was my turn. "You're honest, Rebekkah. And such a hard worker." I remembered the time she'd hurled herself in front of a moving truck to keep it from hitting me. "And, of course, loyal to the very end."

I was on a roll. *Why stop with my sister?* I decided. So that week, whenever I had a few minutes with a friend, I talked about my recent funeral experiences. And before I knew it, we were sharing feelings that might otherwise have gone unexpressed.

Those thank-yous felt so good that I followed them up with notes on old-fashioned stationery. I like to think of those second thank-yous being unfolded again and again on down days when a friend's heart needs the lift that, even in these days of e-mail, only handwritten correspondence can bring. They're the best buy ever for forty-one cents. I should know; my sister said that I'm a great bargain hunter.

Lord Jesus, thank You for the gift of a letter from a friend.
And thank You again for Your Word, Your love letter to each of us.
—ROBERTA MESSNER

NOVEMBER 29

Say to those with fearful hearts, "Be strong, do not fear."
—ISAIAH 35:4

At work, when they needed someone to dress up as a bear for Saturday story time, guess who volunteered? Yes, anything to distract me from the phone call I knew I had to make to apologize to a friend for an unsolicited criticism. While I struggled to don the heavy fake-fur costume, the long feet—that is, paws—and the hairy hands with four-inch nails, I had visions of how happy the children would be to see me.

While I yanked and pulled on the enormous head, I glowed. Maybe some kids would even ask for my "paw-tograph"! Plus, I'd be postponing that dreaded call!

As I lumbered through the store, I could see that out of the twenty or so children who were there, only two or three appeared actually happy to see me. The others? They scattered in terror. Some cried. Some wailed. Some leapt into their parents' arms for safety. I guess a six-foot-tall bear was five more feet than they'd bargained for.

Since bears aren't supposed to speak, I could only watch silently and couldn't say what I wanted to: "I came to make you happy! I won't hurt! Come up to me, please!" But even if I could have given voice to my words, they wouldn't have been heard over the shrieks and tears.

Inside my hot furry cage, I had to laugh, although ruefully. *Wasn't I that way too many times with God?* A difficult phone call to mend a friendship, my former fear of driving—maybe God was handing me those challenges as loving gifts. And there I was screaming, "No! Go away!"

As I made my way to the back room to pull off my furry head, I knew that as soon as I yanked off my paws, I'd be dialing my friend's phone number to make that overdue apology.

Thank You, God, for putting loving challenges in my life.
Help me not to run from them screaming!
—LINDA NEUKRUG

His compassions fail not. They are new every morning.
—LAMENTATIONS 3:22–23 (KJV)

*M*y aunt, at one hundred years old, doesn't string her present moments together as she used to. She says her memory's getting "thin." That's hard for her to accept when her reasoning still works fine.

Each experience is a first-of-its-kind for Aunt Betty, a "fresh first." Whether it's a tree she's seen dozens of times, a neighbor she's greeted often, or a gift she was given weeks ago, she extends her full delight as if it's entirely new. Watching her is like riding a Ferris wheel and rediscovering the same exhilarating sights every time it goes around.

One of my favorite "fresh firsts" is the pie that her daughter Margy gives her. Every morning Aunt Betty is surprised to find pie on her kitchen counter. "Where'd this come from?" she asks. When she learns it's from Margy, she gets another surprise. "How dear of her," she responds.

Why do I allow my daily life to become dull with familiarity? Why can't I catch a ride on the Ferris wheel and see the same things with new enthusiasm? How long since I've felt stirred by God's gifts of sight and sound and movement, of sun and rain and sky, of friends and faith and purpose?

Aunt Betty's wheel of "fresh firsts" is a sweet spin of gratitude and joy, eagerness and surprise. It's the best ride going, whether you're one or one hundred.

Creator God, lead me in circles of recurring wonder
for things that seem commonplace.
—CAROL KNAPP

December

And behold, you will conceive in your womb and bear a son,
and you shall call his name Jesus.
—LUKE 1:31 (RSV)

*T*have often wondered if the angel Gabriel's visit to Mary seemed like a dream to her once he had departed. She must have pored endlessly over his every word, trying to make sense of them. Above all, the one thing she could cling to was a name: Jesus. Mary was the first to hear the name of God's incarnate Son.

I can imagine Mary repeating that name throughout her pregnancy, trying out the sound, saying it over and over until Jesus was a name more familiar than her own. Perhaps holding her baby's name in her heart comforted her when she felt overwhelmed by the magnitude of being His mother.

I learned how truly important a name can be when I discovered I was to become a grandmother for the first time. At first the news was shocking. I wasn't ready to step back a generation. My solution was not to think about it, which was easy to do because my daughter and her husband lived far away.

A few months later, however, my daughter called to tell me that they'd settled on names for their baby-to-be. If the baby was a boy, he would be named Zachary Peter. If it was a girl, Hannah Ruth. My ambivalence disappeared in an instant. The baby, boy or girl, had a name, and I had a connection. This unknown baby sprang to life for me. And when red-headed Zachary finally arrived, Grandma was ready to love him—fiercely and forever.

Mary believed God's promise, but that doesn't mean that she never felt confused or scared. How wonderful for her to have been given her child's name right from the beginning as a personal connection with the great miracle God was creating within her!

Heavenly Father, in Your tender mercy,
You have sent us a Savior, and His name is Jesus.
—CAROL KNAPP

And do not neglect doing good and sharing,
for with such sacrifices God is pleased.
—Hebrews 13:16 (NASB)

*W*hen our daughter Gae and son Glen were preschoolers, they were given an Advent calendar. Behind each little door marking off the days until Christmas was a tiny picture depicting some aspect of Christ's nativity. Every morning Gae and Glen jostled for the chance to open the day's door and tell me how the picture behind it fit into the Christmas story: "That's the star that led the wise guys to Baby Jesus." "That's the angel who singed to the shepherds." "That's Jesus' mommy. She wears a scarf over her head because it's cold in the barn."

While their innocent explanations were delightful, their daily squabble about who should open the door often carried over into playtime. "It's my turn!" "No it's not!" "Yes it is!"

I issued an ultimatum. "From now until Christmas, neither of you opens the Advent door if you bicker about it. Not only that, but if you misbehave during the day, you also lose your turn."

Interesting remarks soon started filtering out of the playroom.

"We've only got a few days left, Glen. I'll share my toys."

"Not many days left, Gae. You can have my cookie."

This year when I opened the door on December, I thought back to Gae and Glen's Advent calendar, only now I was the one who didn't want to share. "I know it'll soon be Christmas, Lord, but I just don't feel like baking for shut-ins this year, or sewing stocking stuffers for singles, or taking the elderly shopping. Can't You find somebody else to do it?"

That's not how my Son responded, God seemed to say.

A few minutes later my husband Leo came in from outside, where he had been clearing a neighbor's driveway with the snowblower. "Mmmm, what's that I smell?"

"Christmas cookies for Vera and Betty," I replied. "Not many days left."

Father God, remind me of the ways You've given me
to share Your love with others.
—Alma Barkman

DECEMBER 3

And suddenly there was with the angel a multitude of the heavenly host.
—LUKE 2:13 (KJV)

Mom had just arrived at our home for a holiday visit. As she stared at an angel ornament on my tree, she said, "My mother saw an angel when I was a girl." Then she told me this story:

"When I was young, I had severe asthma. One night I couldn't breathe. Mama was begging and praying that I wouldn't die. Suddenly she looked up in the open doorway to the hall and saw a beautiful dark-haired woman. The woman didn't say a thing. She just smiled and gave a friendly wave. Afterward Mama told me, 'I think it was an angel telling me that you would live and grow up to be a woman like the one I saw standing in the doorway.'"

Mom's story has challenged my conventional ideas about angels. Her angel looked like an ordinary person. Mom's angel didn't do anything remarkable; she didn't even say anything. Yet in the hour of deepest need, my grandmother had drawn strength and hope from this being who did absolutely nothing except stand there and wave. Sometimes the whole mission of angels is simply to appear.

Angels are spiritual beings who are invisible except when they choose otherwise; we humans are visible beings whose spiritual side is invisible until we choose to let it show. This Advent season, I can imitate the angels by letting someone glimpse my spiritual side. Maybe it will be seen as I drive to church or when I help a person in need. Maybe it will be heard when I sing a carol or write a Christmas letter telling about the wonderful things God has done for me during the past year.

This Advent, let's be angelic. Let's become visible!

Lord, I pray that Your light will so shine in my heart
that it will be seen by everyone I meet.
—KAREN BARBER

A man who refuses to admit his mistakes can never be successful.
But if he confesses and forsakes them, he gets another chance.
—PROVERBS 28:13 (TLB)

*M*istakes. I seem to make lots of them. I call someone by the wrong name. I say something when I should say nothing...or nothing when I should say something. I throw a red sock with the white laundry or forget to turn off the horses' water so it runs down the hill for hours. Usually, when I realize my mistake, I get mad and start carrying around a grudge—*against myself.*

But a friend recently told me a story about mistakes that changed my response. Her father visited a Persian rug factory where exquisite, one-of-a-kind rugs are handwoven. He asked what happened when the weavers made a mistake. "Do they have to go back and start over again?" he questioned.

"Oh no," came the answer. "They call in the master weaver who weaves the mistake right into the pattern."

The very next time I made a mistake, I tried the Persian rug formula. After writing two important letters, I dropped them in the corner mailbox and then discovered I'd sealed them in the wrong envelopes. Instead of standing there and scolding myself, I mentally raised my hand to the Master Weaver. "I goofed, God, and this could be embarrassing. Please weave the mistake into something good."

Two days later, the telephone rang. "I just got your friend's letter in my envelope," a merry voice said. "You don't know how much I needed a reminder today that *everyone* makes mistakes. Thanks."

Into Your hands, Master Weaver,
I commit my mistakes—big ones and little ones.
—CAROL KUYKENDALL

December 5

*I pray that you...may...grasp how wide and long and high
and deep is the love of Christ, and to know this love that surpasses knowledge.*
—Ephesians 3:17–19

*S*eeking some Christmas cheer one day in early December, I drove to a plant nursery. All five of my children lived far away and would not be coming home this year, and my mother had been admitted to the hospital for cancer surgery. Mom had told me once, "When life is hard, plant some flowers. They'll speak of God's love to you." So taking her advice, I asked the clerk for an amaryllis bulb that would have bright red blossoms at Christmastime. She found one eager bulb already forming a bud at the end of a thick green stalk.

I put my potted plant into a bay window facing west, and eagerly watched the bud unfold. By Christmas it sported four radiant bell-shaped blossoms, each one eight inches in diameter. Two weeks later, just as the blossoms were drooping, a bud on a second stalk began to burst open. This time six brilliant red blooms crowned the plant. I used an old windshield wiper to support the drooping stalk.

But there was more: a third stalk appeared and grew to a height of thirty inches. Soon another cluster of four giant red trumpet-flowers appeared.

"Is it unusual for one bulb to grow fourteen blossoms?" I asked a clerk at a nursery.

"You definitely got a bonus," she said with a smile.

My mother, who'd recovered enough to visit me, agreed with the clerk. "I've never seen anything like it," she said.

I'd wanted a sign of God's love, and He had given me an extravagance. From Christmas Day until Valentine's Day, fourteen times over, God said in the most exquisite way, "I love you." But then, He never stops saying, "I love you." I just have to tune my heart to receive His tokens of love all year round.

Thank You, Father, for sending me Your love in a way I can grasp.
—Helen Grace Lescheid

DECEMBER 6

What wilt thou give?
—HOSEA 9:14 (KJV)

T tried to think of something special to make my husband's face light up at Christmas. Gene had once shared a childhood memory about the boy who lived down the hill from him back in Indiana. His friend had received a new bicycle for Christmas and Gene had even ridden it a few times. But Gene had never been able to have one of his own.

We happened by a store, and I pointed out a spiffy bicycle in the window. "I just might get you one," I said teasingly.

"I do *not* need a bicycle. *Do not* get me one," Gene said emphatically. Deflated, I said nothing.

Later that week we were reading our mail in the living room, Gene with his pile, me with mine. "Here's the bicycle I want, honey," he announced loudly. *Was he teasing me?*

I moved over next to him and looked at the catalog he was holding. It showed a bike surrounded by an overjoyed father, a smiling mother, and seven skinny, happy children. They lived in an underdeveloped country, and the bike would provide transportation so the father could get a job. The catalog explained that anyone could give a bicycle, garden seeds, or even an ox.

Gene got his bicycle for Christmas—and halfway around the world, lives would be changed forever.

Father, I have so much to learn about true giving. Teach me.
—MARION BOND WEST

DECEMBER 7

And this day shall be unto you for a memorial.
—EXODUS 12:14 (KJV)

I'd heard about Pearl Harbor all my life...in every US history class I took, and from my father and father-in-law, both of whom served in the navy. But when Gary and I visited Hawaii and took a day trip to see Pearl Harbor for ourselves, I was amazed at the emotion I felt.

A gleaming white structure rested out in the bay, a memorial built over the sunken *Arizona*. We boarded a boat with other tourists and listened as the guide talked about December 7, 1941. "The USS *Arizona* is the final resting place for many of the 1,177 crewmen who lost their lives. In the shrine room of the memorial, you will find the names of those killed."

As we walked onto the memorial, I looked over the side. I could see the sunken ship! Its outline was visible in the clear water below us. I imagined the sailors that morning, roused from their sleep. Young, confused, frightened, brave. Did they have mothers, sweethearts, wives? I sensed someone standing next to me at the rail. I looked up to see a Japanese woman. For a moment I stiffened. What right did she have to be here? Then I realized what she was doing: dropping flower petals into the water. In that instant I knew that death— like bravery and love—knows no national boundaries, that we are all enlarged by the noble and diminished by the tragic.

The water lapped quietly against the sides of the memorial, and when the lady looked my way, I smiled.

Forgive us, Father, for the tragedies we inflict on each other.
May we be inspired by brave men and noble causes.
—MARY LOU CARNEY

"They shall call His name Immanuel," which translated means, "God with us."
—MATTHEW 1:23 (NASB)

t was a Wednesday night in early December. I was downstairs in church preparing for the weekly children's story hour. At home I'd left boxes of unpacked Christmas decorations and mounds of greenery on the floor. The annual struggle to get my house just right had started, and the tension was building. Christmas brings it out in me: I scrub, I bake, I clean, I decorate, I sigh.

Now, getting ready for the children, I pulled out a large laminated picture of a white, steepled church, which had been our theme for the last few weeks. As I turned it in the light, I gasped. There was the Christ Child in the stained glass window! *Why have I never seen Him there before?* I wondered.

When the children came in, I held up the picture. "Do you see who's looking at you from this window?" I asked.

They looked blank. "We don't see anything, Miss Shari."

The culprit was the glare on the laminating. When I shielded the picture from the light, they spotted Baby Jesus right away. "He's in there. He's looking at me," a boy said. "And I never even noticed."

When the story hour was over, I returned home to the holiday tension, carrying a larger truth. In our Christmas celebrations, Christ was beckoning to me. But He was hidden by the glare of my pride—the pride that wanted a beautiful, flawless house; the pride that was desperate to impress my guests; the pride that feared I'd never be good enough.

Now, driving through the darkness, I heard Christ whisper, *Let go of your pride, your need to hide behind perfection, and let Me shine in your imperfect house—and in you.*

> *Lord, may all those who come through my door*
> *this Christmas know Your presence.*
> —SHARI SMYTH

DECEMBER 9

Blessed is he that waiteth.
—DANIEL 12:12 (KJV)

*T*hought I knew about waiting. Especially December waiting. I waited in line at the post office to mail my Christmas packages. I waited my turn at the florist's. And I waited to open that big package under the tree with my name on it. But last year's Advent season was different. Our daughter Amy Jo was going to have a December baby, and waiting took on a whole new intensity.

As her time got closer, we all went on "baby standby." If I didn't hear from Amy Jo by the end of every day, I called her. I started charging my cell phone, carrying it with me and actually turning it on—three things I seldom did before being on baby standby. I bought and wrapped my presents early. I saved up my vacation days at work. I made sure the car had a full tank of gas. And I waited—in a more heightened state of expectancy than any I could remember experiencing, even during my own pregnancies. And on December 22, when Amy Jo gave birth to a healthy baby boy, I knew it had been well worth the wait!

This Advent, I want to remember that expectancy, the happy hope embodied in the waiting. I want to realize that this year—and always and forever—a Child is born. But only if I'm on baby standby can I really know the joy His coming brings. Only if I'm watching with breathless longing will I find my waiting rewarded with a fresh sense of wonder, with a heightened awareness of love. With Christmas!

I praise You, Father, for the miracle of birth and the miracle
of Your love made flesh to dwell among us. I wait for Your coming.
Welcome, welcome, welcome, Baby Jesus!
—MARY LOU CARNEY

"Blessed are those who mourn, for they shall be comforted."
—MATTHEW 5:4 (RSV)

*M*arc-James Manor bed and breakfast here in Bellingham, Washington, has an antique china collection boasting 323 teapots that date back as far as 1740, and more than 1,400 teacups and saucers, salt boxes, coffee "cans," and pieces of table decor. Two of the sets absorbed my attention: they were completely black. "See how elaborately they're decorated?" Marc pointed out. "The mother and child, the shrouded windows—they're for mourning."

Mourning tea sets, I thought. How wonderful it would be to live in a culture that allowed sadness without spiritual or psychological condemnation. When my fifteen-year-old brother snapped his neck and was paralyzed, I was told to stop grieving; this was God's will. When my grandmother died, I was told to stop weeping; she was in heaven. When I broke into tears while telling of my sister's death several years earlier, I was told to get over it; let the dead bury the dead. It isn't "Christian" to lament. Lamentation reveals a bankrupt faith.

Over the years, though, I've not been good at hiding my grief, and after seeing Marc's collection, I confessed my struggle to my youngest child, then twenty. Blake challenged me to find a scriptural basis for tears and weakness, futility and dependency. "Culturally, we give no value to the sick and poor and the bereaved," he explained, "and so our Christianity mirrors the same sorry mistake. Yet didn't Jesus preach, 'Blessed are those who mourn'?"

So I spent the year getting reacquainted with David, Jeremiah, Isaiah, and Job—men who wept and wailed, who dressed in sackcloth and sat in ashes and denied themselves food whenever they found themselves dismayed by turmoil, torn apart by grief, or terrified out of their minds. Even Jesus wept. Reading on, I realized that their tears were not a sign of a bankrupt faith, but the prism through which they saw clearly. Jeremiah saw his mandate, Job his confusion, David his fear, Jesus His sorrow. And in seeing, they found comfort.

*Dear Lord, thank You for tears. They open my eyes to what
I need the most, and in You I find the comfort I need.*
—BRENDA WILBEE

DECEMBER 11

Thanks be to God for his indescribable gift!
—2 CORINTHIANS 9:15

*I*t was the last school day before Christmas break. Just home from school, my brother Paul was taking off his jacket.

"So what did you get?" my mom asked.

Mom and Paul had spent the previous evening at the local five-and-dime looking for a Secret Santa present. The teacher's note about the gift exchange had been lost in my brother's coat pocket and found miraculously at the last moment. It had read: "Purchase a present for a boy. Please spend five to ten dollars."

Paul and Mom had walked the aisles looking for something good and finally settled on a Duncan butterfly yo-yo. Yo-yos were the rage at school, and at seven dollars, this one was well within the suggested amount.

"So," Mom asked again, "what did you get?"

Paul opened his hand and showed her a battered miniature car, its paint worn from handling.

My mother held it in her hand. "Really?" she asked. "Who gave it to you?" She tried to cover up her disappointment. Who would give a beat-up old toy car when the instructions had clearly said, "Spend five to ten dollars"?

"Andy," Paul said, looking down at the car. "Isn't it great? It's his favorite. And he gave it to me!"

Lord, help me always to give generously
and to receive thankfully—from my heart.
—SABRA CIANCANELLI

He turned to the woman and said to Simon.
"She has kissed my feet again and again...her sins—
and there are many—are forgiven, for she loved me much...."
—LUKE 7:44–45, 47 (TLB)

*R*ecently I received a letter with SWALK written across the flap on the back of the envelope. It had been ages since I'd seen the once popular slogan. Sure enough, it was from a friend I have known since the 1950s, who reminded me that her note was "Sealed with a Loving Kiss."

The *X* we use to denote a kiss comes from the Middle Ages, when the cross of Saint Andrew (the white cross on a blue background that is now the Scottish part of the Union Jack) was used for a signature on important documents by those who couldn't write. This was a sign of binding honesty, and after writing the *X*, it was kissed to further guarantee faithful performance of the obligation. Hence *X* became associated with a kiss.

How I treasure the love letters from the man I was to marry, always signed with many *X*'s, some wandering around the borders of each page. I have kept them bundled with blue ribbon. Over our forty-five years of marriage, I frequently untied them and wiggled against my husband in our oversized armchair and read them out loud. "Good heavens," John would tease, making a wry face, "did I write all that mush?" We'd cuddle and kiss and reaffirm our love.

Now that he is dead, I sit alone in the big armchair and fill the empty space with a chunky cushion. I once again read his letters. They give me the strength that only love can give. They ease my hurting heart. As I tie them back up, I kiss them. The *X* seal reminds me that love is eternal.

Jesus, Your never-ending love strengthens and sustains me.
Thank You for those You have given us to love.
—FAY ANGUS

"From now on I will tell you of new things, of hidden things unknown to you."
—ISAIAH 48:6

I was excited about my first trip to Scotland last spring. I'd see new vistas, meet new people, try new food. In Edinburgh, I savored *cock-a-leekie* (a soup of chicken, leeks, and prunes). In the fishing village of Plockton, I had *cullen skink* (pungent chunks of salty haddock simmered with potatoes in cream). There were stick-to-your-ribs *tatties* (potatoes) and bashed *neeps* (mashed turnips). And from the bakeries came a celestial concoction of butter and sugar called *tablet*. Best of all I enjoyed the oatmeal we had for breakfast, grainy and honey-hued and delicious.

But there was one dish I couldn't cozy up to: *haggis*, the legendary Scottish favorite—the innards of a sheep, chopped fine, mixed with oatmeal and spices, and boiled in a sheep's stomach. *My* stomach recoiled.

One night at dinner I saw haggis on the menu. "I've been intending to try it," I bravely told my traveling companions. "But I'm squeamish about the ingredients."

"I know," the woman across from me said with a shiver. An American from Austin, Texas, she clearly shared my aversion. "*Eeeww*, oatmeal."

"Oatmeal? You're yucked out by the oatmeal? What about the other stuff?"

She looked at me as though I were the strange one. "I don't mind organ meats," she said matter-of-factly. "But mixing in oatmeal is too weird."

My whole notion about what was yummy and what was not turned upside down. I ordered the haggis without hesitation. It came steaming and fragrant, and when I dug in, it was spicy and delicious, like sausage or hash or meatloaf with a zing. What had I been afraid of?

It's not just the big new vistas that open up our lives. It's the daily little ones that also surprise.

Dear God, keep my heart open to new experiences—
and keep my taste buds open too.
—MARY ANN O'ROARK

December 14

*Give unto them beauty for ashes...the garment
of praise for the spirit of heaviness.*
—Isaiah 61:3 (kjv)

C an we put up a tree?" Cindy, our assistant clinic director, asked at our
Friday morning staff meeting in mid-December.

Our social service agency often receives Christmas trees and decorations for
clients who wouldn't otherwise have them. I hoped we'd given them all away
the previous year, for even a small tree would make the congestion worse in the
crowded waiting room.

But I didn't say no, and I returned from a late afternoon meeting to find
Cindy and Helen, the office manager, placing delicate silver ornaments on a
flocked white tree. "Looks fine," I said.

Cindy shook her head. "It needs lights."

I fished a string out of the decoration box. "Tiny and twinkling," I told her.

She eyed me sternly. "They're on a green cord," she said. "This tree needs
silver lights on a white cord." The next morning she brought the right lights
plus a delicate tree skirt for the gifts of mittens, caps, and candy we give
neighborhood children.

It was beautiful. Still, I felt a twinge of irritation over the waste of time
and space...until I walked out to see a small boy staring at it, transfixed. "Es
muy bonito," he said softly to his mother. "Sí," she responded. "Hermoso."
Throughout the days that followed, that scene was repeated over and over, in
English and Spanish and German: "Beautiful." "Lovely." "Perfect."

This year I won't argue over the tree. Instead, I'll encourage those who
lovingly bring beauty into others' lives. Thank you, Cindy and Helen, for
honoring the newborn King with a Christmas gift of beauty!

Beautiful Savior, thank You for the loveliness of this holy season.
—Penney Schwab

December 15

So we, being many, are one body in Christ.... Having then gifts differing according to the grace that is given to us...
—ROMANS 12:5–6 (KJV)

Last Sunday, the choir director came up to my daughter Karen, who, like her mother, doesn't carry a tune very well. "I've noticed that you don't sing the hymns," he told her.

"I can't sing!" she said.

"It doesn't matter," he replied. "Really! Some voices are right on pitch, and we need those people. But in the congregation, we also need the voices that aren't perfectly pitched in order to round out the sound. All of them blend together *and God hears it whole!* So please, go ahead and sing!" Karen decided to do just that next Sunday...and her mom might even get up the courage to do it, too.

Maybe it's the same with any other ability. The world surely needs the very talented ones, those who truly excel. But perhaps, just as in the singing of hymns, those with average talent still have a contribution to make. So, with my writing and teaching, I will quit comparing myself to others. Instead, I'll work hard at what I do. I'll sing my own part of the song, knowing that "God hears it whole!"

Thank You, Lord, for giving each of us valued parts in Your inclusive song.
—MARILYN MORGAN KING

DECEMBER 16

"For to the snow he says, 'Fall on the earth'...that all men may know his work."
—JOB 37:6–7 (RSV)

On a Sunday afternoon in December our church holds its annual Bethlehem Day. With temperatures in the seventies in Arizona, we turn the courtyard outside the sanctuary into our idea of old Bethlehem. Families enjoy Christmas music and cookies while little costumed shepherds and angels tromp on the straw-covered ground from one craft booth to the next, making star-shaped candles or a clothespin Baby Jesus in a wooden manger.

The day is usually sunny and bright, but a few years ago an uncharacteristically blustery morning had turned cold by afternoon. And as my little daughter Maria and her Sunday-school choir rehearsed "Away in a Manger," I looked out the windows of the choir room in delighted shock. A soft, wet snow was falling, blanketing Bethlehem Day in dazzling white.

"It's snowing!" someone shouted, and folks ran to the windows and then outside, giddy at this incredible sight. It's hard to say who was more excited, the kids or the grown-ups, as we stood with our arms outstretched, heads tilted toward the sky and mouths open, literally drinking in God's wonderful surprise. The snow in Phoenix lasted only a short time, but it brought a joy that carried well beyond the day.

Christmas began with a wonderful surprise from God, too. The world awaited its Messiah but no one expected a tiny baby to be the One. Christ's actual birth was a small moment, unnoticed by all but a few shepherds. But the joy He brought into the world is everlasting. And unlike our once-in-a-lifetime desert snowfall, Christ comes again and again—each year at Christmas, and every time we invite Him into our hearts.

Come, Lord Jesus, as I stand with my arms outstretched, ready to welcome You.
—GINA BRIDGEMAN

When all the people saw it, they shouted for joy.
—LEVITICUS 9:24

I love books, and I like people. At least I thought I did, until I got caught in the holiday rush in the giant bookstore where I staffed the information desk during the holiday season. "Please, God, give me patience," I'd murmur when yet another customer would come up to the counter and say, "I don't remember the author, but someone was talking about it on the radio the other week."

I'd force a cheery smile. "Do you know the title?"

"Well...it had something about golf in it. At least I think it did."

That was when I'd think, *Well, why didn't you write down the name when the guy on the radio was talking about it?* But usually a silent prayer would keep me patient.

One night, however, near closing, a man came in with a long list of gifts to buy. He said, "Now, I don't know any of these titles, but my wife said there was a new biography that she wanted and it was on display near the front of the store."

I stared. We moved merchandise around daily. "Don't you have any more information than that? There are hundreds of biographies."

"Oh, sure," he said. "She said it had a blue cover."

That was it. "Oh, sure," I snapped. "We keep the books arranged by color in the warehouse." It was meant to be a joke, but it sure didn't sound funny when I said it.

He stared at me, and I wondered if he would report me to the manager for having a bad attitude. But he laughed. "I guess you've been pretty busy finding stuff for people who don't have a clue."

"And I guess you've been pretty busy, too, trying to get the right gift for the right person. Come on, I'll help you find something your wife will like." We headed off to the biography section, and all the while I was thinking:

Lord, thank You for kind people. Help me to be as forgiving and patient with other people as You are with me.

—LINDA NEUKRUG

Love is the fulfilling of the law.
—Romans 13:10 (kjv)

*I*n the latter part of the nineteenth century, a devout young Quaker named Annie Barrow lived in a town called Kendal, in the English midlands. One day she went to an elder in her church to ask for prayer. "I fear," she told him, "that I have no talent at all for serving God!"

The elder studied her for a moment and replied, "Methinks thou hast a talent for loving!"

Apparently he was right. Annie eventually married a young man who became one of the great commissioners of the Salvation Army, and Annie herself became the legendary matriarch of several generations of devoted Christian missionaries, preachers, doctors, nurses, and teachers who have wrapped themselves around the globe like the Savior's arms, helping, healing, comforting, serving, and, above all, loving.

I think of Annie Barrow when I'm in one of my "worthless me" moods. I get this way when I'm sick or exhausted from overworking, and right now I'm in the throes of an illness that will probably require major surgery. I don't like being out of commission. *What good am I,* I ask myself, *when I can't work? When I can't contribute?* I try to remind myself, at times like this, that God doesn't measure me only according to my works.

That's when I open my Bible and find this little story about Annie Barrow inside the cover. I'm reminded that "a talent for loving" has been given to everyone—including me—and that I can find ways to use it no matter how I feel, no matter where I am. Even in a hospital bed or right here at home.

Father, today I will use my "talent for loving" with everyone You send my way.
—Susan Williams

And as thy days, so shall thy strength be.
—DEUTERONOMY 33:25 (KJV)

*M*y daughter gurgled as I fastened the last pin in her clean diaper. After seven years of waiting for a child, finally ours squirmed on the changing table we'd purchased so long ago. Our baby—*ours!*—so tiny, sweet and beguiling, but also noisy and needy. *Feed, change, feed, change, change, change, change!* A parent for only two days, I had changed nearly two dozen diapers. *How can I do this for the next two years? Will I have time for anything else? Will I have the stamina?*

Perhaps it's just as well that I didn't know then that I'd be changing diapers not for two years, but for ten. My extended tour of duty would include three children in diapers at the same time and at least five years of laundering cloth diapers before disposables became readily available.

Once I tried to compute the number of diapers I had changed: Five thousand? Ten thousand? More? It was impossible to determine. Yet by the time I changed the last diaper, I felt sad to be giving up the task that I had once dreaded. I missed the special face-to-face time, the song-and-tickle time, the special closeness with my children. To console myself, I invited my closest friends—all mothers, of course—to my Ditch-the-Diaper-Pail party.

Now, twenty-seven years later, I chuckle as I remember how a distasteful task turned special, how my dread turned to smiles. Once again, God gave me strength gift-wrapped with joy.

Help me to remember, dear Lord, that whatever the task, I can do it with You.
—GAIL THORELL SCHILLING

Who can withstand his icy blast?
—PSALM 147:17

It would have been such a nice photo—my husband John making his way across the yard after a record snowstorm—if only I hadn't gotten those ugly phone and electric lines in the picture! A cat's cradle of wires stretched right across the pristine snowscape, from the street to the side of the house. And then, holding the snapshot, I remembered another wintry scene....

That year, it had been an ice storm—house, trees, telephone poles sheathed in an inch-thick coat. John was attending a conference in balmy Orlando, Florida, when the wind began that night. It screamed around the house, and with it came the rifle-shots of cracking wood.

I woke in the morning to a frigid house and a bizarre landscape. Weighted with ice, tall trees had snapped in two, jagged spars erect and treetops strewn over the ground. A dozen lay across the driveway like a giant heap of jackstraws.

After the uproar of the night, the house was eerily quiet. There was no rumble from the oil burner, no hum from the refrigerator, no radio or TV to tell me how widespread the storm had been or when road crews might reach our suburb. And there was no phone to let John know I was okay.

Sort of okay: there was no coffee—it's an electric pot; no hot oatmeal—electric stove; no power for the toaster; not even a way to count the passing hours on our four electric clocks. For nearly two days, before the road was cleared and a volunteer firefighter crawled over and under the obstacle course in the yard to get me to his truck and a motel, I kept a fire going in the living room and ate canned tuna.

I looked at the photo again. And thanked God for the blessings carried by those ugly wires.

Don't let me take the conveniences of modern life for granted, Father—or forget that human inventiveness is a gift from You.
—ELIZABETH SHERRILL

In him was life, and that life was the light of men.
—JOHN 1:4

In 1978 we lived on eighteen rolling acres in Pennsylvania. We'd acquired a cow, a few sheep, a horse, and Susie, our wooly, nine-hands-high Shetland pony. Susie was past due to give birth. In her stall, her fetlocks deep in fresh straw, she waddled to me, round as a ripe pear. Her big, soft eyes were trusting. It was her first foal. Mine, too.

That night I slept in our barn. It was cold and dark and smelled of fresh hay and stale dirt and dusty cobwebs. The cow mooed. The sheep stamped and stirred. I got up and shined a light in Susie's stall, careful not to hit her eyes. She was lying down, looking miserable. She nickered softly. I shuffled back to my pallet and lay down. A growing anxiety gripped me. *What will I do if something goes wrong with the birth?* I tried to pray, but the words wouldn't come.

The next day went by. Nothing. That night I was back in the barn. The cow and sheep were strangely quiet. Moonlight flooded through the open doors. I tiptoed to Susie's stall, and there it was: just born, lying on wet straw, tiny, dark hooves flailing out of its birth sack. The new mother gently cleaned her baby with her rough tongue. It was a filly, a girl.

Like a pro, Susie nudged and nickered her filly to its thin, gangly legs. A fuzzy tuft of mane waved over a downy cinnamon coat. Gumming her way across her mother with squeals and sucking noises, the filly latched on to a nipple.

Leaning on a rough post, I breathed the tart stable air in deep, relieved gulps. I bowed my head and, with sudden clarity, the light of Christmas shone like the stars. It really happened; the majestic, holy Creator was born a baby on a night like this, in a place like this, among His lowly animals, amid straw and dirt and the darkness of our sin.

Thank You, Jesus.
—SHARI SMYTH